Shakespeare and Celebrity Cultures

This book argues that Shakespeare and various cultures of celebrity have enjoyed a ceaselessly adaptive, symbiotic relationship since the final decade of the sixteenth century, through which each entity has contributed to the vitality and adaptability of the other.

In five chapters, Jennifer Holl explores the early modern culture of theatrical celebrity and its resonances in print and performance, especially in Shakespeare's interrogations of this emerging phenomenon in sonnets and histories, before moving on to examine the ways that shifting cultures of stage, film, and digital celebrity have perpetually recreated the Shakespeare, or even the #shakespeare, with whom audiences continue to interact.

Situated at an intersection of multiple critical conversations, this book will be of great interest to scholars and graduate students of Shakespeare and Shakespearean appropriations, early modern theater, and celebrity studies.

Jennifer Holl is an Associate Professor of English at Rhode Island College, USA.

Routledge Advances in Theatre & Performance Studies

Opera in Performance
Analyzing the Performative Dimension of Opera Productions
Clemens Risi

Performances that Change the Americas
Stuart Day

Staging Detection
From Hawkshaw to Holmes
Isabel Stowell-Kaplan

Poetic Images, Presence, and the Theater of Kenotic Rituals
Enikő Sepsi

Barrie Kosky on the Contemporary Australian Stage
Affect, Post-Tragedy, Emergency
Charlotte Farrell

American Cultures as Transnational Performance
Katrin Horn, Leopold Lippert, Ilka Saal and Pia Wiegmink

Rabindranath Tagore
from Page to Stage
Abhijit Sen

Surviving Theatre
The Living Archive of Spectatorship
Marco Pustianaz

For more information about this series, please visit: www.routledge.com/Routledge-Advances-in-Theatre–Performance-Studies/book-series/RATPS

Shakespeare and Celebrity Cultures

Jennifer Holl

LONDON AND NEW YORK

First published 2021
by Routledge
2 Park Square, Milton Park, Abingdon, Oxon OX14 4RN

and by Routledge
605 Third Avenue, New York, NY 10158

Routledge is an imprint of the Taylor & Francis Group, an informa business

© 2021 Jennifer Holl

The right of Jennifer Holl to be identified as author of this work has been asserted by her in accordance with sections 77 and 78 of the Copyright, Designs and Patents Act 1988.

All rights reserved. No part of this book may be reprinted or reproduced or utilised in any form or by any electronic, mechanical, or other means, now known or hereafter invented, including photocopying and recording, or in any information storage or retrieval system, without permission in writing from the publishers.

Trademark notice: Product or corporate names may be trademarks or registered trademarks and are used only for identification and explanation without intent to infringe.

British Library Cataloguing-in-Publication Data
A catalogue record for this book is available from the British Library

Library of Congress Cataloging-in-Publication Data
Names: Holl, Jennifer, 1974- author.
Title: Shakespeare and celebrity cultures / by Jennifer Holl.
Description: New York : Routledge, 2021. |
Series: Routledge advances in theatre and performance | Includes bibliographical references and index.
Identifiers: LCCN 2021009654 | ISBN 9780367407698 (hardback) | ISBN 9781032050591 (paperback) | ISBN 9780367808976 (ebook)
Subjects: LCSH: Shakespeare, William, 1564-1616--Appreciation. | Shakespeare, William, 1564-1616--Influence. | Fame--Social aspects. | Theater--England--History. | Literature and society--England--History. | English drama--Early modern and Elizabethan, 1500-1600--History and criticism.
Classification: LCC PR2976 .H545 2021 | DDC 822.3/3--dc23
LC record available at https://lccn.loc.gov/2021009654

ISBN: 978-0-367-40769-8 (hbk)
ISBN: 978-1-032-05059-1 (pbk)
ISBN: 978-0-367-80897-6 (ebk)

DOI: 10.4324/9780367808976

Typeset in Bembo
by Taylor & Francis Books

Contents

Acknowledgements   vi

   Introduction   1
1 Stars in deed   23
2 A commodity of good names   59
3 The celebrity's two bodies   92
4 A Shakespeare that looks like Shakespeare   124
5 #shakespeare   159

Index   188

Acknowledgements

As I insist throughout this book, celebrity is not a single person, but a sprawling network of collaborative enterprise, and as I have discovered here, writing a book about celebrity is, too, a highly collaborative endeavor. This book would not exist without the motivation, support, and guidance of mentors, teachers, colleagues, students, and loved ones.

I begin by thanking my supportive editors at Routledge, Laura Hussey, and Swati Hindwan. Their kind encouragement over the course of this project's development has been extraordinary and most appreciated.

This project began as my dissertation, 'Stars Indeed: The Celebrity Culture of Shakespeare's London,' completed at the City University of New York Graduate Center under the supervision of my mentor and friend, Mario DiGangi. I am deeply indebted to Mario, whose offhand comment about stardom in his Shakespearean Economics course first inspired me to consider the overlaps between our contemporary culture of celebrity and the early modern theater. As Mario mentored me through term papers, exams, and, ultimately, my dissertation, I doubt he knows that my most abiding research project of the last decade sprang from his tangential observation about a popstar, even as he wisely and steadily guided me in the dissertation process to always think harder, research further, and write better on a topic that he unwittingly inspired.

During the course of my studies and dissertation at the CUNY Graduate Center, I was privileged to work not only with Mario, but with Rich McCoy, Will Fisher, and Clare Carroll, all of whom encouraged and mentored me throughout the process. While this book has changed substantially from the dissertation that provides its basis, the work I do today would not be possible without the thoughtful attention and guidance that the CUNY faculty provided and the support of an English Program Dissertation Fellowship that helped me launch this project.

Over the years, as I have refined and expanded this project, I have benefitted from the feedback and suggestions I've received in various Shakespeare Association of America seminars, where I have shared early drafts of portions of this book as seminar papers; at Renaissance Society of America and Blackfriars conferences, where I have likewise presented ideas that now feature in this book; and from a grant from the Folger Shakespeare Library to attend the "Shakespeare and the

Problem of Biography" conference, which provided invaluable insights into the collaborative construction of Shakespeare's life story that inspired much of my thinking in Chapter 4 of this book. As these various conferences and seminars have led to publication and collaboration opportunities, I am indebted to the support, feedback, and motivation of a number of collaborators who have further propelled, refined, and encouraged my work: Sujata Iyengar, Louise Geddes, Valerie Fazel, Laury Magnus, Devin Byker, and the late and wonderful Christy Desmet.

I would also like to thank Robert van Krieken, who reached out to me shortly after I completed my dissertation to express his admiration for my historical inquiry into celebrity and invited me to contribute to a special issue of *Historical Social Research* on "Celebrity's Histories." Robert's encouragement, along with the feedback he provided for my essay on Richard Tarlton's early modern celebrity, have helped me hone and refine my thinking on celebrity as a whole. Portions of Chapters 1 and 2 first appeared in this essay, "'The wonder of his time': Richard Tarlton and the Dynamics of Early Modern Theatrical Celebrity" for the *HSR* Special Supplement.

As an Associate Professor of English at Rhode Island College, I could not ask for a more supportive, collegial department from which to continue my work. I am indebted to RIC for the sabbatical leave I was provided to write this book, as well as to the Faculty Research Grants that have facilitated my continued research. I am especially grateful for my colleagues in the English Department—especially the dear, late Daniel M. Scott, III—as well as Alison Shonkwiler, Stephen Brown, and Carrie Shipers, who have all provided me with assistance and encouragement along the way. I am also thankful for the amazing students I work with at RIC. They never cease to offer new and exciting ways to think about Shakespeare.

I have many friends to thank—friends like Jeff, Elle, and Amy who have always cheered me on and provided a sounding board—but I reserve my most profound and humble gratitude for my family, without whom I would never have been able to complete a dissertation, much less this book. My husband, Noel; my parents, Gary and Maria; and my parents-in-law, Karen and Brent, have provided me support in ways too great and diverse to adequately acknowledge here, but I am deeply grateful for their unceasing presence, motivation, and assistance. I also thank the star of my universe—my son, Cooper—who inspires me every day in ways he cannot understand.

Introduction

> Now, now, you stars that move ...
>
> (King John 5.7.74)[1]

In an exquisitely piquant moment of dialogue from Billy Wilder's iconic 1950 meditation on stardom, *Sunset Boulevard*, William Holden's Joe Gillis finds himself in the opulent home of a glamorously attired and strangely familiar figure. He studies her face before asking, "Haven't I seen you before? I know your face." She, in turn, threatens to call her servant on her impudent intruder, but Joe presses on. "You're Norma Desmond," he exclaims in sudden realization. "You used to be in silent pictures. You used to be big!" Then, with a haughty stare and eyebrows arched in indignation, Gloria Swanson's Norma responds coolly yet emphatically, "I am big. It's the pictures that got small" (Wilder 1950).

It is not only Norma's delusional audacity, but her poignant acknowledgment of an unavoidable reality that offers up what is perhaps the second-most oft-quoted line of Wilder's classic film-about-film (right after "Alright, Mr. DeMille, I'm ready for my close-up."). Norma's immovable belief in her lasting star power in an industry that has moved onto new frontiers confers both a tragic fantasy and an inevitable truth—not only that stars rise and fall, but that the very media through which stars are born likewise evolve, and with that shift in platforms assuredly come new audience demands, expectations, and dynamics of engagement. Norma's lament is an enduring one that has propelled similar elegies for fallen stars and the fallen media upon which they had once ascended, from Charlie Chaplin's washed-up stage clown on the cusp of an emerging film industry in *Limelight* (Chaplin 1952) to Paul Thomas Anderson's 1997 *Boogie Nights,* which charts the end of the theatrical-release porn industry, and with it the box-office porn star, in light of porn's migration to VHS. Each of these films echoes the reality that Norma, in her steadfast denial, refuses to confront: that star power is not only a highly ephemeral phenomenon, but a highly contingent one as well, reliant upon the medial structures from which it emerges.

While *Sunset Boulevard* may provide one of the most iconic iterations of this common entertainment-industry lament, similarly fraught requiems for fallen formats extend well beyond the confines of the film era. Consider, for example, Robert Greene's 1592 polemic upon recent developments in the early

DOI: 10.4324/9780367808976-1

modern London theater scene. Like Norma, Greene "used to be big," specifically as the self-professed, former "Arch-plaimaking-poet" (Sig. E1). If Norma refuses to adjust to her diminished star power in a changing industry, the university-educated playwright Greene wallows in his now depleted status in his biting and now nearly canonical *Greenes Groats-worth of Witte*. As the author analogously relays his own theatrical journey from desperate impoverishment to fame and fortune and back again, he recalls how the theater "famozed" (Sig. E1), then forsook him. Offered as a deathbed lament of his own moral failings in response to the seductive and corruptive capacities of the theater, Greene begs his contemporary playwrights to avoid a similarly fraught path and renounce the stage. Chief among the perils they face is an "upstart Crow beautified with our feathers" (Sig. F1v). Of course, that upstart Crow, outwardly adorned with the elegant plumage Greene has provided through his verse, is the actor-turned-playwright William Shakespeare, legibly rendered through the thinly veiled attack that follows:

> with his *Tygers hart wrapt in a Players hyde,* supposes he is as well able to bombast out a blanke verse as the best of you: and being an absolute *Iohannes fac totum,* is in his owne conceit the onely Shake-scene in a country.
>
> (Sig. F1v)

In Greene's invective, Shakespeare is figured as both the most pernicious and visible of a new class of "Puppets" reshaping the parameters of playmaking fame and robbing Greene, and his fellow University Wits, of their former eminence. The newly arrived player-poet, a hybrid "painted monster" (Sig. F2), has demeaned both the profession and Greene's place within it. "Remember Robert Greene," he directs his readers, "whom they have so often flattered" (Sig. F2).

Separated by time, space, and medium, both Norma Desmond and Robert Greene point to one of the few reliable givens in celebrity's long and variable history: to riff on Heraclitus, one of the few constants in the phenomenon of celebrity is change. Consumer tastes and cultural conditions that make one "big" or "famozed," even intra-medially, are volatile forces that operate through a consistent pattern of displacement. In *Sunset Boulevard,* Norma goes on to skewer the now-dominant talking film's insistence on "voices" over "faces." She asks Joe, "Have they forgotten what a star looks like?" It's an enduring question, and one that I would argue extends to the history of celebrity as a whole. The question notably does not ask if audiences have forgotten Norma specifically; what Norma asks is whether the unnamed "they" have forgotten what defines a star, just as her precise question attempts to frame celebrity only by the mechanisms that produced her own. For Norma, stars "look like," but stars must now *sound like* as well, and this discrepancy renders her question unanswerable, as looking like no longer makes a star; an entirely new ethos of celebrity has forced her, and the platform upon which she established her stardom, into obsolescence. Her desperate plea is not so much a lament for her own fallen star as it is an elegy for an entire mode of stardom lost to the progress of industry. That stars come and go is a common-sense adage; what Norma illuminates here is that systems of stardom are just as fleeting.

Greene, too, bewails the changing landscape of fame when he asks,

> Is it not strange that I, to whom they al have beene beholding: is it not like that you, to whome they all have beene beholding, shall (were yee in that case that I am now) bee both at once of them forsaken?
>
> (Sig. F1v)

That Greene reaches out to his contemporary playwrights in his dire warning suggests that, like Norma, he views his theatrical usurpation as not only a personal, but an existential crisis of industry. Have they forgotten, Greene seems to be asking, what an arch-playmaking-poet sounds like? But his focus on Shakespeare's and other player-poets' visibility and deceptive appearance—these "painted monsters," those "buckram Gentleman" wearing "our feathers" (Sigs. F1v, F2)—suggests that, as is the case with Norma, the ethos of engagement has similarly shifted, but in the opposite direction: poets don't just sound like now; as actor-writers, they must look like, too.

Both Norma's lament for the silent-film star and Greene's invective against the vagaries of the early modern theater offer two disparate discourses of fame that nonetheless converge in their mutual insistence on the inconstancy of celebrity. It is precisely this inconstancy that propels the central inquiries of this book. Even if Julius Caesar swears to be "constant as the Northern Star" (3.1.61), the stars, Polaris included, never stop moving. This unceasing mobility is just one of the many attributes that have allowed stars to provide such a fitting and enduring metaphor for the phenomenon of celebrity. Stars sparkle. They exert a gravitational pull. They arouse our wonder and compel our imagination, yet their light is easily eclipsed—by encroaching clouds or competing light equally—and the stars themselves remain in perpetual motion. This book is about the volatility of the stars, and one star in particular, William Shakespeare—"thou starre of Poets" (Jonson 1623, Sig. A4v), as Ben Jonson famously labeled him—who is, like all stars, a variable, mobile, and aggregated entity.

Shakespeare and Celebrity Cultures examines the robust relationship between the two enigmatic, notoriously unstable, yet undeniably puissant cultural forces of Shakespeare and celebrity, not only Shakespeare-as-celebrity, but Shakespeare's variant roles, from thoughtful inquisitor to paradigmatic model, within evolving cultures of celebrity. Beginning with the early modern culture of theatrical celebrity and continuing through Shakespeare's prominence in film, television, and our contemporary culture of digital stardom, this book argues that Shakespeare and celebrity have enjoyed a ceaselessly adaptive, symbiotic relationship since the final decade of the sixteenth century when Greene launched his polemic against the caprices of theatrical fame that favored Shakespeare. Just as the concepts, structures, and dynamics of celebrity participate in a ceaseless evolution informed and shaped by cultural and technological development, Shakespeare, too, is always in motion. As Valerie M. Fazel and Louise Geddes note, "what is collectively represented or defined as Shakespeare is continuously being reimagined or reconstructed in accordance with the affordances of the medium in which he appears and the purposes to which he is put to task" (Fazel and Geddes 2017, 2). In mapping out the overlapping terrains of two strikingly variable yet unquestionably potent cultural entities, this book aims to shed light on both Shakespeare's and celebrity's remarkable durability through ever-changing cultural and medial landscapes, illuminating the ways each entity has contributed to the vitality and adaptability of the other. Celebrity offers us new ways of thinking about Shakespeare, and Shakespeare offers insight into the phenomenon of celebrity.

In charting Shakespeare's relationship to celebrity from its early modern origins, this book quite consciously steps outside the generally acknowledged chronological parameters that circumscribe the preponderance of celebrity studies, which generally allow for a celebrity culture to exist no earlier than the eighteenth century. Partially due to the perceived modernity of the phenomenon of celebrity, to date, there has been little dialogue between the substantial and dynamic bodies of Shakespeare and celebrity studies. Michael D. Bristol offers one of the earliest and most important inquiries into the relationship between Shakespeare and celebrity in his 1996 *Big-Time Shakespeare*, in which he makes the provocative claim that Shakespeare has "achieved contemporary celebrity" as "the result of his circulation as a mass-cultural icon" (Bristol 1996, 3, 5). Following Bristol, other important investigations of Shakespearean celebrity have done much to uncover the intricate relations between Shakespeare and contemporary film- and new media-driven celebrity cultures: Jennifer Barnes's *Shakespearean Star: Laurence Olivier and National Media* (Barnes 2017) analyzes the ways that both twentieth-century film stardom and the ceaseless search for Shakespearean meaning resulted in Olivier's unique brand of celebrity; Anna Blackwell's *Shakespearean Celebrity in the Digital Age: Fan Cultures and Remediation* (Blackwell 2018) explores the ways both Shakespearean stars and fans digitally interact to shape Shakespeare's enduring legacy. However, these illuminating treatments of the intersections between Shakespeare and celebrity focus, as does the bulk of celebrity inquiry, on modern and contemporary paradigms of celebrity.[2] In turn, the handful of accounts of early modern celebrity, including Nora Johnson's *The Actor as Playwright in Early Modern Drama* (Johnson 2003), Alexandra Halasz's essay exploring the commercial aspects of Richard Tarlton's fame in posthumous circulation (Halasz 1995), S.P. Cerasano's discussion of Edward Alleyn's early modern celebrity (Cerasano 2005), and Louise Geddes's essay on the celebrity of the early modern stage clown (Geddes 2015), hold little dialogue with the contemporary celebrity theories that have thus far generally precluded early modernity from consideration. As this book aims to bring the early modern theater, Shakespeare and Shakespearean appropriation, and the substantial insights offered through contemporary celebrity studies into conversation, this book first and most critically insists on the existence of multiple and mutable celebrity cultures—that there is, in fact, no such thing as celebrity culture, or at least, a monolithic one with clearly defined parameters, able to be transposed from one time and place into another. To the contrary, with every technological and industrial development—from page to stage to screen, from the silent film to the talkie, from limited-release cinematic event to repeatable movie rental, from big screens to little ones and to even littler, transportable ones (where the pictures quite literally got small)—the dynamics that facilitate celebrity have evolved along with them. As David C. Giles has argued, "'celebrity' will manifest differently according to the different *affordances* of […] media" (Giles 2018, 21), and audience expectations of access and the thresholds for identificatory relationships are always contingent on the available modes of dissemination, along with a whole host of similarly evolving cultural and social factors. Thus, celebrity's contemporaneity demands, in some ways, exactly what Norma and Greene lament: an almost ritualized process of forgetting or forsaking. Celebrity can only maintain its currency through a perpetual process of palimpsestic displacement, not only by trading in yesterday's star for a newer, hotter one, but in restructuring celebrity dynamics at the pace of technological and cultural development even while holding firm to celebrity's central, core mechanisms of intense audience identification with and trade in its stars. In fact, the aforementioned woeful laments invite us to consider alternate modalities of celebrity that may have likewise faded into obscurity, and subsequently arisen, upon the advent of new tastes and technologies, as celebrity need not have looked like, nor sounded like, our own contemporary structures in order to play a vital role within any particular cultural or medial landscape.

Of course, such instability and perpetual adaptation begs an essential question of celebrity that has in the past decade proven a compelling if somewhat contentious inquiry regarding Shakespeare as well: given the capacity for ceaseless permutation, is there a stable entity at its core? A recent proliferation of work in Shakespeare and adaptation and appropriation across a range of media has provoked compelling debates as to what, exactly, we are discussing when we discuss Shakespeare, especially given the vast constellation of cultural products—from performance to artifact to the critical and creative enterprise engendered through social media—all travelling under the capacious name of Shakespeare. As Maurizio Calbi and Stephen O'Neill note, it is a question that "Shakespeare scholars […] never tire of asking: what constitutes 'Shakespeare'?" (Calbi and O'Neill 2016), and whether and where we might carve out the lines between what we label as Shakespeare, Not Shakespeare, or the cultural pastiche generally signaled as "Shakespeare." As Calbi and O'Neill explain,

> The indicative scare quotes around 'Shakespeare' often function as a performative gesture, our field's way of delineating the historical figure from a wider cultural phenomenon that encompasses adaptations across a range of cultures, genres and media, as well as citations and appropriations in popular culture.
>
> (Calbi and O'Neill 2016)

This "wider cultural phenomenon" points to what Douglas Lanier has called "Shakespearean rhizomatics": a concept modeled on Deleuze and Guattari's theory of the rhizome that describes

> the aggregated web of cultural forces and productions that in some fashion lay claim to the label 'Shakespearean' but that has long exceeded the canon of plays and poems we have come to attribute to the pen of William Shakespeare.
>
> (Lanier 2014, 27)

As Lanier explains, "Shakespearean meaning is available in the present only through processes of appropriation that actively create, rather than passively decode, the readings and values we attribute to the Shakespearean text" (25), and thus, a rhizomatic approach acknowledges that Shakespeare has never existed as a stable or undisputed text or field and that Shakespeare's perpetuity depends upon active reconstruction.

As *Shakespeare and Celebrity Cultures* subscribes to this rhizomatic formulation of Shakespeare that dispenses with the notion of an authoritative Shakespearean source at the core of the aggregated entity understood as Shakespeare (rendered here and throughout without the traditional winking air-quotes), I apply a similarly rhizomatic model to celebrity to suggest that celebrity, too, operates as an "aggregated web of cultural forces and productions" that resists singular, authoritative definition, or a somehow "pure" construction of celebrity beset by imitation, likeness, or prototype. Celebrity is, like Shakespeare, a continuously evolving, collaborative enterprise between famous figures; cultural, political, and economic conditions; medial environments; and variously defined publics. Celebrity is a process in a perpetually fluid state of active renegotiation, and this book aims to chart the significant and consequential overlays between two perpetually morphing and moving fields. Moreover, this book aims to demonstrate that the processes of celebrity have played, and continue to play, an important role in the production of Shakespearean meaning throughout the past four centuries and that celebrity is one of the integral cultural forces involved in Shakespeare's ceaseless regeneration. In turn, Shakespeare's cultural force likewise continues to shape the aggregated tensions encapsulated in the concept of celebrity. Just as the celestial stars emanate not from a solid, stable core, but a highly charged fusion of particles, the terrestrial stars, too, are fueled through a matrix of competing tensions.

Locating celebrity

"Celebrity," writes Simon Morgan, "is a notoriously difficult concept to pin down" (Morgan 2011, 96). In recent decades, the celebrity has been variously defined as "narrative" (Gabler 2009); a "system for valorizing meaning and communication" (Marshall 1997, x); "a known individual who has become a marketable commodity" (Morgan 2011, 98); and "a genre of representation and a discursive effect; it is a commodity [...]; and it is a cultural formation" (Turner 2014, 10). Much of the difficulty in isolating a coalescent definition or even a stable referent lies in celebrity's absolute refusal to stagnate. Celebrity is an amorphous process that hinges on contemporaneity, always contingent upon the technological platforms from which the stars emerge and the ever-shifting cultural conditions of celebrity production and consumption. Celebrity "espouses the rapid rhythm of current events," writes Antoine Lilti (2017, 6); it is a phenomenon "dedicated to the ephemeral" (Gabler 1994, xiii) and marked by "peculiar fragility" (Rojek 2001, 16). Paradoxically, the very immediacy of celebrity that prevents it from being pinned down is, to a large degree, precisely what distinguishes it from other systems of fame. As Sharon Marcus commonsensically but nonetheless imperatively emphasizes, "Celebrities are people known *during their lifetimes*" (Marcus 2019, 9), and this important distinction resonates throughout a number of components frequently cited as requisites of a celebrity culture, including the public's identification with and expansive dissemination and commoditization of famous contemporaries. Unlike cults of hero- or legend-worship that cluster around the great and honored dead, celebrity is bound by a mortal architecture, and whether celebrity is viewed primarily as a mode of storytelling or commodities exchange, it remains grounded in the necessarily ephemeral realm of human-to-human interaction, mediatized as that interaction may be. Celebrity requires dialogue, though the nature of that dialogue is highly contingent on the affordances of available platforms and the cultural conversations that sustain public interest. Further, celebrity dialogue takes many forms, from the literal dialogic exchanges between the famous and their admirers on Twitter, to the flesh-to-flesh encounters in theaters and concert halls, to the production and consumption of celebrity media. In all its patterns of exchange, celebrity happens in real time between human agents, which means that celebrity exchanges are both highly charged and fleeting, subject to the potentially volatile intensities, imbalances, and disruptions of all human relationships.

Faced with the inevitable hurdle of celerity's immediacy and unpredictability, the history of celebrity theory has operated less as an exercise in pinning down a precise definition than an examination of an ever-shifting series of relationships, juxtapositions, and tensions aimed at demystifying a phenomenon almost unanimously recognized as a potent and meaningful component in modern— and as this book argues, early modern—social, political, cultural, and economic relations. Fittingly reflective of their target of inquiry, celebrity studies, or star studies, remain in a perpetual process of revision, but even the earliest treatises on celebrity, largely preoccupied with discrediting what was deemed a troubling innovation of the mass-media age, tended to eschew direct definition in favor of distinctive juxtaposition if not outright oxymoron. Leo Lowenthal, for example, never used the term *celebrity* in his 1944 denunciation of "mass idols," but he carefully contrasted the dispiritingly visible "idols of consumption," or movie stars and athletes, to the traditional "idols of production," or politicians and successful professionals, who once enjoyed eminence (Lowenthal 2006

[1944], 130). The difference between the mass idol and traditional icons for Lowenthal and other early theorists lay in notions of deserved versus undeserved fame, and this relationship between notions of authentic, earned status and a fabricated, public sham propelled much early work in celebrity. In 1962, Francesco Alberoni oxymoronically defined the celebrity as the "powerless elite": prominent individuals who, though highly visible, held no institutional power and offered only "an escape into fantasy and an illusion of mobility" (Alberoni 2006 [1962], 119–120).

Such derisive condemnations, of course, speak to the recognition of celebrity's cultural potency, thereby necessitating forceful disavowal, and Daniel Boorstin's landmark 1961 *The Image* provides perhaps the most thorough and resonant entry in this early catalogue of disdain. Like his predecessors, Boorstin contrasts the deserved, time-tested fame of the socially productive, or "the hero," to an illegitimate, immediate, media-generated fame of celebrity. Also like his contemporary theorists, he describes the celebrity through a juxtaposition he terms "the human pseudo-event" (Boorstin 1992 [1961]), positioning the celebrity as the human embodiment of a staged, public-relations stunt. Unlike his cohorts, however, Boorstin also offered what is likely still the most oft-cited, though often glossed, definition of the celebrity: "a person known for his well-knownness" (Boorstin 1992 [1961], 57).

If Boorstin's definition and overall treatise drip with derision and emerge from a nostalgically mired belief in a foregone era of authentic greatness, this early work in celebrity theory also highlights two important features of celebrity worth re-examining. First, in describing the celebrity as a human pseudo-event, Boorstin usefully charts celebrity as a process-in-motion between various actors, rather than a firmly structured entity. Likening celebrity to an event underscores its mobility and immediacy, which underlie a number of subsequent explorations of celebrity: Robert Van Krieken, for example, points to the "constantly changing social practices" that inform celebrity society (Van Krieken 2012, 4); Ulinka Rublack deems "notions of celebrity" as "instances of fame" (Rublack 2011, 400); and Marcus likens celebrity to an ongoing "drama," dependent on a wide cast of players (Marcus 2019). Second, Boorstin's circular definition points to one of celebrity's central ambiguities and actually echoes the term's etymological origins: *celebrity*, which entered the English lexicon in 1831 to denote public persons, traces its origin to the Latin *celebritās*, meaning both "fame" and "the state of being crowded" (OED Online n.d.(a), *s.v.* celebrity, n.3). Unlike other icons of fame such as the hero or the legend, both posthumously bestowed honors that originally signified either superhuman strength or saintly piety respectively, the term *celebrity* speaks only to the mechanisms of fame, indifferent to causation. Therefore, the etymological origins of celebrity are similarly reflexive and place primary focus on the role of the public, or the crowd, through which the celebrity's fame circulates. Though Boorstin's definition is undeniably cynical, it usefully shifts attention from the famous figure to the socially interactive processes of well-knownness that sustain the figure's relevance, even as it highlights the ambiguity that might most distinguish celebrity from other modes of fame. Unanchored to any specific causative propellant, celebrity exists solely within the tensions of process, open to endless speculation, mutation, and variant revision.

While celebrity studies have, for the most part, long since dismissed the distinctions between celebrities and heroes, or between the value-laden notions of earned versus fabricated fame, it is fair to say that the frivolity and inauthenticity with which early theorists coded the celebrity still permeate public perception. As Su Holmes and Sean Redmond acknowledge, if "the term celebrity is ambiguous in its meanings [...] it can also imply (or confer) judgments about the topic or figure under discussion" (Holmes and Redmond 2006, 12), as the vacuity at the heart of the processes of celebrity—that is, its lack of a specific causative agent, or its ambiguous relationship to any verifiable notion of achievement—continues to color the concept of celebrity as "being acknowledged simply for being famous" (Bell-Metereau and Glenn 2015, 16). As Graeme Turner points out, such judgments are part of an "elite critique of the popular" that has often been particularly suspicious of publicity and promotion practices and the corporate ends they serve (Turner 2014, 19), and the absence of a stable core of accomplishment can lead to an over-simplified calculation of celebrity as merely the product of the publicity machine. But as Turner clarifies, celebrity "is not just the consequence of an accumulation of publicity handouts, advertisements, [or] chat show interviews" (19). Marcus, too, notes that while "no one can become a celebrity without media attention, [...] media coverage alone does not a celebrity make," and instead depends upon an interdependent relationship between media, publics, and the celebrities themselves (Marcus 2019, 3–4). Put simply, what Turner and Marcus helpfully elucidate is the commonsense truism that if celebrity were so easy to construct, if the celebrity could be cast at will through purposeful publicity, it would likely be far less exclusive and fickle, and lamentations on the caprices of stardom like Norma's and Greene's would not exist.

Of course, not every publicized performer becomes a star, nor are the factors behind certain celebrities' rises to prominence always readily apparent, and this central mystery of celebrity allure has long provoked critical speculation. In 1979, Richard Dyer provided both a provocative response to this enduring mystery and a compelling new direction in the study of celebrity with his highly influential *Stars*, in which he introduced a semiotic approach to celebrity. Stars, according to Dyer, function as cultural signs that can be read as texts, and thus, their significance can only be understood when historically and culturally contextualized (Dyer 1998 [1979]). Building off Max Weber's notion of *charisma,* in which certain individuals are thought to exude a set of "gifts [...] believed to be supernatural, not accessible to everybody" (Weber 1946, 55), Dyer argues that stars' "superhuman" capacities lie in a perceived ability to embody contemporary cultural tensions. The overarching tension embodied by stars, Dyer explains in *Heavenly Bodies* (1986), is the tension of being human in a capitalist society, as stars probe the boundaries between the private individual and the public roles the individual must perform. According to Dyer, "Stars articulate what it is to be a human being living in contemporary society" (Dyer 2004 [1986], 7).

Dyer's formulations of the star-as-text, celebrity's relationship with the capitalist structures that promote it, and stars' situatedness within cultural concern and social movement have influenced much subsequent writing on the subject of celebrity (this book included), perhaps most directly in P. David Marshall's *Celebrity and Power*, which expands beyond the world of the film star to consider the cultural roles of television, music, and political celebrities as well. Here, Marshall posits that the celebrity embodies the twin pillars of democracy and capitalism and, as with Dyer, operates as a sign that articulates value; specifically, "The celebrity embodies the empowerment of the people to shape the public sphere symbolically" (Marshall 1997, 7). Thus, much like the term's etymological origins and Boorstin's early circular definition, Marshall assigns primary agency in the production of celebrity to the public who also consumes the celebrity. Such democratizing capacities provide significant currency to the celebrity's theoretical distinction from other forms of fame, especially in its insistence on spectacular individualization and self-promotion, along with what Turner calls the "from below" mode of consumption: a consumer-producer relationship in which the public wields considerable power over the star's image and value through their active consumption and circulation (Turner 2014, 101–102).

In further attempting to atomize the celebrity and strip down its myriad cultural and discursive processes to an identifiable core, Lilti isolates "the curiosity elicited among contemporaries by a singular personality" as "the source of celebrity" (Lilti 2017, 6), and Turner gestures toward this same root of curiosity when he maps out "the precise moment a public figure becomes a celebrity" as the moment when popular interest in the figure shifts from public role to private life (Turner 2014, 8). Always embedded within notions of celebrity is a recognition that the public presentation of the self is an incomplete personal narrative, that there exists, as Chris Rojek explains, "a split between the private self and a public self" (Rojek 2001, 11), and that there is a fuller, more genuine, and more captivating narrative waiting to unfold behind the veneer of persona. But this curiosity, this intense desire to locate a celebrity's authentic personhood, is, too, an inherently unstable set of tensions, spurred on by piqued interest and sustained through a necessary absence that compels the desire to know more.

Joseph Roach has labeled these tensions "public intimacy": the interactions that render the celebrity "at once touchable and transcendent" (Roach 2006, 16), as "the very tension between their widespread visibility and their actual remoteness creates an unfulfilled need in the hearts of the public" (17). Fred Inglis similarly cites a dialectic of "knowability and distance" as central to celebrity allure (Inglis 2010, 11).[3] This precarious positioning between antipodal forces, which I will explore more fully as the "strange intimacy" of celebrity in Chapter 1, involves a ceaseless push-and-pull between celebrities and their audiences and maps out a fraught, fragile space for the perpetuation of celebrity dynamics, as forays too far into either the knowable or the distant threaten to disrupt the tensions that hold celebrity bonds in place. As Edgar Morin offers, the star must remain "*almost* at the disposition of her adorers" (Morin 2005 [1960], 25, emphasis mine), tantalizingly just out of reach in order to whet the public appetite, yet never satiate it.

Strange intimacy, as I will discuss in this book's first chapter, provides the heart of what Marshall has labeled the "affective economy" of celebrity (Marshall 1997, 75), as this persistent renegotiation of revelation and concealment facilitates the identificatory bonds between stars and their publics. For as much as celebrity necessitates processes of mass-dissemination for the star to reach ubiquity and commoditization to facilitate both open exchange and communal ownership of the celebrity image, perhaps celebrity's most central dynamics lie in the highly personal arenas of desire and identification. Audiences make affective investments in celebrities as much as they make financial ones, and celebrity consumers authorize their sites of personal, identificatory investments to speak on their behalf to become what Lawrence Grossberg calls a "surrogate voice" with the authority to "organize their emotional and narrative lives and identities" (Grossberg 2006, 587). However, as Gary C. Woodward has argued, "Identification thrives on first impressions and limited knowledge [and] withers in the glare of sustained attention" (Woodward 2003, 69), as genuine intimacy, or the unimpeded reciprocal exchange of desires and vulnerabilities, invariably reveals the distancing gulfs between persons that thwart empathic identification. This brittle meeting space between celebrity and public, sustainable only in the space of limited disclosure, explains in part why the never-truly-knowable celebrity can become a locus of impassioned identification in what scholars have variously referred to as the "pseudo-social" (Caughey 1984) or "para-social" (Horton and Wohl 1956) interactions between stars and their publics. These relations between distant persons, in which sustained but generally one-way intimate revelations are exchanged between people who never meet, can become the foundational structures upon which consumers establish their identities.

The intensely human basis of celebrity dynamics is part of the reason why such strict chronological barriers have been erected around the phenomenon's existence. In *The Frenzy of Renown*, Leo Braudy offers a sweeping history of fame since Alexander the Great and traces the kind of individualized fame that informs celebrity to fifth-century Athens (Braudy 1986, 585); however, he is careful to distinguish contemporary forms of popular mediatization from the fame of legendary figures hailed from antiquity through the middle ages that spread through the public consciousness quite gradually, "when the means of communication were slow and the methods primitive" (1986, 15).[4] Because celebrity rests upon, as Rublack has argued, "imaginary relationships with well-known people" (Rublack 2011, 400), and as celebrity must remain ever tethered to a live body, it requires a rather extensive and rapid means of dissemination to facilitate bonds between living persons as well as to allow the famous figure to reach such pervasive representation. Nearly all critical accounts hold an organized mass-media as a fundamental requisite of a celebrity culture, as celebrity hinges upon an immediate and repetitious relevance substantial enough to reach ubiquity, which has generally precluded the early modern era from consideration. Inglis's *A Short History of Celebrity*, for example, lists the circulation of newspapers as one of the necessary conditions for celebrity to emerge (Inglis 2010); Boorstin deems celebrity the byproduct of the "Graphic Revolution" (Boorstin 1961, 47); and Rojek holds "mass-media representation [as] the key principle in the formation of celebrity" (Rojek 2001,13). Perhaps cultural and film historian Neal Gabler sums up these arguments most succinctly: "No media, no celebrity" (Gabler 2009).

A number of celebrity treatises further pare down the mass-media requisite to particular forms of mass-media, notably film, and much foundational work in celebrity theory claims celebrity as either the exclusive property of film or a derivative offshoot of the old Hollywood studio star system. In 1960, Morin argued that, "A stage actor has never become a star" to the degree of the film star (4), even though the very terminology he employs—*star*, as denoting famous performers—emerged from the eighteenth-century London theater (OED Online n.d.(b), *s.v.* star n.4c). But as Norma demonstrates in *Sunset Boulevard*, new medial formats invariably give rise to new audience expectations and dynamics of engagement, and the affordances of any particular medium actively restructure the processes of identification at the heart of celebrity. If audiences forgot Norma, audiences and critics alike can easily forget the structures once capable of forging strong affective bonds between stars and their publics. Though celebrity studies have certainly grown much more expansive in scope, a great deal of criticism continues to circumscribe the phenomenon within the temporal, if not the medial, borders of the film era. Richard Shickel argues that "there was no such thing as celebrity prior to the beginning of the twentieth century," with any similarly premodern structures only "celebrity-like" (Schickel 1985, 23), and Turner speaks for the contemporarily dominant strand in celebrity theory when he acknowledges his inclination toward the "standard view—which is that the growth of celebrity is historically linked to the spread of the mass media" (Turner 2014, 11).

In recognition of the celebrity's shifting dynamics of engagement, a small but growing body of historical inquiry has emerged to investigate cultures of premodern celebrity and frequently looks to the long eighteenth century as the genesis of celebrity, even as such work tends to cling to the same kind of rigorous temporal bordering its historical probes initially resist: Lilti cites the mid-eighteenth century as the "first age of celebrity" (Lilti 2017, 12); Inglis deems celebrity a "no more than 250-year-old phenomenon" (Inglis 2010, 8); and Stella Tillyard argues that "celebrity appears to have been made in the eighteenth century" (Tillyard 2005, 61).[5] Other scholars locate celebrity's inception in the nineteenth century (McDayter 2009; Mole 2007; Ponce de Leon 2002) and tie the phenomenon to the spread of urbanization, photography, and mass-circulating newspapers. A handful of outliers have stepped beyond the historical boundary of 1660 to consider celebrity structures, or at least what are deemed as productive forebears, in the cult of medieval saints

(Kleinberg 2011), or in the publicity strategies of sixteenth- and seventeenth-century monarchs (Sharpe 2009).

As one of the most important voices in expanding the strict historical parameters often imposed upon celebrity scholarship, Van Krieken has advanced the argument that an overly restrictive model of celebrity precludes serious and important inquiry into the phenomenon's long history of social significance. Contrary to the aforementioned medially circumscribed models, Van Krieken compellingly argues that, "Celebrity has had a variety of configurations, purposes, and effects" and that, "Seeing how celebrity operates in very different historical contexts and configurations reveals key aspects of its inner logic, mechanisms, and dynamics that would otherwise not be apparent" (Van Krieken 2018, 26). Morgan, too, suggests that the "the insights of modern celebrity theory" offer valuable tools through which we can "identify particular historical moments" outside of modernity in which "an identifiable celebrity culture existed" (Morgan 2011, 95). To this end, Rublack proposes some provocative and potentially expansive questions:

> How has the phenomenon of transient fame itself been reflected on and how have ideas about what makes people famous or infamous changed? In other words: why assume that there is a definition of celebrity or fame as stable referent? The point of critical history for me is to render the very idea that there should be a definition of celebrity as a clear conceptual category problematic.
>
> (Rublack 2011, 400)

Like Van Krieken, Rublack adopts a fluid conceptual view of celebrity, uncircumscribed by medial parameters but framed instead by broader questions of the episodic, unstable, and fleeting instance of fame, which in turn allows for a broader scope of historical inquiry. This enhanced scope offers numerous insights into the shifting nature of celebrity and to its most central mechanisms, especially as the radical departures of our contemporary culture of digital celebrity force a reckoning on mass-media-centered models.

The proliferation of digital celebrity through social-media platforms underscores the limitations of celebrity paradigms set too firmly upon the pillars of unidirectional mass-media, as the one-way, traditionally commoditized flow of mass-media cannot account for the highly conversant, and data- rather than dollar-driven publicity strategies of the Twitterati, much less the rise of the net-star understood as the "influencer." But if today's digital celebrity landscape offers new structures of celebrity production-consumption, such developments invite further scrutiny of celebrity structures that do not resemble those built upon film, fanzine, or newspaper circulation, and to consider, as Morgan offers, how the insights of celebrity theory might find broader historical applicability in celebrity cultures that look very different from the ones that spawned critical inquiry into the phenomenon in the first place. For example, as I explore in this book's final chapter, an exploration of the social medium of Shakespeare's early modern theater offers valuable insights into the tensions of social-media-driven celebrity today, and a broader scope of historical interrogation may help to uncover, more generally, some of the key tensions of celebrity replicated and adapted in alternate medial environments.

As the title of this book conveys through its pluralizing "s," *Shakespeare and Celebrity Cultures* subscribes to a fluid model of celebrity yet operates through the considerable insights offered in modern celebrity theory, as well as valuable contributions in performance, economic, and digital culture theories. Perhaps most abidingly, however, this book adopts a rhizomatic approach, as formulated by Deleuze and Guattari, that resists the hierarchical organization, medial parameters, and chronology of origination and acceleration in favor of an interconnected web of signs and processes. A system of fame that both responds to and articulates contemporaneity and perpetuates through active economic, medial, and affective exchange cannot be frozen in time, pinpointed to specific media, or confined to a stagnant or even, as Rublack notes, a stable definition. But a rhizomatic model that resists rigid historical or medial borders in favor of a web-like assemblage of cultural forces illuminates some central workings of celebrity just as it disperses its productions. According to Deleuze and Guattari, the rhizome "ceaselessly establishes connections between semiotic chains, organizations of power, and circumstances relative to the arts, sciences, and social struggles" (Deleuze and Guattari 1987, 7). Appropriated from the botanical model of web-like root systems, the rhizome, Deleuze and Guattari write, "has no beginning or end; it is always in the middle, between things" (25). This book similarly locates celebrity as always an active process in motion "between things"—between famous figures and publics, between production and consumption, between intimacy and estrangement, between materiality and fantasy. Like the stars, celebrity is an intermediary between our known world and a transcendent beyond, and also like the stars, celebrity never stops moving.

Amongst the growing body of historical inquiries into the emergence of celebrity, one dominant trend has been to extend the commonly accepted twentieth-century parameters of celebrity, including its reliance on an organized mass-media, backward in order to demonstrate that the phenomenon's putative medial requisites can be found earlier than previously understood. However, even as this historical operation moves in reverse, it works ultimately in service of a linear story of celebrity, originating in a big-bang event of origin and gradually expanding forward and outward to the star systems of the twentieth century and beyond. In this book, I propose a view of celebrity that does not chart a clear trajectory from the inklings of prototype to its fully realized potential, nor one that necessitates any particular mediatizing structure, but instead recognizes that any celebrity culture—from the early modern culture of theatrical celebrity to the social-media-driven culture of digital celebrity—is a culturally, historically, medially contingent rhizomatic offshoot in the larger web of cultural production we call celebrity. While the Hollywood star system may have launched the field of celebrity studies, it is but one galaxy in an expansive universe of celebrity, with its particular structures no more fundamental to the mechanisms of celebrity than any other. So while celebrity can certainly emerge within the formations of mass-media, it can and does emerge through structures of theater, literature, social media, and other pathways of production as well. As Deleuze and Guattari argue, "The rhizome is reducible neither to the One nor the multiple" (Deleuze and Guattari 1987, 21), but instead depends upon the "collective assemblages" of the whole (9). Systems of stardom may appear and disappear, as both Norma and Greene lament, but as Deleuze and Guattari theorize of the rhizome, "A rhizome may be broken, shattered at a given spot, but it will start up again on one of its old lines, or on new lines" (9). That is, individual paradigms of stardom may wither in the face of technological, medial, or cultural development, but celebrity has proven amply capable of regenerating along new lines and by repurposing old ones, and this book explores both old and new lines of celebrity and the inner logic that compels its ceaseless adaptation.

As I chart a series of relationships between the variable and aggregated entities understood as Shakespeare and celebrity throughout this book, I return to a foundational theoretical text rightfully dismissed for its derision but valuable in its understanding of celebrity as a process: Boorstin's highly polemical *The Image*. Like Boorstin, though with none of the contempt that compels his treatise, I offer here that celebrity is an event, a momentary convergence of persons and tensions. This event specifically offers a potent and immediate intersection of three powerful forces often cited in contemporary celebrity theory—dissemination, commoditization, and identification—through which fame, public ownership, and strong affective bonds meet, allowing public individuals to rise like stars in the popular imagination and providing the publics that produce and consume them a vehicle for the negotiation of their cultural environments. Celebrity, then, is neither strictly person, nor narrative, nor sign, nor commodity but, like a star, a highly charged fusion of elements. As events, however, these momentary meetings of various social forces are by necessity fleeting, as modes of dissemination, processes of economic exchange, and thresholds of identification are invariably contingent processes. But celebrity is a capacious and highly adaptable cultural form, as even a scant survey of recent texts in the field demonstrate, from Crystal Abidin's *Internet Celebrity: Understanding Fame Online* (Abidin 2018) to Edward Berenson and Eve Giloi's *Constructing Charisma: Celebrity, Fame and Power in Nineteenth-Century Europe* (Berenson and Giloi 2013) to Guy Davidson's *Categorically Famous: Literary Celebrity and Sexual Liberation in 1960s America* (Davidson 2019). As this small sampling of the proliferation of highly compartmentalized celebrity studies attests, the social and affective forces that intersect in the event of celebrity can converge within various temporal and medial landscapes.

Shakespeare and celebrity cultures

As Lucy Riall offers in a 2007 article for *History Today*, "The history of celebrity has still to be written" (Riall 2007) and while this book does not claim to offer a definitive point of origin for the phenomenon of celebrity, nor does it claim that one even exists, it does aim to expand celebrity's putative historical parameters and contribute to ongoing historical inquiry as it maps a constellation of relationships between Shakespeare and various cultures of celebrity. I pair celebrity with Shakespeare here not in service of a linear trajectory nor to suggest a birth for the phenomenon, but with the aim of uncovering through proximal, shared, and intersecting relations some of what Van Krieken labels the "inner logic, mechanisms, and dynamics" of each entity (Van Krieken 2018, 26). As any history of Shakespeare can readily profess, Shakespeare's trajectory from his birth to today is not a linear narrative, nor even a gradually expansive and intensifying set of practices; Shakespeare exists today as an aggregate of thousands of texts and artifacts, rises and falls in popularity and prominence, variable technologies, adaptations and appropriations, popular fantasies and fabrications. There is no single story of Shakespeare, nor is there a single story of celebrity. Both are sites where multiple processes meet; both possess a keen, chameleon-like capacity for adaptation; and both arrive for us today as indeterminable assemblages of the bodies, narratives, images, and practices that have sustained them.

In acknowledgment of both Shakespeare's and celebrity's aggregatory variability, this book is organized as a series of intersections and relationships between Shakespeare and various arenas and modes of celebrity. While this book begins with the early modern stage and concludes in digital frontiers, it is not meant to suggest a teleological chronology but rather a map of the ways Shakespeare and celebrity have intersected on the stage, in print, through political structures, in Shakespeare's own body, and in digital platforms. The first three chapters are concerned primarily with early modernity, where a yet-living Shakespeare and celebrity first interacted on pages and stages, while the final two chapters examine Shakespeare's enduring relationship with celebrity once he shuffled off this mortal coil.

Chapter 1, "Stars in Deed," takes a remarkable proclamation in Shakespeare and Fletcher's *Henry VIII* as both the chapter's and this book's initiating inquiry. When, in the play's dramatization of Anne Boleyn's coronation procession, a group of gentlemen onlookers pronounce the figures parading before them to be "stars indeed" (4.1.54), they bestow a new, lively, and theatrical twist upon a classical signifier of posthumous renown and, thus, offer up a provocative point of entry into Shakespeare's relationships with the stars. This chapter then explores the theatrical dynamics that converge upon the early modern stage to facilitate the presence of stars indeed, including the wonder and strange intimacy between audience and actor engendered through performance and the ways that theatrical celebrities coalesce and enfranchise the playgoing public to elevate momentarily spectacularized individuals into stars. As this chapter explores, primarily through the guidance of performance theories, Shakespeare and his contemporaries regularly interrogated the star-making processes that *Henry VIII* encapsulates in the aggregated construction of "stars indeed."

Chapter 2, "A Commodity of Good Names," begins with Shakespeare's lament in Sonnet 111 that his "name receives a brand," as he bemoans one of the troubling consequences of theatrical celebrity: his famous name has become a publicly traded commodity, molded through circulation and public assessment. This chapter examines the ways that the names, images, and narratives of early modern theatrical celebrities, including Shakespeare, detached from their persons to become commoditized goods on the market as it traces the tangled journeys of several notable early modern theatrical celebrities, including Richard Tarlton and Will Kemp, through various stages, pages, and goods. Building from the theoretical principles of consumption, production, and social circulation of Arjun Appadurai and Michel de Certeau and the historical research of Jean-Christophe Agnew, this chapter posits that the celebrity trade assigned a human face to the invisible tensions of market exchange and credit culture for early modern Londoners. This chapter thus concludes with an analysis of *The Comedy of Errors*, in which Shakespeare probes the ways famous names can spiral outside of individual control in the market, and individuals, as he laments in Sonnet 111, are then forced to negotiate their social identities amidst competing public projections.

With analyses of the 1995 Richard Loncraine-directed adaptation of *Richard III* as well as Shakespeare's *Richard III* and *1 Henry IV*, Chapter 3, "The Celebrity's Two Bodies," considers both the conference and conflict between the seemingly inverted models of authority encapsulated in king and celebrity. In this chapter, I suggest that celebrity offers a demotic re-articulation of the king's divinely appointed second body, and that Richard, Henry, and Hal court their publics to project upon their persons a popularly appointed second body of celebrity as a substitute for the *character angelicus* that their shaky birthright claims do not afford them. Contextualized within an early modern culture of what David Scott Kastan has called "spectacular sovereignty" as well as striking historical confrontations between royal and celebrity power on the stage and in royal presentation, this chapter argues that Shakespeare's histories offer the playwright's most extended meditations on the structures of celebrity, with staged kings who calculatedly withhold their royal presence in order to solicit the public's collaboration in the cultivation of their celebrity.

While the first three chapters deal primarily with early modern celebrity structures and Shakespeare's relationship to those structures as both active contributor and probing inquisitor, Chapter 4, "A Shakespeare that Looks Like Shakespeare," shifts focus to consider Shakespeare's own status as a celebrity and, specifically, the status of his corporeal, celebrity body. As this chapter argues, Shakespeare's audiences have, since his own lifetime, participated in a ceaseless pursuit of an appropriately Shakespearean somatic body to house his body of work—shaping that body out of words and images or in the bodies of the actors who bring his work to stage and screen. This hunt for Shakespeare's body, I argue, is a function of his enduring celebrity: a second, collaboratively crafted self perpetually made and re-made flesh through the projection and speculation of readers, admirers, scholars, and fans. Beginning with the work of Shakespeare's contemporaries, who versified his body into being from the raw materials of his plays and poems; continuing through the Shakespearean celebrities who offered Shakespeare's disembodied legacy a new human home; and concluding with the fictionalized character of Shakespeare on TV, this chapter argues that, as an inversion of typically understood celebrity dynamics, Shakespeare's publics have been participating in a centuries-long project to craft a public face to anchor the complex interiorities with whom they have grown attached.

This book's final chapter, "#shakespeare," continues discussions of Shakespeare's celebrity as it moves into today's ever-fluid domains of digital culture. Digital celebrity Shakespeare positions Shakespeare—as the print page, stage, big screen, and little one have done before—on the forefront of emerging technology and its distinct affordances, and this chapter explores the various incarnations Shakespeare's celebrity has assumed online, from Twitter handle to AI-generated chatbot. However, as this final chapter argues, digital celebrity's unique affordances find little precedent in the twentieth-century celebrity structures that so often take center stage in celebrity scholarship, and thus, I look back to the collaborative environment of early modern theatrical celebrity for navigational guideposts through the matrix of digital Shakespeare's participatory networks. Here, I position new media celebrity as a rhizomatic offshoot of theatrical stardom—"new lines," as Deleuze and Guattari suggest, spawned of old ones—and a particularly revelatory one at that. Digital celebrity, and digital celebrity Shakespeare in particular, offer a meta-articulation of established celebrity paradigms, rendering apparent through identifiable links, hashtags, and self-reflexive content the processes of performance, strange intimacy, and collaboratively constructed second selves. Digital celebrity offers up previously unseen processes to pixelated visibility and new modes of critical scrutiny. This final chapter also offers a rhizomatic offshoot of this one, in that it reiterates in practice the theoretical assertions outlined here—that not only are celebrities ephemeral entities, but celebrity cultures are as well, as entire star systems flicker in and out of existence at the rate of technological innovation, changing cultural fixations, and patterns of social exchange.

As this map of the stars charts various resonances, overlaps, and intersections between Shakespeare and celebrity, it is important to note here at the onset that this book uses the terms *celebrity* and *star* interchangeably, even as I acknowledge that these terms can hold quite different meanings in various scholarly treatments. While *star* remains the predominant terminology in film studies, and *celebrity* is often figured as encompassing a much broader scope of applicability—extending, for example, to prominent chefs, notorious criminals, or famous business leaders—this book consciously rejects the "less prestigious lineage" often ascribed the celebrity as opposed to the star (Holmes and Redmond 2006, 10, 11), as this divide in many ways resuscitates the value-laden judgments that mark early celebrity treatises and position celebrity as superficial, frivolous, or unworthy of serious critical inquiry. The term *star*, as the first chapter will explore more fully, predates the term *celebrity*, as it metaphorically invokes connotations that would later attach to the concept of celebrity, such as the celestial stars' elevated visibility, magnetism, and capacity to provoke the public's contemplation. These capacities apply to celebrities of various arenas, regardless of the relative value assigned their public status. As Rebecca Bell-Metereau and Colleen Glenn argue, "the difference between a star and a celebrity remains […] nebulous" and that, "Attempts to distinguish between the two categories of star and celebrity reflect academia's tendency to perpetuate boundaries no longer recognized in public discourse" (Bell-Metereau and Glenn 2015, 16).

Despite the frivolity often attributed the stars, and even more so when housed under the category of celebrity, as Holmes and Redmond argue,

> Stars and celebrities *do* matter; they 'house' our dreams and fuel our fantasies; they address and represent (often implicitly) some of the most important political issues of the day, and they can give us both ephemeral and lasting pleasure, even if, in the end, this is a pleasure built on artifice and the lie of the possible.
>
> (Holmes and Redmond 2007, 8)

To add, I'd also suggest that celebrity matters in many of the ways that Shakespeare matters, as a rich interplay of words and images, an amalgamation of people and performances, a cross-section of the convergence of social, cultural, political, and affective forces. As each of these targets of inquiry snakes its way through time and media, each both inflects and becomes inflected by the passions and processes of the landscapes in which they emerge, as both Shakespeare's and celebrity's diverse audiences collaboratively reshape and become shaped by them. A deep dive into the core mechanisms and interactive processes of both Shakespeare and celebrity can offer us insight into platforms through which publics negotiate their cultural environments and glimpses into the unrecoverable forums of the ever-morphing popular imagination.

Notes

1 Unless otherwise noted, all citations from Shakespeare's plays and poems come from *The Norton Shakespeare*, 3rd edition (2016), edited by Stephen Greenblatt, Walter Cohen, Suzanne Gossett, Jean E. Howard, Katharine Eisaman Maus, and Gordon McMullan.
2 Blackwell also includes a chapter on "Pre-Digital Shakespearean Celebrity," which discusses the notable stardom of Shakespearean actors beginning with David Garrick and continuing through Kenneth Branagh (Blackwell 2018, 31–53).
3 Chris Rojek similarly argues that "celebrities seem, simultaneously, both larger than life and intimate confrères" (Rojek 2001, 16–17), and Richard Schickel's *Intimate Strangers* (Schickel 1985) explores a similar phenomenon in which audiences share an "affectionate—if slightly distant—regard" for celebrities (10).
4 Boorstin likewise notes of the fame enjoyed by past heroes: "his gestation required at least a generation" (1992 [1961], 62).
5 In *Theatre and Celebrity in Britain, 1660–2000*, Mary Luckhurst and Jane Moody similarly argue that "celebrity is above all a media production: only in the eighteenth century does an extensive apparatus for disseminating fame emerge" (Luckhurst and Moody 2005, 3).

References

Abidin, Crystal. 2018. *Internet Celebrity: Understanding Fame Online*. Bingley: Emerald.

Alberoni, Francesco. 2006 [1962]. "The Powerless 'Elite': Theory and Sociological Research on the Phenomenon of the Stars." Translated by Denis McQuail. In *The Celebrity Culture Reader*, edited by P. David Marshall, 108–123. New York: Routledge.

Anderson, Paul Thomas (dir.). 1997. *Boogie Nights*. Performed by Mark Wahlberg, Julianne Moore, and Burt Reynolds. New Line Cinema.

Barnes, Jennifer. 2017. *Shakespearean Star: Laurence Olivier and National Cinema*. Cambridge: Cambridge University Press.

Bell-Metereau, Rebecca and Colleen Glenn. 2015. "Introduction." In *Star Bodies and the Erotics of Suffering*, edited by Rebecca Bell-Metereau and Colleen Glenn, 1–28. Detroit: Wayne State University Press.

Berenson, Edward and Eve Giloi, eds. 2010. *Constructing Charisma: Celebrity, Fame and Power in Nineteenth-Century Europe*. New York: Berghahn.

Blackwell, Anna. 2018. *Shakespearean Celebrity in the Digital Age: Fan Cultures and Remediation*. New York: Palgrave Macmillan.

Boorstin, Daniel. 1992 [1961]. *The Image: A Guide to Pseudo-Events in America*. New York: Vintage.

Braudy, Leo. 1986. *The Frenzy of Renown: Fame and Its History*. New York: Vintage.

Bristol, Michael D. 1996. *Big-Time Shakespeare*. London and New York: Routledge.

Calbi, Maurizio and Stephen O'Neill. 2016. "Introduction" to #SocialMediaShakespeares. *Borrowers and Lenders: The Journal of Shakespeare and Appropriation* 10: http://www.borrowers.uga.edu/.

Caughey, John L. 1984. *Imaginary Social Worlds: A Cultural Approach*. Lincoln: University of Nebraska Press.

Cerasano, S.P. 2005. "Edward Alleyn, the New Model Actor, and the Rise of Celebrity in the 1590s." *Medieval and Renaissance Drama in England* 18: 47–58.

Chaplin, Charlie. 1952. *Limelight*. Performed by Charlie Chaplin and Claire Bloom. United Artists.

Davidson, Guy. 2019. *Categorically Famous: Literary Celebrity and Sexual Liberation in 1960s America*. Stanford: Stanford University Press.

Deleuze, Gilles and Felix Guattari. 1987. *A Thousand Plateaus: Capitalism and Schizophrenia*. Translated by Brian Massumi. Minneapolis: University of Minnesota Press.

Dyer, Richard. 1998 [1979]. *Stars*. London: British Film Institute Publishing.

Dyer, Richard. 2004 [1986]. *Heavenly Bodies: Film Stars and Society*, 2nd ed. London: Routledge.

Fazel, Valerie M. and Louise Geddes. 2017. "Introduction: The Shakespeare User." In *The Shakespeare User: Critical and Creative Appropriations in a Networked Culture*, edited by Valerie M.Fazel and Louise Geddes, 1–22. New York: Palgrave Macmillan.

Gabler, Neal. 2009. "The Greatest Show on Earth." *Newsweek*, December 11. http://www.newsweek.com/tiger-stalking-defense-our-tabloid-culture-755772009.

Gabler, Neal. 1994. *Winchell: Gossip, Power and the Culture of Celebrity*. New York: Vintage.

Geddes, Louise. 2015. "Playing No Part but Pyramus: Bottom, Celebrity, and the Early Modern Stage Clown." *Medieval and Renaissance Drama in England* 28: 70–85.

Giles, David. C. 2018. *Twentieth-Century Celebrity: Fame in Digital Culture*. Bingley: Emerald.

Greene, Robert. 1592. *Greenes, Groats-worth of Witte, bought with a million of Repentance.* London.

Grossberg, Lawrence. 2006. "Is There a Fan in the House? The Affective Sensibility of Fandom." In *The Celebrity Culture Reader*, edited by P. David Marshall, 581–590. New York: Routledge.

Halasz, Alexandra. 1995. "'So beloved that men use his picture for their signs': Richard Tarlton and the Uses of Sixteenth-Century Celebrity." *Shakespeare Studies* 23: 19–38.

Holmes, Su and Sean Redmond. 2006. "Introduction: Understanding Celebrity Culture." In *Framing Celebrity: New Directions in Celebrity Culture*, edited by Su Holmes and Sean Redmond, 1–16. London: Routledge.

Holmes, Su and Sean Redmond. 2007. "Introduction: What's in a Reader?" In *Stardom and Celebrity: A Reader*, edited by Su Holmes and Sean Redmond, 1–12. London: Sage.

Horton, Donald and R. Richard Wohl. 1956. "Mass Communication and Para-Social Interaction: Observations on Intimacy at a Distance." *Psychiatry* 19 (3): 215–239.

Inglis, Fred. 2010. *A Short History of Celebrity*. Princeton: Princeton University Press.

Johnson, Nora. 2003. *The Actor as Playwright in Early Modern Drama*. Cambridge: Cambridge University Press.

Jonson, Ben. 1623. "To the Memorie of the deceased Authour Maister W. Shakespeare." In *Shakespeare's Comedies, Histories, & Tragedies*. London.

Kleinberg, Aviad. 2011. "Are Saints Celebrities?" Some Medieval Examples." *Cultural & Social History* 8 (3): 393–397.

Lanier, Douglas. 2014. "Shakespearean Rhizomatics: Adaptation, Ethics, Value." In *Reproducing Shakespeare: Shakespeare and the Ethics of Appropriation*, edited by Alexa Huang and Elizabeth Rivlin, 21–40. New York: Palgrave Macmillan.

Lilti, Antoine. 2017. *The Invention of Celebrity*. Translated by Lynn Jeffress. Cambridge: Polity.

Lowenthal, Leo. 2006 [1944]. "The Triumph of Mass Idols." In *The Celebrity Culture Reader*. Edited by P. David Marshall. London: Routledge. 124–152.

Luckhurst, Mary and Jane Moody. 2005. "The Singularity of Theatrical Celebrity." In *Theatre and Celebrity in Britain, 1660–2000*, edited by Mary Luckhurst and Jane Moody, 1–14. New York: Palgrave Macmillan.

Marcus, Sharon. 2019. *The Drama of Celebrity*. Princeton: Princeton University Press.

Marshall, P. David. 1997. *Celebrity and Power: Fame in Contemporary Culture*. Minneapolis: Minnesota University Press.

McDayter, Ghislaine. 2009. *Byromania and the Birth of Celebrity Culture*. Albany: SUNY Press.

Mole, Tom. 2007. *Byron's Romantic Celebrity: Industrial Culture and the Hermeneutic of Industry*. New York: Palgrave Macmillan.

Morin, Edgar. 2005 [1960]. *The Stars*. Translated by Richard Howard. Minneapolis: University of Minnesota Press.

Morgan, Simon. 2011. "Celebrity: Academic 'Pseudo-Event' or a Useful Concept for Historians?" *Cultural & Social History* 8 (1): 95–114.

OED Online. n.d.(a). "celebrity, n." Oxford University Press, https://www-oed-com.ric.idm.oclc.org/view/Entry/29424 (accessed March 14, 2019).

OED Online. n.d.(b). "star, n." Oxford University Press, https://www-oed-com.ric.idm.oclc.org/view/Entry/189081 (accessed March 14, 2019).

Ponce de Leon, Charles L. 2002. *Self-Exposure: Human Interest Journalism and the Emergence of Celebrity in America, 1890–1940*. Chapel Hill: University of North Carolina Press.

Riall, Lucy. 2007. "Garibaldi: The First Celebrity." *History Today* 57 (8): https://www.historytoday.com/archive/garibaldi-first-celebrity.

Roach, Joseph. 2005. "Public Intimacy: The Prior History of 'It'." In *Theatre and Celebrity in Britain, 1660–2000*, edited by Mary Luckhurst and Jane Moody, 15–30. New York: Palgrave Macmillan.

Rojek, Chris. 2001. *Celebrity*. London: Reaktion.

Rublack, Ulinka. 2011. "Celebrity as Concept: An Early Modern Perspective." *Cultural and Social History* 8 (3): 399–403.

Schickel, Richard. 1985. *Intimate Strangers: The Culture of Celebrity in America*. Chicago: Ivan R. Dee.

Shakespeare, William. 2016. *Julius Caesar*. In *The Norton Shakespeare, Third Edition*, edited by Stephen Greenblatt, Walter Cohen, Suzanne Gossett, Jean E. Howard, Katharine Eisaman Maus, and Gordon McMullan, 1685–1750. New York: Norton.

Shakespeare, William. 2016. *King John*. In *The Norton Shakespeare, Third Edition*, edited by Stephen Greenblatt, Walter Cohen, Suzanne Gossett, Jean E. Howard, Katharine Eisaman Maus, and Gordon McMullan, 1097–1164. New York: Norton.

Sharpe, Kevin. 2009. *Selling the Tudor Monarchy: Authority and Image in Sixteenth Century England*. New Haven: Yale University Press.

Tillyard, Stella. "Celebrity in 18th-Century London." *History Today* 55 (6): 20–27.

Turner, Graeme. 2014. *Understanding Celebrity*, 2nd ed. Los Angeles: Sage.

Van Krieken, Robert. 2012. *Celebrity Society*. New York: Routledge.

Van Krieken, Robert. 2018. "Celebrity's Histories." In *Routledge Handbook of Celebrity Studies*, edited by Anthony Elliott, 26–43. London: Routledge.

Weber, Max. 2006 [1946]. "The Sociology of Charismatic Authority." In *The Celebrity Culture Reader*, edited by P. David Marshall, 55–60. London: Routledge.

Wilder, Billy. 1950. *Sunset Boulevard*. Performed by William Holden, Gloria Swanson. Paramount.

Woodward, Gary C. 2003. *The Idea of Identification*. Albany: State University of New York Press.

1 Stars in deed

Amid the sumptuous display and elaborate pageantry of Anne Boleyn's coronation procession in Act 4 of Shakespeare and Fletcher's *Henry VIII (All Is True)*, a group of unnamed gentlemen gathers to marvel at the illustrious individuals parading before them. With "the list/ Of those that claim their offices this day" in hand (4.1.14–15), the onlookers narrate the noble march across the stage with unbound glee:

SECOND GENTLEMAN: A royal train, believe me. These I know.
      Who's that that bears the sceptre?
FIRST GENTLEMAN: Marquis Dorset.
      And that, the Earl of Surrey with the rod.
SECOND GENTLEMAN: A bold brave gentleman. That should be
      The Duke of Suffolk?
FIRST GENTLEMAN: 'Tis the same: High Steward.
SECOND GENTLEMAN: And that, my lord of Norfolk?
FIRST GENTLEMAN: Yes.
                                    (4.1.37–42)

When the Second Gentleman finally spies Anne, he cries out, "Heaven bless thee!/ Thou hast the sweetest face I ever looked on" (4.1.42–43), before inquiring about the duchess, barons, and countesses fortunate enough to travel alongside her. Enraptured by the dazzling spectacle, he proclaims, "These are stars indeed" (4.1.54), to which his cynical companion adds, "And sometimes falling ones" (4.1.55).

   This brief but highly charged exchange between raptly attentive gentlemen spectators offers a provocative point of entry into Shakespeare's long and dynamic relationship with celebrity—most notably, in the remarkable, two-word construction the gawking gentlemen employ in designation of the noble entourage: *stars indeed*. While the term *star* as denoting "a very famous or popular actor, singer, or other entertainer" emerged only in 1751, the term had long functioned as a signifier of exceptional renown, tracing its roots to the classical notion that the gods could transform certain exalted mortals' souls, after death, into new stars (OED Online n.d.(c), *s.v.* star, n. 4c, 1d). In Book 15 of Ovid's *Metamorphoses*, for example, Jupiter commands Venus to fetch the soul "from Caesar's murdered corpse" in order to:

DOI: 10.4324/9780367808976-2

make it a bright star,
So that great Julius, a god divine,
From his high throne in heaven may ever shine.
(Ovid, 838–841)

Chaucer revivified this classical tradition in *The House of Fame* when the narrator, pondering what seems his imminent death, asks if Jove will "stellifye" him (Chaucer, 586), to which his eagle companion quickly assures, "Joves is nat theraboute [...] To make of thee as yet a sterre" (597, 599). Shakespeare, too, makes regular employ of this classical trope: in *1 Henry VI*, Bedford mourns the death of King Henry V and declares, "A far more glorious star thy soul will make/ Than Julius Caesar" (1.1.55–56); the Chorus's epilogue in *Henry V* apologizes for its imperfect tribute to "This star of England" (Ep. 6); Pericles proclaims on word of King Simonides' death, "Heav'n make a star of him!" (22.102); and at the conclusion to *Henry VIII*, Cramner predicts the baby Elizabeth's glorious reign and eventual demise by prophesizing that upon her death, she will "star-like rise as great in fame as she was, /And so stand fix'd" (5.4.46–47).

In the early English tradition, then, as in Ovid, the label *star* functioned not only as a marker of brilliant renown, but a strictly posthumous honor as well.[1] Thus, the Second Gentleman's assignation of *stars* upon the mobile and very much in-the-flesh parading nobles of *Henry VIII* offers up a strangely polytemporal and metatheatric twist on an otherwise fairly consistent trope. For the play's 1613 theatrical audience, many of the individuals enacted in the royal procession might well have been considered stars in the classical sense: their lives extinguished, their names and exploits continued to decorate the annals of English history. The Duke of Suffolk, Charles Brandon, for example, was a two-time commander of the English army and, according to the seventeenth-century antiquarian William Dugdale, "a person comely of stature and high of courage" (Dugdale 1675, 299). But the First Gentleman's sly addendum that these stars are "sometimes falling ones" complicates these figures' easy categorization as stars in the classical sense. For Ovid, and generally for Shakespeare as well, the honor was an indissoluble one: Jupiter places Caesar in the heavens so that he may "ever shine," and Cramner's prediction about the newborn Elizabeth later in the play stresses the permanence of her celestial positioning, as she will "so stand fix'd." To the contrary, the First Gentleman calls attention to the liquid nature of the nobles' fame, though he can only do so by stepping outside the diegetic space of the play to acknowledge a historical reality unavailable within. With a rhetorical wink to his contemporary playgoers, his quip calls up the eighty-year historical span between the 1553 event and its 1613 theatricalization, during which several of the processional nobles would descend quite sharply from their elevated positions to become relegated to the margins of English history. The "bold brave" Earl of Surrey, Henry Howard, would be accused of treason and generally regarded as a proud fool; he fell swiftly out of the king's favor and was beheaded at his order in 1547. Queen Mary would likewise have the Marquis Dorset's head for treason in 1554. Of course, the procession's most luminous star, Anne, enjoyed a complicated legacy during the play's initial staging, as her reputation remained haunted by charges of adultery while she was simultaneously hailed as the mother of one of England's most beloved monarchs.[2] All of these figures' stars, unlike the baby Elizabeth's, are unfixed and, in fact, quite certain to decline from their processional peak.

The First Gentleman's playfully sardonic, yet indisputable observation warrants a brusque "No more of that" from his companion (4.1.57), as his cold dousing of historical certitude dampens the Second Gentleman's otherwise unrestrained delight in the pageantry. Played off as an unsavory joke, the pointed rejoinder also calls attention to the gentlemen's liminal position both within and beyond the spectacle, at once both the onstage contemporaries to the marvelous procession they behold and, as evidenced by the First Gentleman's prescient foreknowledge, the savvy contemporaries to the theatrical audience with whom they share information unavailable to the onstage processors. It is from this temporal and theatrical limbo that the Second Gentleman proclaims the parading nobles to be *stars indeed*, adding a fitting qualifier to Shakespeare's only reference to live, staged individuals as stars. For as much as *indeed* may function adverbially to affirm the assessment—that is, these are truly and assuredly stars—it also simultaneously subverts the designation by declaring these stars to be *in deed*, or "in action, in actual practice" (OED Online n.d.(a), s.v. deed, n. 5b). Here, the modifying *indeed* assigns a definitionally impossible vitality to a strictly posthumous, fixed honor, but one particularly compatible with the stars' fleshly, mobile presence and mutable legacies. Unlike Ovid's, the procession's stars are yet active, motile, and fluid, with the First Gentleman's barbed retort all but negating the affirming potential of *indeed* with the irrefutable historical realities of *in deed*.[3] In pairing these linguistic incompatibilities, *stars indeed*, much like our contemporary *living legend*, becomes an oxymoron, allowing the Second Gentleman to enthusiastically exclaim in self-conscious contradiction what no existent word can aptly denote: a living star.

In *The Invention of Celebrity*, Lilti notes that long before the term *celebrity*, as denoting famous persons, made its nineteenth-century lexical debut, the "*topic of celebrity*," if not the specific title, emerged discursively through various media to "testify to a collective effort to think about a new phenomenon and provide the foundations, narrative or linguistic, with which individuals tried to navigate the strangeness of the social world" (Lilti 2017, 7–8). Lilti locates the dawn of this "new phenomenon" in the eighteenth century, but as I offer here, *stars indeed* provides one of many early modern examples of a discourse on the *topic of celebrity*. To be sure, the topic of celebrity, even and perhaps especially in the absence of a ready signifier to encapsulate it, is a complex and sprawling concept that speaks to a conflation of social, cultural, and economic interactions and developments that meet in the body of a famous individual. However, the concise, two-word construction *stars indeed* and the highly theatrical context within which it is spoken isolate and juxtapose a few particularly salient strains of its early modern theatrical incarnation: namely, the magnified and exalted presence of *stars*, the striking contemporaneity and fluidity embedded within their *in-deed* status, the theatrical context of the proclamation, and the vital role that the audience of gentlemen plays in their assignation. In its reorientation of a posthumous designation of eternal renown to a contemporary assessment of living, momentarily spectacularized individuals, *stars indeed* restructures a paradigm of enduring, celestial distinction into one of fleeting, terrestrial fame.

As this chapter explores, the oxymoronic construction, *stars indeed*, participates in a long tradition in the discourse of celebrity in its juxtaposition of competing tensions in order to capture through aggregate a process that resists easy definition. Like Alberoni's "powerless elite" (Alberoni 1962), Schickel's "intimate strangers" (Schickel 1985), or Van Krieken's "democratized aristocrats" (Van Krieken 2012, 8), Shakespeare and Fletcher pair incongruous elements in order to capture a special convergence of forces that transforms live, mortal bodies into stars. In this way, *stars indeed* holds a mirror to a larger cultural junction of competing forces taking place on the stage and proliferating beyond it—a momentary fusion of tensions that both enraptures and collectivizes an audience around the amplified significance of a spectacularized individual. This chapter aims to demonstrate and distill the aggregated theatrical dynamics that *stars indeed* both responds to and names: the dazzling presence that enraptures, the wonder and speculation such presence provokes, the intimacy of audience-actor exchange, and the manner by which audiences collectivize in their communal experience in the presence of their contemporary stars. As this chapter asserts, *stars indeed* is part of a wide-ranging early modern conversation on the *topic of celebrity* taking place on and around Shakespeare's theater.

Star presence/star absence

When the term *star,* as denoting famous performers, first appeared in print in the mid-eighteenth century, it arose from the English stage, specifically in the context of the "Theatric star" (OED Online n.d.(c), *s.v.* star, n. 4c). In 1761, David Garrick was hailed as "a Star of the first magnitude" (Victor 1761, 62), and again in 1765 as a "bright star" who "flew with the rapidity of lightning through the town" (Memoirs 1765, 224). Embedded within the designation of person as star is a forceful assertion of presence that outshines others in the star's midst—an exuded presence more lustrously magnified, more powerfully magnetic, and more keenly felt by audiences. "Being a star," writes Richard Schechner in *Performance Theory*, "is to be a person whose very presence transcends whatever activity s/he may be absorbed in" (Schechner 1988, 232). The theatrical celebrity's presence, according to Michael L. Quinn, is a quality of actors "that exceeds the needs of the fiction" (Quinn 1990, 155), a kind of extra-dramatic personal excess that spills out over the confines of character to pique the audience's curiosities and tease their desires. In the theatrical star, the partially obscured playing body unable to be constrained by the played part confronts the audience's desires in the intense yet fleeting experience of shared performance in the theatrical event. The result is, as Quinn says, "a bewildering flow of persons and images" (154)—a brief, but electric episode, captivating as it is disorienting, and one that leaves audiences in a state of "fascination" (Zazzali 2016), if not in the "experience of being overwhelmed" (Marcus 2019, 45).

When the Second Gentleman appropriates and modifies the classical *star*, he speaks to a similarly entrancing theatrical experience. Perched at the margins of a metatheatric play-within-a-play, he gawks and marvels at the spectacularly arrayed processors, eager to know who stands behind what part. He may also mirror the external audience's response to the opulently arrayed actors parading across the stage, reported to include in its initial staging the highly celebrated Richard Burbage, Henry Condell, John Lowin, and John Hemminges.[4] The Second Gentleman's enraptured experience is hardly without early modern precedent; a number of early modern theatrical commentaries attest to similarly potent and magnetic dynamics between audiences and actors. "He charmes our attention," Sir Thomas Overbury writes of the "Excellent Actor" in 1615. "Sit in a full theatre and you will thinke you see so many lines drawne from the circumference of so many eares, while the actor is the center" (Overbury 1615, Sig. M5v).[5] As Overbury positions the actor as the gravitational nexus around which the playhouse audience orbits, John Earle extends the actor's allure beyond the theater walls in his 1628 *Micro-cosmographie* when he writes of the player, "The eyes of all men are upon him" and that "waiting women spectators are over-eares in love with him, and Ladies send for him to act in their chambers" (Earle 1628, Sigs. E3, E5). Tributes to individual actors describe similarly beguiling magnetism. A funeral elegy for Burbage pays homage to the player's "enchaunting tongue" and "charming art" ("On the Death" 1825, 499); Charles Fitzgeoffrey describes the "thunderous roar of laughter [...] From all who saw" Richard Tarlton, such that "The heavens were all astonished" (Fitzgeoffrey 1881 [1601], xxiv). Long before the advent of the term *star* to describe the theatrical luminary, contemporary accounts of early modern actors demonstrate highly charged, visceral responses to the presence of players, suggesting that "audiences had as much interest in the player as they did in his character" (Tribble 2013, 185).

While the relations between celebrities and their publics involve a vast network of affective, cultural, and economic exchanges that extend well beyond the confines of a single medium, the star's genesis arises from what Lilti has called "the curiosity elicited among contemporaries by a singular personality" (Lilti 2017, 6). But if curiosity is a quotidian feature sustaining all manner of interpersonal relationships, the curiosity theatrical stars arouse in their audiences reflects the magnified circumstances of the theatrical encounter, where curiosity, under pressure, can translate to something more akin to enchantment—which the aforementioned "charmes" and "enchaunting tongue" seem to suggest. "To be enchanted," writes Jane Bennett in *The Enchantment of Modern Life*, "is to participate in a momentarily immobilizing encounter; it is to be transfixed, spellbound" (Bennett 2001, 5). In the presence of celebrities, we call that experience *starstruck*—a sudden flash of stunned entrancement when confronted with those whose personal excesses seem to surfeit the confines of their person. Gary Backhaus has discussed such aesthetic enchantment in the theater as a kind of "hyper-awareness": a heightened state of attention in which experiences and emotions can resonate more forcefully than in the mundane world of day-to-day living (Backhaus 2000, 26). As audiences must hang upon the actors' words and motions in the unrepeatable and unpredictable unfolding of the dramatic presentation, Backhaus argues that, "the unexamined suspension of doubt of the everyday life-world is existentially called into question" (28). In the theater, everyday expectations become fractured into worlds of innumerable and uncertain potentialities, and the actor, the magnified target of a thousand gazes, serves as the primary conduit through which these possibilities register.[6] Thus, the audience's hyper-awareness projects onto the body of the actor a kind of hyper-presence, an amplification of his or her being and significance as the center of aesthetic enchantment, and audiences can then become starstruck—transfixed, fascinated, perhaps even disoriented—by the larger-than-life presence of a human body endowed with the capacity to house the tensions of the theater.

Perhaps the most pointed and sustained meditation on the early modern actor's capacity to enchant his audience lies in Philip Massinger's *The Roman Actor*, first performed in 1626. In this Caroline tragedy, Domitia, a young mistress of Caesar Domitian, becomes so enraptured by the tragedian Paris that she claims an out-of-body experience during his performance. "What I saw presented/ Carried me beyond myself," she explains of her unrestrained behavior during performance. "I feel myself much indisposed" (3.2.291–292). The concubine Canis quickly confirms that it is the actor, Paris, rather than his verse or the character he performs, who has so aroused Domitia's fervor. Domitia, she explains, is "so taken" with "the tragedian's shape,/ that is to act a lover" (3.1.91, 92–93).

The Roman Actor participates in an ongoing early modern conversation regarding spectators', and particularly women spectators', susceptibility to the player's charms. Middleton's *A Mad World, My Masters* similarly includes a Courtesan who confesses in an aside during a performance, "an I were not married, I could find in my heart to fall in love with that player now" (5.2.32–33). But *The Roman Actor* stands apart in its atomization of the distinctly theatrical mechanisms that propel spectatorial desire to the point of disorientation. As Domitia reveals, she has designated Paris as the sum accumulation of theatrical experience. As she explains to her beloved,

> [...] thou whom oft I have seen
> To personate a gentleman, noble, wise,
> Faithful, and gamesome, and what virtues else
> The poet pleases to adorn you with,
> But that (as vessels still partake the odour
> Of the sweet precious liquors they contained)
> Thou must be really, in some degree,
> The thing thou dost present.
> (4.2.32–39)

Here, Domitia confesses that she believes Paris must contain within his person some part of every part he has ever played, as she renders his body a mere vessel where the lingering traces of all his variant roles converge. In short, she offers that, "Our Paris is the volume in which all [...] are curiously bound up" (4.2.41–43), as she projects onto him a larger-than-life presence—many lives in one, in fact. But this projection is not solely the product of the immediacy and intensity of the theatrical event, but a response to Paris's chameleon-like capacity to embody multiple roles within a single human frame. In his repeated performances, Domitia has become fixated on the constant of Paris's body, or the excesses of his person that enticingly sneak past role, even as she remains unable to discern a firmly locatable Paris amidst his many guises. She opts instead to fill those vacancies with her own projections, so that Paris becomes not only a selective accretion of every character he has ever embodied, but an accumulation of Domitia's projected desires as well.

As Domitia boils down her out-of-body experience and enchanted infatuation to a distinct set of theatrical impulses, *The Roman Actor* dramatizes a dynamics of engagement central to the theatrical star's allure, yet one that travels under multiple descriptors. As Domitia demystifies her desire, she ultimately centers on a paradoxical conflation of the presence of Paris's body in performance and the absence of a knowable person amidst his enacted characters. This confounding dialectic is, according to Schechner, at the heart of star "presence," which simultaneously "becomes a kind of absence," if not an entirely "blank screen" (Schechner 1988, 232, 233). As the curiosity and enchantment stars arouse hinge on an always as-of-yet unknown quality that stars exude, the self that peeks beyond the veneer of disguise but never fully reveals itself thus invites the audience's speculation and associations. Roach labels this interplay of "self-expression and self-erasure" simply as *It* (Roach 2007, 9):

> It is the power of apparently effortless embodiment of contradictory qualities simultaneously: strength *and* vulnerability, innocence *and* experience, and singularity *and* typicality among them. The possessor of It keeps a precarious balance between such mutually exclusive alternatives, suspended at the tipping point like a tightrope dancer on one foot; and the empathic tension of waiting for the apparently inevitable fall makes for breathless spectatorship.
>
> (8)

In Domitia's eyes, then, Paris might be said to have It: an alpha-and-omega capacity to be all things at once, and the gentlemen onlookers of *Henry VIII* likewise subscribe to a similar formulation when the Second Gentleman, overcome in the presence of Anne, declares her at once an "angel" as well as "all the Indies" (4.1.44, 45). She becomes, through the simultaneously revealing/concealing enchantment of spectacle, a figure of both heaven and Earth, with all the treasures of this world conflated with a transcendence of the next one.

As both Roach and *The Roman Actor* reveal, the stage provides a particularly conducive environment for the flourishing of these antipodal dynamics through the actor's repeated presence in multiple guises, allowing one actor to seem "all those gifts [...] bound up" in one body, even as the actor himself becomes erased in a maze of performance and projection (4.2.42–43). Paradoxically, Domitia's fixation demonstrates how an actor's larger-than-life excesses can translate to personal vacancy; being everything at once means being nothing specifically, and Paris becomes, in her eyes, precisely what she would like him to be: a living reification of her own desires. As Joanne Rochester argues, in *The Roman Actor*, the person of the actor is erased, rendering Paris "a blank slate, a field for the projection of concepts and desires" (Rochester 2010, 40). His intoxicating star presence fuses the presence of his spectacularized, staged body through multiple characters with the absence of the knowable actor, available only in the sporadic and seductive glimpses that emerge from behind the veil of performance.

Stars and wonder

As the star operates as a point of contact between a live, magnetic body and the recognition of the limits of ever truly knowing it, the star remains perched at the fragile intersection of audience desire and the performance that continues to solicit the desire it can never adequately sate. As a predecessor to It or star presence, the early modern English, too, offered an encapsulating signifier for this mesh of competing dynamics: the multivalent *wonder*, which similarly captured in aggregate the interplay of presence and absence that converge in the theater and in the person of the star performer. Wonder, as Philip Fisher theorizes, is akin to enchantment: it is a moment of "pure presence," he writes, "in which the mind does not move on" (Fisher 2003, 131). As both noun and verb, *wonder* denotes both marvels and the emotional response to them, as well as the desire to know more fully that which remains concealed (OED Online n.d.(d), *s.v.* wonder, n., v.).[7] Thus, in *wonder*, various strands of amplified presence and its disorienting absences intertwine; however, as Stephen Greenblatt relays, the term held a complex and tangled web of early modern connotations:

> Wonder—thrilling, potentially dangerous, momentarily immobilizing, charged at once with desire, ignorance and fear [...] the sign of heightened attention. The expression of wonder stands for all that cannot be understood [...] and at the same time insists upon the undeniability, the exigency of experience.
>
> (Greenblatt 1991, 20)

Wonder was also, according to Greenblatt, "yoked to possession" in its "unappeasable desire" (xi). In its vast array of affective properties, *wonder* stood in for much of what celebrity now encapsulates: it aroused passions, desires, and curiosity; it was urgent; it appeared as both apparent and unknowable; it elicited possessive, consumptive impulses that could never be fully satiated. And while Greenblatt's focus is the wonder generated in New World encounters, the term was strongly linked to the theater as well.

Wonder features prominently in early modern treatments of both theater more broadly and the specific persons who populate it. Jonson, for example, labels Shakespeare the "wonder of our Stage" in the First Folio (Jonson 1623, Sig. A4), and in 1640, the poet Leonard Digges describes Shakespeare's audiences as "ravish'd, with what wonder they went thence" (Digges 1640, Sig. Pilcrow 3v). Will Kemp titled the chronicle of his Morris dance from London to Norwich his *Daies Wonder* (Kemp 1600), and his clowning predecessor, Tarlton, one of the earliest and perhaps most consequential celebrities to emerge from the early modern theater, is described by the chronicler John Stowe as "the wonder of his time" (Stowe 1615, 697). As these various examples illustrate, wonder was neither the sole possession of player, playwright, or audience, but a fluid term attributable to all participants of performance. According to T.G. Bishop, wonder functions as an especially "potent gift" in theatrical production, and in Shakespeare's theater specifically, in that "it foregrounds the difficulty of [...] distinguishing a subject and an object of perception [...] and wonder becomes a kind of high-level 'switchpoint' for transactions between emotional and rational responses" (Bishop 1996, 4). In Bishop's formulation, theatrical wonder occupies a liminal space between cognitive and affective processes, not unlike Greenblatt's assessment of wonder's position between "all that cannot be understood" and "undeniability." Further, as Bishop notes, wonder is a phenomenon that even obscures the boundaries between the looker and the looked upon, the self and other selves, potentially facilitating an intimacy of communion and shared identificatory processes through its utter indecipherability. Fittingly, Bishop positions theatrical wonder primarily "with the actors who inhabit and enliven the play's 'parts' and who actively adjust the fit between self and role moment by moment" (170). Wonder, then, occupies a space between the spectating subject and the spectacular object, through which empathic transference takes place, facilitating the bonds that allow audiences to project speculation into the uninhabited middle ground forged between persons onstage and off.[8]

Shakespeare offers an extended meditation on the workings of theatrical wonder, though by omission rather than demonstration, in the rude mechanicals' farcical presentation of *Pyramus and Thisbe* that concludes *A Midsummer Night's Dream*. Like the coronation procession of *Henry VIII*, this play-within-a-play offers a metatheatric reflection on the practices of performance, but with a notable difference: if the internal audience to Anne's procession respond to the spectacle with delight and wonder, here the gathered audience to the players' inept performance of *Pyrmaus and Thisbe* demonstrates the stark opposite. As the stage-managing Quince offers a jumbled prologue to properly foreground the ensuing drama, he points out which actors are assuming which parts:

> Gentles, perchance you wonder at this show,
> But wonder on till truth makes all things plain.
> This man is Pyramus, if you would know,
> This beauteous lady Thisbe is, certain.
> This man with lime and roughcast doth present
> Wall, that vile wall which did these lovers sunder;
> And through Wall's chink, poor souls, they are content
> To whisper—at which let no man wonder.
>
> (5.1.126–133)

Immediately upon the prologue's conclusion, a spectating Theseus muses, "I wonder if the lion be to speak" (5.1.151), to which Demetrius responds, "No wonder, my lord; one lion may when many asses do" (5.1.152). In this moment of metatheatricality, in which the word *wonder* is spoken five times in a span of fewer than thirty lines, it is clear that, as Demetrius retorts, this is a play that involves "no wonder," not only through the ineptitude of its performers, but in Quince's purposeful demystification of theatrical process. As Quince informs his audience, his intent is to make "all things plain" so that his audience is no longer suspended in the wonder of the theater; thus, he highlights which actors play which parts before previewing the plot. Of course, this play-within-a-play offers a discernible counterpoint to the larger play that works primarily through the wonders of the disorienting and enchantingly dream-like fairy realm that calls the central characters' realities into question—the inarticulable "wonders" that Bottom struggles to "discourse" (4.2.26). To the contrary, this play's internal audience, as rendered apparent through numerous snide asides, never misrecognize the play as anything other than a fiction nor the players for anyone other than their unconcealed offstage identities. If assured unambiguity is Quince's goal in his prologue, it is also the end of wonder. The artisans' unskilled performance of *Pyramus and Thisbe* aims to make all things known and his players perpetually present, never absented in the shroud of role, and thus, Snug the joiner will inform his audience that he is not actually a lion, Bottom in the role of Pyramus will interject with a note about the actors' cues, and Starveling will announce, "Myself the man ' th' moon do seem to be" (5.1.236). Full disclosure combined with unconvincing dramatic display are here figured as antithetical to the kind of wonder that sustains the larger play and forges the beguiling bonds between actor and audience.

As the unskilled players halt the wondrous possibilities of misrecognition, projection, or enchantment by making all things plain, their exit from the stage is greeted as a welcome cessation of the audience's burdensome obligation to watch, rather than an invitation to speculation. Such dismissal of interest is sharply antithetical to Francis Bacon's formulation of wonder in his 1605 *The Advancement of Learning*, in which he deems wonder "the seede of knowledge" (Bacon 1605, Sig. B2v)—not knowledge itself, but the inspiration to grow and cultivate it. Bacon cautions against relying on wonder as a means of knowing;

wonder, he writes, is not "perfect" but only "broken" knowledge (Sig. B3), and thus, he positions wonder in much the same way as do Greenblatt and Bishop: as a cognitive middle ground that propels further discovery but has yet to reach it. Such is the dynamic at work in a snippet of verse from the poet Edward Guilpin who, years after a theatrical event, remains immobilized in the speculative space of wonder. In a 1598 epigram, Guilpin describes his memory of seeing the famed tragedian Edward Alleyn in the role of Cutlack the Dane, staged in 1594: "What humours have possess'd him so I wonder," Guilpin muses of "Allens Cutlack." "His eyes are lightning, and his words are thunder" (Guilpin 1598, Ep. 43). In this passage, the fiery intensity of the star meets an insatiable curiosity centered squarely on the person of Alleyn, to the extent that the poet probes the actor's humoral physiology to unravel the mystery of the actor's electrifying performance.[9] Even years after the performance, Guilpin remains suspended in the middle space between the desire to know and true knowing as he contemplates the intersection between the limits of his own understanding and a body so potent it is imagined as erupting in thunder and lightning. As Quinn notes of the theatrical celebrity, Alleyn is here remembered for his personal excesses that surpass the confines of character to arouse the spectator's curiosity, and Guilpin testifies to this curiosity's staying power, which has similarly slipped beyond the confines of the playhouse walls to become firmly lodged in the spectator's memory of performance.

The strange intimacy of theatrical celebrity

If *wonder* speaks, in early modern parlance, to that momentary convergence of bodies, enchantment, desire, and performance so powerfully charged that they initiate the complex affective bonds of celebrity, then Guilpin's recollection and persistent wonder suggest something of the manner by which these transient encounters can translate to lasting relations between stars and their publics. Celebrity theorists regularly term these bonds as the para-social interactions of celebrity, or the means by which audiences sustain relations with the stars who have captivated their attention yet remain socially and spatially distant from them. In 1956, Donald Horton and R. Richard Wohl coined the term "para-social" to describe "the simulacrum of conversational give and take" as occurs between celebrities and their admirers (Horton and Wohl 1956, 215), as they argue that while celebrity-audience relations originate through the same principles of "direct observation and interpretation" as are found in other social relations (216), the para-social is distinct in its "lack of effective reciprocity" and the interjection of "fantasy" (215). Celebrity studies have since expanded upon and complicated notions of para-social interaction, with treatments ranging from cautionary and pathologizing (Rojek 2012) to apologia (Jenson 1992).

Central to the inquiry into celebrity para-social relations is a question of knowing, or to what extent that speculative arousal of interest can ever actually yield true knowing or only amount, as is the case in *The Roman Actor*, to a projected fantasy. More specifically, para-social relations hinge on the specifically dialogic interactions of intimacy, or the "reciprocal exchange of self-disclosure, vulnerability, or sexuality" (Bennett 2002, xiv). Horton and Wohl clearly favored a formulation of para-social relations rooted in illusory projection and one-sided dynamics, but M.S. Piccirillo offers another way of thinking about such interaction, in that the "collected instances of intimacy" achieved through repetitious interaction can facilitate intimacy "slowly and over time" through "shared history"—not only between spectator and spectacle, but amongst the viewing body as a whole (Piccirillo 1986, 345). "By *intimacy*," Piccirillo emphatically stresses, "I do not mean 'pseudo-experience' or 'illusion' of intimacy [but the] everyday experience of intimacy in interpersonal relationship" (344). While Piccirillo theorizes this genuine experience of intimacy specifically in the context of television, her work is easily appropriable to the theater, as what sustains such relationships in this formulation is "regular interjection" into the lives of the audience (344). As television characters, through repetitious availability, mine and mimic lived experience, Piccirillo claims that such characters create long-lasting, deeply textured relationships not only between viewers and the characters they follow, but within a community of viewership as well.

By the final decade of the sixteenth century, the general stability of London's theaters and the theatrical repertory system likewise provided a means of "regular interjection" into Londoners' lives, with actors appearing daily in different roles, similarly mimicking the world of lived human experience to forge long-lasting bonds with their audiences. As S.P. Cerasano observes, at the close of the century,

> Burbage's Theatre and Henslowe's Rose established not only an easily identifiable location where particular companies performed, but they also provided venues where the most notable players could be seen and enjoyed by their fans, time and again. Given this, it is perhaps no surprise that the 1590s witnessed the rise of the celebrity player as an unprecedented phenomenon on the London stage.
>
> (Cerasano 2005, 47)

Like Piccirillo, Cerasano isolates repetitious familiarity as the key to forging the bonds of celebrity—specifically, here, in an analysis of Alleyn's remarkable cultural and commercial cachet as a star of the early modern theater. As Cerasano observes, the reliability and repeated access facilitated by the Rose theater gave rise to a "new model actor" whose presence became a selling point as audiences increasingly demanded to see their favorite star in the kinds of roles for which he was beloved, as Guilpin demonstrates in his epigram. Repetitious familiarity, therefore, becomes a kind of intimacy, a process through which audiences learn to detect the player's personal excesses that provide a discernible constant through multiple performances. As Nora Johnson argues, "For a player to become known on stage is to become known for working around the script [...], developing a personal reputation while playing a series of roles devised by others" (Johnson 2003, 79). In 1592, Thomas Nashe attested to just such a personal discernibility in his *Strange Newes* when he writes that, "the name of Ned Allen on the common stage [...] was able to make an ill mater good" (Nashe 1592b, Sig. G), thereby suggesting that Alleyn's presence in a show transcended any particular role, or even the show itself.

If repeated access and accruing familiarity sustain the relations forged in moments of theatrical wonder, then the early modern star most overtly and sustainably linked to wonder offers some tantalizing insights into the particular kind of intimacy early modern actors enjoyed with their audiences. Tarlton, the much beloved extemporal clown and first early modern actor to become, as Andrew Gurr recounts, "a national figure" (Gurr 1987, 151), was regularly associated with the wonder he both aroused and, indeed, came to embody. An extant seventeenth-century ballad, for example, features a woodcut of Tarlton with tabor below the title "A Wonder of Wonders" (Miles 1662); Henry Peacham invokes Tarlton as a metaphor for wonder in a 1620 epigram (Peacham 1620, Ep. 94, Sig. C8). In 1615, Stowe's *Annales* eulogizes the deceased extemporal clown as a wonder through repeated emphasis: "For a wondrous plentifull pleasant extemporall wit," Stowe writes, "hee was the wonder of his time" (Stowe 1615, 697). As the *Oxford Dictionary of National Biography* notes, "no other Elizabethan actor was so much spoken and written about" (Thomson 2011), as Tarlton became a regular fixture in the print-stalls for at least a century after his 1588 death, demonstrating to pronounced effect the manner by which he continued to elicit his audience's wonder well beyond his passage on the stage.

While Tarlton was regarded for his skills as a dancer, musician, and author, he was primarily celebrated for his extemporal capacities—"his pugnacious stage presence, his verbal facility, his quick wit" (Preiss 2014, 119)—and the particular demands of his art might have more readily aligned Tarlton with the wonder of theatrical performance in its already liminal position between scripted performance and spontaneous witticism. According to Gurr, one of Tarlton's most celebrated features was his skill in the extra-dramatic performance known as "backchat," in which the actor appeared to doff the restraints of scripted character and engage in witty, sometimes biting repartee with audience members on topics they supplied. As audiences clamored for Tarlton by name to appear onstage and perform his special brand of comedy, Gurr explains that the practice sometimes "spill[ed] into the play itself," as eager audiences demanded to see their beloved clown "as himself," even in the midst of performance (Gurr 1987, 155). Several extant records capture some of Tarlton's specific dialogues with his audiences and "give some sense of the intimate kinship which existed between players and audience" (155).

As recorded anecdotes demonstrate, the exchanges between Tarlton and his public pressed upon, and sometimes may have overtly punctured, the boundaries between good-hearted fun and outright offense. As the crowds laughed at Tarlton, he laughed back at them, and as one story from *Tarltons Jests* recounts, when an audience member pointed at him, he pointed back, but with two fingers derisively suggesting the cuckold's horns. The audience member "tooke the matter more hainously," so that "this matter grew so" until the spectator, unable to save face against the onslaught of Tarlton's witticisms, pulled his hat down over his eyes, and his imagined horns, and left the theater (1613, Sig. B2v). The exchange demonstrates some of the "intimacy" that Gurr attributes to the practice of backchat, with both player and playgoer rendered mutually vulnerable to each other's and the public's assessment, as it likewise probes the extent of the audience's ability to know Tarlton, as Gurr says, *as himself*—that is, not as character, but as the highly capable extemporal clown whose pointed barbs and quick turns of phrase they craved and clamored for. Tarlton's backchat offers a potent site for the interrogation of early modern para-social interaction, as the audience interaction required of this kind of performance hinges on the repetitious familiarity that allowed playgoers to call for him by name and anticipate the thrills of his unpredictable form. Backchat also requires an audience savvy to its conventions; it depends upon Tarlton's "regular interjection" into their lives.

Theatrical intimacy is often conceived as a relationship freer of interrupting obstacles between spectacle and spectator, such as in Josephine Machon's work on the intimacy of immersive theater in which divisional spaces and conventions of audience response are dispensed in favor of a more communal experience (Machon 2013). Intimacy is, likewise, considered a fundamental, though typically qualified, component of the phenomenon of celebrity. Van Krieken, for example, discusses the "long-distance intimacy" of celebrity para-social interaction (Van Krieken 2012, 83); in his analysis of Lord Byron's celebrity, Tom Mole qualifies the engagement between reader and poet as a relationship that only "resembled an intimate connection" (Mole 2007, 23); and Rojek deems relations between celebrities and their audiences a form of "second-order intimacy" (Rojek 2001, 52), with mediatized representation always providing a barrier to genuine interaction. In 1985, Schickel introduced the concept of "intimate strangers" to account for the semblance of intimacy achieved through mediatized relations, arguing that the medial representation often thought to thwart genuine intimate contact is precisely what allows the illusion of intimacy to take place. As Schickel explains, film's capacity to enhance the subtle details of an actor's appearance and performance project an illusion of intimate contact unavailable in other formats. For Schickel, the film close-up is key, as the magnified, enhanced visibility provided via close-up works as the vessel most likely to arouse feelings of intimacy: "We do not see our closest friends so intimately," Schickel argues, "or the people who share our homes, or our lives, except perhaps in the act of making love" (Schickel 1985, 35).

Staged performance can offer a similar sense of intimacy, as audiences clamoring for Tarlton *as himself* suggest, even as such bonds are achieved through somewhat different means from those achieved through filmed close-up. "Put simply," Mary Luckhurst and Jane Moody argue, "the celebrity of performers is about the experience of seeing an actor in the flesh" (Luckhurst and Moody

2005, 3). On stage, the magnification of film is traded for the mortal vulnerability of corporeal exposure, unmediated by the prescriptive gaze of the camera and the restrictive pace and scope of editing.[10] Flesh-to-flesh confrontation more directly mimics the paradigm of human interpersonal relations, even as the parameters of performance may prevent the full and reciprocal disclosure facilitated through private dialogic exchange. This is a process of the theater that I call strange intimacy. Though Schickel isolates the intimate stranger within the amplification and domestication available in film, I invoke here the same linguistic incompatibility to account for the similarly intimate contact between theatrical actor and audience; however, I'd like to suggest, as Piccirillo does within the context of television, that this intimacy is not, as Schickel or others formulate, illusory, or a diminutive adjunct to genuine intimate exchange. Rather, I offer instead that the theater does indeed facilitate intimate contact, if only to subvert it through a simultaneous dynamic of estrangement in a perpetual counterplay of revelation and concealment.

As oxymoron, strange intimacy—not unlike *stars indeed*—captures an interplay of competing, antipodal tensions that propels the relations between stars and their publics. The strange intimacy of celebrity is, I would argue, a central paradoxical dialectic that forges para-social interaction and occurs in the repetitious access, stark vulnerability, and magnified affect of stage performance. Strange intimacy is both presence and absence in motion, a mitigation of intimate exchange and estrangement that allows an audience to come to know, yet never fully know, an actor *as himself*, which is not to suggest that the audience's experience of knowing is by necessity illusory, but instead, that this knowing is always an incomplete narrative never allowed the full satiation of unimpeded consumption. Strange intimacy is a process of perpetual wonder, the seed of knowledge in a ceaseless state of germination, as the countering impulses of estrangement prevent the fruition that would fill the absence of speculation with the distancing presence of a knowable and distinct entity.

Through repertory engagement, early modern audiences came to know their favored actors by sight and name and would eventually attach those names and bodies to specific kinds of theatrical experiences. While Tarlton's audiences celebrated him for his "pleasant plentifull extemporall wit," Alleyn's audiences associated him with his "stalking gait" and "thundring" voice (Hall 1597, 7), and Burbage was remembered for his "tragic parts" ("On the Death" 1825, 499). Each of these actors is described by contemporaries as embodying a particular, discernible ethos of performance that transcends any one role to become a personal marker that speaks to the audience's intimate knowledge of the person who plays beyond any single part. But as theatrical familiarity is achieved not only through repetitious encounter, but live, in-the-flesh exposure, the kind of intimacy enjoyed in the theater is a particularly bodily interaction that puts corporeal identification, and vulnerability, on central display. As Herbert Blau argues,

> The primary architectural space of the theater is and always has been the body of the actor, subject as it is to the dematerializing power of the gaze that dissolves all space into itself. It is, of course, a transient architecture with a breathing skin, subject at any instant to the corrosions of time.
>
> (Blau 2002, 50)

As a testament to the reciprocal, intimate relations engendered in theatrical performance, Blau suggests that in the theater, "actor and spectator breathe each other" (50), as they share that most intimate of revelations: their own human frailties and the common, shared experience of mortality.

Such revelations are only possible in a theater of live bodies. The dead can speak well beyond the confines of mortality in film, just as film actors can speak to an invisible body of spectators across time and space, but the theater depends upon the immediate exchanges between the live bodies of both actors and audiences. In the theater, Brian Walsh argues, the "*lively* encounter" of "fleshly presence" produces a "forced intimacy with the body of the performer in real time" (Walsh 2009, 22). Bodies are not only immediately present but exposed to the critical gaze of visible others. In 1620, Peacham invoked the memory of Tarlton as an emblem of such corporeal vulnerability, as records indicate that Tarlton's reportedly unattractive appearance often provoked audience laughter before the actor even stepped foot on stage:

> Tarlton when his head was onely seene,
> The Tire-house dore and Tapistrie betweene,
> Set all the multitude in such a laughter,
> They could not hold for scarse an houre after.
> (Peacham 1620, Ep. 94, Sig. C8)

Nashe reports a similar audience reaction to Tarlton in *Pierce Penilesse*: "the people began exceedingly to laugh, when Tarlton first peept out his head" (Nashe 1592a, 36). That a Justice reportedly beat the laughing audience members with a staff for "presum[ing] to laugh at the Queenes men" indicates that such spontaneous eruptions at the sight of Tarlton were not solicited through performance (36); they appear to have been laughing upon the mere glimpse of his face, which may explain why, for Peacham, Tarlton became an enduring symbol of exposure and vulnerability. In his epistle to his 1608 collection of epigrams, Peacham anticipated his readers' response and lamented that, "like Tarleton, I see once again I must thrust my head out of doores to be laughed at, and venture a hissing amongst you" (Peacham 1608, Sig. A3). The reference not only positions Tarlton as emblematic of the vulnerability of public scrutiny, but also strongly attests to the identificatory bonds such vulnerability can provoke, through which Peacham appropriated Tarlton's experience as a way to make sense of his own.

Impressive stature, likewise, became part of the theatrical display on the early modern stage. Based upon both the full-length portrait of Alleyn that survives in the Dulwich Picture Gallery and an analysis of a ring he once owned, Cerasano suggests that Alleyn was about 5 feet 10 inches tall, "significantly taller than most men of his time" (Alleyn 1994, 178). He was frequently cited by his contemporaries for his deeply resonant voice and stalking gait, and Cerasano further looks to one of Alleyn's signature roles, that of Marlowe's Tamburlaine, for confirmation:

> Of stature tall, and straightly fashioned,
> Like his desire, lift upwards and divine,
> So large of limbs, his joints so strongly knit,
> Such breadth of shoulders as might mainly bear
> Old Atlas' burden.
> (2.1.7–11, qtd. in Cerasano 1994, 176)

Of course, it is impossible to know how accurately such verses describe the actor's physicality, but lines such as these certainly at least direct the audience to assess Alleyn's body for parallels, rendering his presumably tall, broad body part of the staged spectacle and open to public scrutiny. As the body of the actor provides, according to Jeremy Lopez, "a primary agent of theatrical meaning" (Lopez 2007, 196), early modern plays regularly coax viewers to study and investigate those bodies, further rendering the actor's staged body as vulnerable to external assessment.

"Theater, unlike other art forms, uses living bodies as its media," argues Celia R. Daileader. "Theater literally takes warm flesh as its 'material' […]. And this fleshiness can be rendered visually, as well as rhetorically" (Daileader 2006, 64). A number of plays, like *Tamburlaine*, render flesh simultaneously through visual and rhetorical means as they rhetorically direct audiences to gaze upon actors' bodies—sometimes to physical features easily assumed through strategic costuming, but also to those characteristics less easily faked and more likely the physical characteristics of actors, like Helena's height or Hermia's diminutive stature. In fact, the pointed barbs traded in *A Midsummer Night's Dream*, in which Hermia deems her friend "a painted maypole" (3.2.297), before Lysander demeans Hermia as a "*minimus* of hind'ring knot-grass made,/ You bead, you acorn" (3.2.329–331), rhetorically rest upon the actors' physiques providing the appropriate visual confirmation of the slander. The humor, here, is contingent upon a corresponding tableau of live bodies and works only so far as the audience responds by assessing and laughing at those bodies, rendering the physical bodies of actors exposed and vulnerable to critique and derision. In fact, David Wiles argues that Tarlton's "physical ugliness," frequently referenced in even fond tributes, was "essential to a comic persona that invites mockery from the audience" (Wiles 1987, 17).

As the theater does not only invite, but compels audiences to anatomize the staged body, the actor's corporeal disclosures are not illusory, but a genuine vulnerability to a host of unpredictable responses, from laughing derision to erotic desire—responses which can, in turn, render the audience vulnerable in their spontaneous affective displays. As intimacy hinges on reciprocal vulnerability, in the theater, the bodies of playgoers, too, are exposed and vulnerable, subject to the return gaze of performers, with their responses not only discernible but frequently and publicly criticized. Like actors, early modern spectators' behavior was partially prescribed, by convention rather than script, and audiences regularly shouted, clapped, stood, and hissed throughout performances. Early modern audiences are also reported to have experienced quite visceral reactions to the plays they attended. A 1610 account of a performance of *Othello* records the manner by which the actors, "not only by their speech but also by their deeds they drew tears" (qtd. in Gurr 1992, 226). Matthew Steggle charts how tears—both happy and sad—were regular fixtures in early modern playhouses and discusses how weeping offered "a communal act" and a means of "linking the spectators [...] to the actor" (Steggle 2007, 86), while also signaling the audience's vulnerable emotional state in the theater.

But audiences were also frequently held in contempt for their behavior in the playhouse, and Gurr counts at least 34 complaints by dramatists regarding playgoer response (Gurr 1992, 227). The most notable of those complaints is likely Thomas Dekker's *The Gull's Hornbook*, in which the playwright satirically instructs playgoers in obnoxious behavior, especially the "over-weening Coxcombe" seated on the onstage gallant's stool who makes himself a spectacle and interrupts productions (Dekker 1609, 29). But playgoers suffered the sting of their fellow audience members' rebuke perhaps just as readily. In 1617, London law student Henry Fitzgeffrey published a scathing collection of character sketches in his *Notes from Black-Fryers*, in which he singled out specific spectators for ridicule. From a viewing box in the Blackfriars, he and a friend scan the crowd for amusement, transforming the audience into a spectacle staged for their laughter; there, they find a "plumed Dandebrat," a "Monstrous [...] Woman of the Masculine Gender" (Fitzgeffrey 1617, Sig. F2), and an "Affecting Asse/ That never walks without his Looking-glasse" (Sig. F4v). Anecdotes recording Tarlton's performances, too, including the previously recounted episode involving the playgoer's offense at the clown's cuckolding gestures, demonstrate the means by which audiences could find themselves not only scrutinized and mocked in the moment of the theatrical event, but purposefully publicized as laughing-stocks through print. Such condemnation and derision cast a withering return gaze upon the audience, demonstrating the extent to which they, too, were being watched, rendering the audience vulnerable to the same assessment actors face.

Entwined in the mutual vulnerability of external assessment and evaluation, the intimacy between audience and actor was not, I would argue, an imaginary substitute for genuine exchange, but a deeply felt, reciprocal recognition of exposure within the playhouse. The theater was a place, as Lopez has argued, "to see and be seen by others" (Lopez 2002, 44), but if that was part of its appeal, the potential for reciprocal exhibition and estimation was also chief amongst its risks. Actors and audiences alike opened themselves up to visceral display and public scrutiny, with their appearances and actions subject not only to immediate appraisal but the indefinite prospect of publication. This intimate interaction was only further enhanced by the intensely personal nature of their mutual disclosures. Audiences, as noted, responded with tears and laughter to the fiercely evocative experiences and affects performed on stage. On stage, the early modern player enacted moments of betrayal, lust, heartbreak, anxiety, reconciliation, mourning, love, and what Julia Kristeva labels as the most intimate of all experiences, death (Kristeva 1992, 229). On stage as well as off, human life, like the theatrical event itself, proves fleeting, and early modern audiences witnessed hundreds of theatrical deaths—sometimes, as an elegy for Burbage suggests, rather convincingly represented:

> Oft have I seen him leape into the grave
> Suiting the person (which hee us'd to have)
> Of a mad lover, with so true an Eye
> That there I would have sworne, hee meant to dye,
> Oft have I seene him play this part in jeast,
> So lively, that Spectators, and the rest
> Of his crewes, whilst hee but seem'd to bleed,
> Amazed, thought hee had bene deade indeed.
> ("On the Death" 1825, 499, 50–57)

Though the poet may be hyperbolizing Burbage's effective enactments of death in posthumous tribute, he is not alone in singling out Burbage's stagecraft as believable. Overbury's "An Excellent Actor," which is likely modeled on Burbage, notes, "what we see him personate, we think truely done before us" (Overbury 1615, Sig. M6). As any audience's capacity to respond empathetically rests, at least in part, on convincing representation, the credibility Overbury assigns Burbage's performance further provokes intimate engagement; however, convincing enactment simultaneously shields the actor as himself behind a veil of credible characterization, thereby facilitating the inverse theatrical interaction of estrangement.

According to the *OED, personation*—the term Overbury chooses to distinguish successful playing—first appeared in print in 1589 (OED Online n.d.(b), *s.v.* personation, n.1), with its verb form emerging a few years later and soon displacing traditional words like *played* and *acted* on print-play title pages, such as in the 1608 publication of Jonson's *Masque of Blackness*, "personated by the most magnificent of queenes Anne [...] With her honorable Ladyes" (Jonson 1608, Sig. A1). The term frequently appears in association with successful or credible performance, such as when Thomas Heywood notes that the good actor can "qualifie everything according to the nature of the person personated," as he contrasts successful personation to both the lackluster performance of the "stiffe starchte man" as well as the "overacting trickes" of histrionic performance (Heywood 1612, Sig. C4).

Personation, according to Travis Curtwright, "signifies how well an actor's imagination envelopes language, movement, intonation, fluency, and becomes internalized" (Curtwright 2017, 80). It proposes "that one whole human being

(Hamlet, say) can be represented by another whole human being (Burbage)" (Thomson 1994, 329). In personation, a strong emphasis on the dramatic character's interiority meets the exteriority of the actor's physical form, such that his staged body can project—visually, aurally, affectively—the interior life of the person personated. The term *personation* also suggests that the embodied character as appears on the stage only exists once made person through the body of the actor. Leanore Lieblein labels this fusion of character and actor an "intersubjective relationship" whereby the actor's perception of the "person to be personated [...] is informed by his own corporeal history" (Lieblein 2009, 123); thus, personation more profoundly obscures the boundaries between player and part. Intertwined in the physical and affective hybridity between person who personates and person personated, the staged character becomes an irretrievable conflation, with neither entity fully effaced by the other but neither distinctly isolatable through their mutual interdependence.[11]

The enmeshed relationship between actor and character in personated performance facilitates a more deeply resonant audience experience in that playgoers may more readily recognize the embodied conflicts on stage as congruous to their own and, thus, empathetically connect to the persons involved. But the blurry line between character and actor in personated performance likewise alienates playgoer from player, distancing and veiling the actor *as himself* from the audience in favor of the hybridity of personation. Here, the very processes that forge intimate contact in shared, empathic experience simultaneously estrange; that which reveals also conceals to propel the mutually resistant bonds of strange intimacy and suspends the relationship between audience and actor in the midst of processes of desire and revelation.

If personation facilitated the actor's shape-shifting capacities to become different, relatable persons in different performances, Thomson argues that Tarlton, to the contrary, always "remained Richard Tarlton, and was loved for it" (Thomson 1994, 334). Distinguishing Tarlton's art from the unrecoverable intersubjectivity of personated performance, Thomson suggests that a large part of Tarlton's appeal was that audiences never lost sight of their beloved clown behind the veil of character and, thus, never experienced the resistant force of estrangement pressing upon the otherwise intimate interactions they shared with him. While Tarlton took on scripted roles, such as the role of Derrick in *The Famous Victories of Henry the Fifth,* it is his capacity for spontaneous jest that is most frequently cited by contemporaries and in remembrance; in fact, Tarlton was so thoroughly associated with his extemporal witticisms that the English scholar and writer Gabriel Harvey conflated the man and his art by referring to extemporizing as "Tarletonising" in a 1592 pamphlet (Harvey 1592, 19). But certainly, even in his extemporal capacities for which he was primarily known and celebrated, the jigging, rhyming Tarlton was, too, in a sense, a person personated; that is, as he appeared in the prescribed homespun of the stage clown to engage the audience with a mix of quick wit and studied performance, he inhabited a character: the character known as Richard Tarlton. In 1590, Roger Williams observed that, "Our pleasant Tarleton would counterfeite many artes, but he was no bodie out of his mirths" (Williams 1590, Sig. A4); not only does Williams's use of the word "counterfeite"—a term frequently linked to personation—suggest that he recognized Tarlton's stage appearances as theatrical performances, but he similarly invokes a model of personation by suggesting that Tarlton became "bodie" only through his performed "mirths." Outside of performance, Tarlton is figured here as "no bodie," as Williams indicates that the actor's offstage presence may have been somewhat less dazzling than his onstage persona.

Though personation is a concept generally reserved for tragedians, the extemporal clown's subtle embodiment of persona may have provided the blurriest of all distinctions between actor and role, rendering his performance so convincingly authentic that he seemed not to act at all, but rather, to appear *as himself*. This performance of self, or self-personation,[12] is regularly recognized as a fundamental component of celebrity today. As Marshall notes, "Celebrities perform in their primary art form […] as well as the extra-textual dimensions" of celebrity (Marshall 2010, 39), with performances of self that extend beyond the stage or screen to the varied and placeless arenas of public presentation. The performance of self is, perhaps, the celebrity's most abiding role, and the one most germane to the strange intimacy the celebrity participates in with audiences, with the very stagecraft that exposes the self to the public's identificatory impulses preventing reciprocal self-disclosure. A number of early modern accounts attest to just such indistinguishability between an actor and his various personations outside the boundaries of the stage. As Earle observes of the player in his *Micro-cosmographie*:

> He is like our painting Gentle-women, seldome in his owne face, seldomer in his cloathes […] Hee do's not only personate on the Stage, but sometime in the Street, for hee is mask'd still in the habite of a Gentleman—His parts find him oaths and good words, which he keepes for his use and discourse, and makes shew with them of a fashionable Companion.
> (Earle 1628, Sigs. E3v–E4)

John Stephens's 1615 *Essayes and Characters* similarly remarks that the player "hath beene familiar so long with the out-sides, that he professes himselfe, (being unknowne) to be an apparent Gentleman" (Stephens 1615, 295). In both accounts, the fuzzy line between player and part is further obscured in its placelessness; personation, including costume and scripted oratory, is not relegated to the stage, but a fluid performance of self that permeates even material boundaries. Stephens's assertion that the player, despite his high visibility, remains "unknowne," further testifies to the antipodal dynamics of strange intimacy; he is, at once, recognizable from his appearances on the stage, visually identifiable as a gentleman, yet a stranger, as he sustains in unscripted performance the contradictory exchanges that propel his relations with the public.

A public in deed

In Heywood's *Apology for Actors*, the playwright-turned-apologist notes that amongst the actor's many virtues, his performance has the power to shape his audience into a morally upright body. As he argues,

> [In] prosperous performance, as if the Personater were the man Personated, so bewitching a thing is lively and well spirited action, that it hath power to new mold the harts of the spectators and fashion them to the shape of any noble and notable attempt.
>
> (Heywood 1612, Sig. B4)

As Heywood figures successful performance as that which bewitches and renders the person personated indecipherable from the person personating, he calls attention to the empathic resonances of personation—namely, here, that the performance of nobility inspires nobility in its audience, and that performance prospers when it solicits mutual performance from its beholders. As such, Heywood iterates a position espoused by Blau, wherein audiences and actors "breathe each other" and respond in kind to the transformative power of personation.[13] Key to Heywood's assessment is not only the transformational affective power of the theater, but its capacity to coalesce a multitude—actors and spectators alike—into a performing body, all fashioned to singular shape.

In Piccirillo's model of para-social relations, the shared history among viewers who share in the same spectatorial relations achieves a kind of community that extends the bonds of intimacy amidst the collective of the audience. Gurr speaks of a similarly coalescing effect in regard to Tarlton's backchat, as the crowd became a "gathering of like-minded pleasure-seekers" (Gurr 1987, 156), held together in their shared experience of Tarlton's unpredictable witticisms. *Henry VIII* similarly folds its audience into a collective through the staged internal audience, who stand in for the external audience and speak the enraptured voices of the audience's wonder through a gathering of emblematic onlookers. Perhaps most importantly, it is these gentlemen spectators, rather than the gods, who transform the staged processors into stars through their assessment and assignation, thereby signaling through surrogate voice the audience's capacity to similarly narrate the celebrity of onstage performers. As the marginalized gentlemen spectators speak the ascents and declines of the parading nobles, they reflect upon the deliberative body of the public who likewise fashions its celebrated actors into stars.

If celebrity originates in the fusion of wonder, and perpetuates through the shared dynamics of strange intimacy, the phenomenon likewise necessitates a collaborative public for the widespread saturation that transforms interpersonal bonds into social and cultural ones. Thus, the collectivization of audience is as vital a component of theatrical stardom as are the highly personal, highly charged relations engendered between individual spectators and performers. As Jeffrey Doty argues in *Shakespeare, Popularity and the Public Sphere*, the idea of the public sphere now features regularly in early modern scholarship, modifying and historically resituating Jürgen Habermas's foundational model, in which private persons, through their active consumption and evaluation of political discourse, congregate into a more powerful public body capable of effecting political change (Habermas 1989, 30). While Habermas traces the idea of a public sphere to the eighteenth century and its proliferating print culture, much like celebrity's history is frequently linked to this era of mass-print, Peter Lake and Steve Pincus have influentially argued that the "post-Reformation period can fairly be said to have fostered public spheres of sorts," as the disseminations of "print, the pulpit, performance, and circulating manuscripts" gave rise to the notion of "an adjudicating public or publics" (Lake and Pincus 2006, 276–277). Doty builds upon this notion of early modern public spheres in his monograph and aims focus specifically at Shakespeare's theater "as an emergent space of political uptake and public deliberation" (Doty 2017, 64), through which "ordinary people came together through shared interests" and were invited to contemplate "how they could be imagined and addressed as a group despite being innumerable strangers, and how voluntary participation in a public might affect one's identity and relation to others" (19).

While Doty's exploration of popularity and publichood in the early modern theater centers on the political engagement of the playgoing public, post-Habermasian formulations of variously constituted publics extend notions of the public beyond the political realm into a wide array of shared concerns and interests. Gerard Hauser, following a post-Habermasian model, argues for the existence of multiple public spheres centered around a diverse array of issues, while still maintaining the public's active participation and ability to effect change in the issues they discuss. The public sphere then becomes:

> a discursive space in which strangers discuss issues they perceive to be of consequence for them and their group. Its rhetorical exchanges are the bases for shared awareness of common issues, shared interests [...] and self-constitution as a public whose opinions bear on the organization of society
>
> (Hauser 1999, 64)

It is this latter model that offers the most insight into the early modern theater's role as a public space, and a great deal of scholarship has demonstrated the means by which the theatrical event drew a disparate group of playgoers, through a variety of shared interests, into a participatory collective.[14] The primary shared interest amongst the theatrical public was, of course, attending plays, but as Lopez argues, the playgoing publics also shared an interest in the unique kind of social interaction available in the theater, the ability "to loiter about, to meet members of the opposite sex, to show off new clothes" (Lopez 2002, 44). Lopez further argues that a large share of the pleasure experienced by early modern playgoers derived from being treated as an actively collaborating collective: "They enjoyed thinking of themselves and being thought of as a collective entity, whose collective response quite powerfully determined the value of a play" (44).

Given the theaters' capacity to seat approximately 2,500 spectators, amounting to what Gurr estimates to be about one million theater visits per year (Gurr 1992, 212–213), the theatrical public's reach into London's population of approximately 200,000 (Merritt 2001, 1)[15] was likely both expansive and substantive. But the idea of a public sphere capable of effecting change depends upon more than the size and scope of the public body, but upon its ability to negotiate present, mutable matters. The public sphere is a merger of the public and the present, a communal coalescence around contemporaneity, and this notion is central to the gentleman's proclamation of *stars indeed*, as what modifies the classical signifying power of the star is its reorientation within the present, unfolding moment—its *in deed* status. As contemporaneity involves "a notion of participating in a shared present" (Dooley 2016, xiii), *stars indeed* signifies not only the elevated status of the star, but the shared experience of the public in the present as converges in the body of the star.

"It is hard to say," J. Paul Hunter writes, "when the present time became such an urgent issue in the English cultural consciousness" (Hunter 1990, 169); however, he argues that the seventeenth century, as evidenced in the proliferation of corantos, ballads, and newsbooks, seemed to have given rise to "a developing concern for contemporaneity" and an "urgent sense of now" (168). Of course, the print sources he cites also signify a growing sense of the public, in that, through print, a larger segment of the population could collectively understand and engage in present affairs. Hunter does not include the theater in his exploration of the early modern fixation with the present, as his account overlooks the early theater's position as a center of news, or as Ian Munro puts it, "a place of dissemination" (Munro 2005, 107), and the manner by which the paradigms of the present and the public intersect there. Beginning in the 1590s, the theater became a locus for communal news and current affairs. On stage, plays enacted recent or concurrent goings-on of national importance, like Middleton's satirical take on the proposed marriage of Prince Charles to the Spanish Infanta in *A Game at Chess*; or regional sensationalism, as in Rowley, Dekker, and Ford's dramatization of the execution of purported witch Elizabeth Sawyer in *The Witch of Edmonton*. The theater also became the subject of news, with the nine-day run of *A Game at Chess*, according to Paul Yachnin, becoming the "most newsworthy event in the history of the early modern English theatre" (Yachnin 2001, 187). And though the dramas enacted on stage could both present the news and become news stories in themselves, the greatest source of news at the playhouse may have resided within the stories traded amongst audience members. The centralized forum of the early modern theater facilitated the circulation of information both within and outside its walls. Yachnin adds that the theater provided a space for the circulation of news to those excluded from reports exchanged at court (183), and that playgoers not only dispersed news, but attended performances to become, like courtiers, part of the news. The playhouse, especially its more visible stage seating, provided an avenue of what he calls "self-publication" (184), which not only enhances the affective ties between audience and actor mutually engaged in the staged presentation of self, but also positions the theater as a site where news was relayed, made, and traded, where the collective body of the playgoing public constructed its sphere and their place within it.

Of course, the early modern playhouse's enmeshed association with the news reflects upon the immediacy and collaborative ethos of the theater itself,[16] as theater is always grounded in the temporality of the present moment, always a spontaneous production "co-created by performers and spectators" (Schechner 1988, 230). In the theater, Anne Ubersfeld theorizes, "there is no time to waste; the image is snatched [...], stolen from time; it is being done and undone at the same time" (Ubersfeld 1982, 130). Even when confined to the dialogue and direction of a play-script, live theater is continuously subject to interruption and alteration, and thus, each performance, even of an older play, is a new(s) event.

Early modern drama frequently and self-reflexively celebrates its own innovation and immediacy, for example, in re-inventing historical accounts in the present moment, in the bodies of live, contemporary actors wearing contemporary clothing speaking contemporary English. In this way, staged histories continually displace the past with the present, through each new appropriation and, indeed, through each performance. Jonson offers a stinging critique of theatrical history in his Induction to *Bartholomew Fair*, in which he derides for "staid ignorance" those audience members whose tastes reside "five and twenty or thirty years" behind in that they "will swear that Jeronimo or Andronicus are the best plays" (Ind. 131–136). In an induction that figures the presentation of a new play as an unspoken collaboration between poet and playgoer, Jonson promises a merry time so long as his audience remains, like the production, present-minded, and not fixated on the theatrical past.

The theater's contemporaneity likewise reverberates in the non-dramatic literature it inspired. As Cerasano has observed of sixteenth-century English praise poems, "few *living* individuals of any sort were memorialized in praise poetry before 1590" (Cerasano 2005, 53), yet a remarkable shift occurs during the century's final decade in which contemporaries of all sorts—including aristocrats, poets, and actors—emerge as subjects of commendatory verse to become stars in deed. As the seventeenth century wore on, actors became increasingly commemorated in such poems, and Alleyn became one of the form's more frequent subjects, with John Weever, William Alexander, and Thomas Campion all penning poems in praise of Alleyn's acting ability,[17] years before Jonson's famous 1616 "To Edward Allen". Alleyn's contemporaries, like Robert Armin, likewise became the subjects of praise poetry during their lifetimes. In 1611, John Davies wrote, "Armine, what shall I say of thee, but this,/ Thou art a foole and a knave? Both? fie, I misse" (Davies 1611, 1–2). John Day commended Lord Admiral's man Thomas Downton in his "Acrostic Verses upon the name of his worthie friende, Maister Thomas Dowton," and King's man William Ostler is commended in the 1611 *The Scourge of Folly* as "the Roscius of these times" (Davies 1611, Ep. 205).

A number of early modern poems and prose works praising actors self-consciously acknowledge their own temporality, such as the *The Scourge of Folly*'s assertion that Ostler is the Roscius "of these times." In his 1612 prose commentary *Apology for Actors*, Heywood calls attention not only to Alleyn's talent, but to the author's contemporaneous memorialization of that talent, writing, "Among so many dead, let me not forget one yet alive, in his time most worthy, famous Maister Edward Allen" (Heywood 1612, Sig. E2v). Heywood's insistence that Alleyn is worthy "in his time" offers a subtle counterpoint to the kind words he reserves for the deceased Tarlton, "in his time, gratious with the queene, his soveraigne, and in the people's general applause" (Sig. E2v), as he circumscribes each actor by generational limitations. Jonson, like Heywood, singles out Alleyn as representative of the present:

> If *Rome* so great, and in her wisest age,
> Fear'd not to boast the glories of her stage,
> As skilful ROSCIUS, and grave ÆSOPE, men,
> Yet crown'd with honors, as with riches, then;
> Who had no lesse a trumpet of their name,
> Than Cicero, whose every breath was fame:
> How can so great example dye in me,
> That ALLEN, I should pause to publish thee?
> Who both their graces in thy selfe hast more
> Out-stript, than they did all that went before:
> And present worth in all dost so contract,
> As others speak, but only thou dost act.
> Weare this renowne. 'Tis just, that who did give
> So many *Poets* life, by one should live.
>   (Jonson 1616, 793)

Here, Jonson taxes himself with the responsibility to recognize and record what is extraordinary in his own day, lest it "dye in mee." It is a remarkably present-minded tribute, focused on Alleyn's ephemeral presence in the early modern public sphere, or his "present worth"—a notable departure from the kind of posthumous accolades Jonson would bestow on Shakespeare in 1623, whom he deemed "not of an age, but for all time!" (Jonson 1623, Sig. A4v). Alleyn, to the contrary, is here painted not as an eternal figure, but a symbol for the triumphs of the theatrical present; as the only player that in the present tense "dost act," Alleyn is not merely the new Roscius, but superior in talent to the classical tragedian Roscius and comedian Aesope combined. His enduring legacy is hinted at in the final line, in that, through this poem, he "should live," but the conditionality of the verb construction suggests that his perpetuity remains as of yet untested.

The flourishing of theatrically inspired print testifies not only to the disseminating reach of the theatrical public, but to the means by which the public coalesced in celebration of the figures inhabiting the early modern stage and the ways in which living actors functioned as markers of present innovation. As seventeenth-century praise pieces increasingly commemorated living actors, such commendations were frequently achieved through the kind of displacement Jonson employs, in which the contemporary is lauded in light of theatrical history, sometimes the very recent theatrical past. Heywood, for example, noted how Kempe succeeded Tarlton "in the favour of her majesty, as in the opinion and good thoughts of the generall audience" (Heywood 1612, Sig. E2v). In 1672, Richard Flecknoe closes his poem "The Praises of Richard Burbage," by singling out a noted Restoration actor: "Such even the nicest critics must allow/ Burbage was once; and such Charles Hart is now" (Flecknoe 1672, 19–20). The anonymously penned 1605 *Ratseis Ghost* actually looks ahead to the inevitable demise of Burbage (referenced here as the actor of Hamlet) to suggest his future replacement when he instructs a travelling player:

> Get thee to London, for, if one man were dead, they will have much neede of such a one as thou art. There would be none in my opinion fitter then thyselfe to play his parts [...] I durst venture all the money in my purse on they head to play Hamlet.
>
> (*Ratseis Ghost* 1605, Sig. B1)

The consistent displacement of yesterday's actors for today's (or even today's for tomorrow's) exalts the present, celebrating and claiming the value of the immediate moment through the names of famous actors. It is unsurprising that as seventeenth-century poets increasingly looked to their living contemporaries for their subjects that they would turn so often to the theater. Commendatory verse generally focuses on ephemeral qualities, including youth, beauty, and human mortality, and part of the genre's mission, as made abundantly apparent in countless examples, is to bestow upon its subject a kind of earthly immortality. "So long as men can breathe or eyes can see," Shakespeare writes of the fair youth in Sonnet 18, "So long lives this, and this gives life to thee" (13–14).[18] Embedded within this mission is the assumption that poems outlast their subjects; theater, on the other hand, is not only perpetually present, but by extension, strikingly ephemeral as well. As Macbeth said of the player, he "struts and frets his hour upon the stage/ And then is heard no more" (5.5.24–25), and a great deal of praise poetry for actors seems fixed on rescuing the players from the ephemerality of the stage. Jonson closes his epigram to Alleyn by figuring his verse the just recompense for the actor's gifts: Alleyn, he says, brought his words to life on the stage, so the poet will, in turn, endow the actor with a quality the stage cannot provide: enduring life. Shackerley Marmion expresses similar sentiments when he notes in his commendation of King's Man Joseph Taylor, "while this Poeme shall be read,/ *Taylor*, thy name shall be eternized" (Marmion 1634, Sig. A3). Echoing a similar call for preservation, Heywood deems it "a kinde of sinne to [...] not commit their (almost forgotten) names to eternity" (Heywood 1612, Sig. E2v), as he records the names and achievements of the theatrical stars of his day for posterity. This dedication to concretizing the momentary exchanges of the theater testifies to the collaborative construction of the early modern theatrical celebrity, with writers coalescing to narrate the ascent—much like the gentlemen spectators of *Henry VIII*—of the stars yet in deed.

Stars indeed

Of the gentlemen spectators in *Henry VIII*, the Second Gentleman, who proclaims the parading nobles "stars indeed," most clearly emblematizes the role of the public in the elevation of stars as he demonstrates the exchanges between public and performer that constitute the theatrical phenomenon of celebrity. Before the procession begins, he stands in rapt attention, ever aware that the ensuing spectacle of monarchical pageantry will last but a moment. "The trumpets sound, Stand close" (4.1.36), he orders his companions in heightened anticipation. When the processors arrive, he exclaims, "A royal train, believe me. These I know" (4.1.37), before immediately revealing his ignorance by asking, "Who's that that bears the sceptre?" (4.1.38). In an almost immediate alternation between claiming to know the parade's participants, then confessing not to know who they are, the Second Gentleman remains in a state of wonder, ravenously attentive yet suspended in the in-between spaces of knowing and not knowing. Throughout the procession, he similarly probes the identities of the nobles parading before him, turning to his companion who holds a print program in order to tease out the noble titles from the parts they play, ever in a state of coming-to-know.

When he finally spies Anne, he fawns in admiration and speaks to her in a direct address that he knows she will not hear:

> Heaven bless thee!
> Thou hast the sweetest face I ever looked on.
> Sir, as I have a soul, she is an angel.
> Our King has all the Indies in his arms.
> And more, and richer, when he strains that lady.
> I cannot blame his conscience.
> (4.1.42–47)

In his impassioned declaration to a distant Anne who silently proceeds, certainly unaware of her admirer's effusive praise, across the stage, the Second Gentleman demonstrates the bonds of strange intimacy, not only in that he speaks to her as intimately as if she were his lover, but in that he claims an almost empathic connection to the king who embraces her. In the scant but highly charged interaction between staged spectacle and spectator, the Second Gentleman alludes to the highly intimate matter of the king's adulterous relationship and instantly pardons him, empathically transferring his own enrapture at her dazzling presence to his king. Of course, both king and queen remain strangers to him, but this highly theatrical, flesh-to-flesh confrontation both invites the gentleman's outpour of affection as it provokes his speculations and evaluations of the figures staged before him.

Before he finally proclaims the processing nobles "stars indeed," the Second Gentleman unites the crowd—both processors and spectators alike—as a collective body: "Those men are happy, and so are all are near her" (50). Thus, when he reaches his eventual declaration, he speaks as a happy member of a deliberative public as he offers a concise, two-word, oxymoronic construction to attest to the wonder, strange intimacy, and collectivizing effect of the stars.

Notes

1 Certain exceptions to this general rule include metaphoric uses of stars to describe persons as objects of affection or physical brilliance, such as when Lucrece's eyes are described as "mortal stars" (64).
2 For more on these figures' complicated histories and enduring renown, see William A. Sessions, *Henry Howard, The Poet Earl of Surrey: A Life* (Sessions 1999); James D. Taylor's 2015 *Henry Grey, 3rd Marquis of Dorset, 2nd Duke of Suffolk (c.1500–1554)*; Kevin Sharpe, *Selling the Tudor Monarchy: Authority and Image in Sixteenth Century England* (Sharpe 2009).
3 The homophonic yet divergent potentialities of *indeed/in deed* and their indecipherability when spoken from the stage were already, by 1613, a well-tread rhetorical play; *Antony and Cleopatra*, for example, toys with these contradictions when Cleopatra's eunuch attendant, Mardian, informs her that he experiences affections despite his castration. She responds, "Indeed!" (1.5.14), to which he clarifies, "Not in deed, madam" (1.5.15), differentiating his assured desires from his ability to act upon them.
4 If "A Sonnet upon the Pittiful Burneing of the Globe Playhouwse in London" (ctd. in Chambers 1923, II. 420–422) is to be believed, Burbage, Condell, and Heminges were all at least present in the 1613 staging of *Henry VIII* that razed the Globe to the ground. In 1709, John Downes claimed in his *Roscius Anglicanus* that John Lowin, "who had his Instructions from Mr. Shakespear himself" (Downes 1709, 24), had originally played the titular monarch in *Henry VIII*. While Lowin was reported to play Henry VIII and Burbage is speculated to have portrayed Wolsey, the play's massive *dramatis personae* undoubtedly necessitated role-doubling, and this silent spectacle narrated only by unnamed gentlemen would have provided an ideal moment for even the play's chief actors to assume additional parts.
5 Of Earle's description, Evelyn Tribble observes that, "The actor is imagined as seizing the eyes, ears, and attention of the audience and directing them through an invisible tether" (Tribble 2017, 25).
6 Nandini Das and Nick Davis's volume, *Enchantment and Dis-enchantment in Shakespeare and Early Modern Drama*, offers a variety of perspectives on theatrical enchantment, including the "repeated process by which characters are revealed to be actors as they cross the threshold between the stage and the unseen 'offstage'" (Das and Davis 2017, 2).
7 Chapter 3 offers a detailed examination of celebrity and wonder as employed by the titular monarch in *1 Henry IV*.
8 For more on Shakespeare and wonder, see Adam Max Cohen's *Wonder in Shakespeare*, which, among a number of astute observations, offers the provocative notion that Shakespeare "clouds" distinctions between disembodied spirits and embodied actors in depictions of ghosts (Cohen 2012, 45), thus pointing to a kind of fluidity of personhood and projection as pertains to celebrity. See also Peter G. Platt, *Reason*

Diminished: Shakespeare and the Marvelous, which offers a useful theoretical survey of wonder's formulations since Aristotle (Platt 1997); and the various essays collected in Das and Davis (2017).
9 In an extensive analysis of Edward Alleyn's early modern celebrity, S.P. Cerasano argues that Guilpin's poem relays how "Alleyn's unique swagger and overwhelming voice imprinted the part in the audience's memory" (Cerasano 2005, 50).
10 To the contrary, Schickel argues in *His Picture in the Papers* that "the stage is a less intimate medium (even though the audience is physically in the presence of the actors) because the proscenium has a profoundly distancing effect—no close-ups here" (Schickel 1973, 6). While this point, echoed also in Morin, is debatable, it is irrelevant to the pre-proscenium theatrical structures of the early modern stage, which did not feature such physical barriers.
11 For more on personation on the early modern stage, see also Robert Weimann and Douglas Bruster, "Personation and Playing: 'secretly open' role-playing," in *Shakespeare and the Power of Performance* (Weimann and Bruster 2008); Genevieve Love, *Early Modern Theater and the Figure of Disability* (Love 2018); and Paul Yachnin, "Personations: The Taming of the Shrew and the Limits of Theoretical Interpretation" (Yachnin 1996).
12 Chapter 2 further explores the concept of self-personation by way of self-parody on the early modern stage.
13 Lieblein similarly argues that, "The spectator, too, is a body-subject who is transformed by his or her embodied experience of the actor's performance," and that Heywood illustrates this effect through the audience's emulation of the actor's transformation through personation (Heywood 2009, 130–131).
14 Amongst a substantive body of criticism and research into early modern theatrical audiences, and its potentials for and resistance to collectivization, see Alfred Harbage, *Shakespeare's Audiences* (Harbage 1941); Ann Jennalie Cook, *The Privileged Playgoers in Shakespeare's London, 1576–1642* (Cook 1981); Anthony B. Dawson and Paul Yachnin, *The Culture of Playgoing in Shakespeare's England* (Dawson and Yachnin 2001); and Jennifer A. Low and Nova Myhill, *Imagining the Audience in Early Modern Drama, 1558–1642* (Low and Myhill 2011).
15 Merritt's figures are derived from *Stowe's Survey of London*, first published in 1598 (Merritt 1598).
16 Tarlton was a figure particularly associated with the news, as his name appears in print at least three times during his lifetime, though somewhat questionably, as a reporter of news—of floods (Tarlton 1570), snow (1579), and an earthquake (1580), respectively. While Tarlton's *Devise upon This Unlooked for Great Snow* is now lost (its existence only known from its listing in the Stationers Register), his report on the earthquake appears in Thomas Churchyard's *A warning for the wise*, and his *A very lamentable and Wofull Discours of the fierce fluds whiche lately flowed in Bedfordshire* is entirely attributed to the actor only with a concluding "*Finis.* Richard Tarlton" (Churchyard 1580, Sig. D3).
17 See Weever, "In Ed Allen"; Alexander, "To his deservedly honored friend, Mr. Edward Allane"; and Campion, "In Ligonem"; all included in Nungezer (1929, 9–10).
18 In his "The Portrait of Mr. W.H.," Oscar Wilde popularized the notion that Shakespeare's fair youth was actually an actor—specifically, a young actor named Will Hughes (Wilde 1889).

References

Alberoni, Francesco. 2006 [1962]. "The Powerless 'Elite': Theory and Sociological Research on the Phenomenon of the Stars." Translated by Denis McQuail. In *The Celebrity Culture Reader*, edited by P. David Marshall, 108–123. New York: Routledge.

Backhaus, Gary. 2000. "The Phenomenology of the Experience of Enchantment." In *The Aesthetics of Enchantment in the Fine Arts*, edited by Marlies Kronegger and Anna-Teresa Tymieniecka, 23–48. Dordrecht: Kluwer Academic.

Bacon, Francis. 1605. *Of the Two Books of Francis Bacon: Of the Proficience and Advancement of Learning*. London.

Bennett, Jane. 2001. *The Enchantment of Modern Life: Attachments, Crossings, and Ethics*. Princeton: Princeton University Press.

Bennett, Joel B. 2002. *Time and Intimacy: A New Science of Personal Relationships*. Mahwah, NJ: Lawrence Erlbaum Associates.

Bishop, T.G. 1996. *Shakespeare and the Theatre of Wonder*. Cambridge: Cambridge University Press.

Blau, Herbert. 2002. *The Dubious Spectacle: Extremities of Theater, 1976–2000*. Minneapolis: University of Minnesota Press.

Cerasano, S.P. 1994. "Tamburlaine and Edward Alleyn's Ring." *Shakespeare Survey* 47: 171–179.

Cerasano, S.P. 2005. "Edward Alleyn, the New Model Actor, and the Rise of Celebrity in the 1590s." *Medieval and Renaissance Drama in England* 18: 47–58.

Chambers, E.K. 1923. "A Sonnet upon the Pittiful Burneing of the Globe Playhowse in London." In *The Elizabethan Stage*, by E.K. Chambers. Oxford: Clarendon, 420–422.

Chaucer, Geoffrey. 2007. The House of Fame. In *Dream Visions and Other Poems*, edited by Kathryn L.Lynch, 39–92. New York: Norton.

Churchyard, Thomas. 1580. *A warning for the wise, a feare to the fond, a bridle to the lewd, and A glass to the good*. London.

Cohen, Max Adam. 2012. *Wonder in Shakespeare*. New York: Palgrave Macmillan.

Cook, Ann Jennalie. 1981. *The Privileged Playgoers of Shakespeare's London, 1576–1642*. Princeton: Princeton University Press.

Curtwright, Travis. 2017. *Shakespeare's Dramatic Persons*. Madison: Fairleigh Dickinson University Press.

Daileader, Celia R. 2006. *Eroticism on the Renaissance Stage: Transcendence, Desire, and the Limits of the Visible*. Cambridge: Cambridge University Press.

Das, Nandini and Davis, Nick. 2017. "Introduction." In *Enchantment and Dis-Enchantment in Shakespeare and Early Modern Drama: Wonder, the Sacred, and the Supernatural*, edited by Nandini Das and Nick Davis, 1–17. New York: Routledge.

Davies, John. 1611. *The scourge of folly consisting of satyricall epigramms, and others in honor of many noble and worthy persons of our land*. London.

Dekker, Thomas. 1609. *The Gul's Horne-booke*. London.

Digges, Leonard. 1640. "Upon Master William Shakespeare, the Deceased Author, and His Poems." In *Poems Written by William Shakespeare, Gent*. London. Pilcrow 3–4.

Dooley, Brendan. 2016. "Preface." In *The Dissemination of News and the Emergence of Contemporaneity in Early Modern Europe*, edited by Brendan Dooley, xiii–xiv. New York: Routledge.

Doty, Jeffrey S. 2017. *Shakespeare, Popularity and the Public Sphere*. Cambridge: Cambridge University Press.

Downes, John. 1709. *Roscius Anglicanus*. London.

Dugdale, William. 1675. *The Baronage of England, or An Historical Account of the Lives and Most Memorable Actions of English Nobility*. London.

Earle, John. 1628. *Micro-cosmographie or, A Peece of the World Disovered; in Essays and Characters*. London.

Fisher, Philip. 2003. *Wonder, the Rainbow, and the Aesthetic of Rare Experiences*. Cambridge: Cambridge University Press.
Fitzgeffrey, Henry. 1617. *Satyres and Satyricall Epigrams with Certain Observations at Black-Fryers*. London.
Fitzgeoffrey, Charles. 1881 [1601]. "To Richard Tarlton." In *The Poems of the Rev. Charles Fitzgeoffrey*, edited by Alexander B. Grossart. Blackburn.
Greenblatt, Stephen. 1991. *Marvelous Possessions*. Chicago: Chicago University Press.
Guilpin, Edward. 1598. *Skialetheia, or, A Shadowe of Truth in Certaine Epigrams and Satyres*. London.
Gurr, Andrew. 1987. *Playgoing in Shakespeare's London*. Cambridge: Cambridge University Press.
Gurr, Andrew. 1992. *The Shakespearean Stage 1574–1642*. Cambridge: Cambridge University Press.
Habermas, Jurgen. 1989. *The Structural Transformation of the Public Sphere: An Inquiry into a Category of Bourgeois Society*. Translated by Thomas Burger. Cambridge: MIT Press.
Hall, Joseph. 1597. *Virgidemiarum sixe bookes*. London.
Harbage, Alfred. 1941. *Shakespeare's Audience*. New York: Columbia University Press.
Harvey, Gabriel. 1592. *Four Letters and Certain Sonnets*. London.
Hauser, Gerard A. 1999. *Vernacular Voices: The Rhetoric of Publics and Public Spheres*. Columbia: University of South Carolina Press.
Heywood, Thomas. 1612. *An Apology for Actors Containing three briefe Treatises*. London.
Horton, Donald and R. Richard Wohl. 1956. "Mass Communication and Para-Social Interaction: Observations on Intimacy at a Distance." *Psychiatry* 19 (3): 215–239.
Hunter, J. Paul. 1990. *Before Novels: The Cultural Context of Eighteenth Century English Fiction*. New York: Norton.
Jenson, Joli. 1992. "Fandom as Pathology: The Consequences of Characterization." In *The Adoring Audience: Fan Culture and Popular Media*, edited by Lisa A. Lewis, 9–29. London and New York: Routledge.
Johnson, Nora. 2003. *The Actor as Playwright in Early Modern Drama*. Cambridge: Cambridge University Press.
Jonson, Ben. 1623. "To the Memorie of the deceased Authour Maister W. Shakespeare." In *Shakespeare's Comedies, Histories, & Tragedies*. London.
Jonson, Ben. 1616. "To Edward Allen." In *The Works of Benjamin Jonson*, 793. London.
Kemp, Will. 1600. *Kemps nine daies wonder Performed in a daunce from London to Norwich*. London.
Kristeva, Julia. 1992. *Black Sun: Depression and Melancholia*. New York: Columbia University Press.
Lake, Peter and Steve Pincus. 2006. "Rethinking the Public Sphere in Early Modern England." *Journal of British Studies* 45 (2): 270–292.
Lieblein, Leanore. 2009. "Embodied Intersubjectivity and the Creation of Early Modern Character." In *Shakespeare's Character: Theory, History, Performance, and Theatrical Persons*, edited by Paul Yachnin and Jessica Slights, 117–138. New York: Palgrave Macmillan.
Lilti, Antoine. 2017. *The Invention of Celebrity*. Translated by Lynn Jeffress. Cambridge: Polity.
Lopez, Jeremy. 2002. *Theatrical Convention and Audience Response in Early Modern Drama*. Cambridge: Cambridge University Press.

Lopez, Jeremy. 2007. "Imagining the Actor's Body on the Early Modern Stage." *Medieval and Renaissance Drama in England* 20: 187–203.

Love, Genevieve. 2018. *Early Modern Theatre and the Figure of Disability*. London: Bloomsbury.

Low, Jennifer A. and Nova Myhill, eds. 2011. *Imagining the Audience in Early Modern Drama, 1558–1642*. New York: Palgrave Macmillan.

Luckhurst, Mary and Jane Moody. 2005. "The Singularity of Theatrical Celebrity." In *Theatre and Celebrity in Britain, 1660–2000*, edited by Mary Luckhurst and Jane Moody, 1–14. New York: Palgrave Macmillan.

Machon, Josephine. 2013. *Immersive Theatres: Intimacy and Immediacy in Contemporary Performance*. New York: Palgrave Macmillan.

Marcus, Sharon. 2019. *The Drama of Celebrity*. Princeton: Princeton University Press.

Marmion, Shackerley. 1634. "Unto His Worthy Friend, Mr. Joseph Taylor." In *The Faithfull Shepherdess* by John Fletcher, Sig. A3. London.

Marshall, P. David. 2010. "The Promotion and Presentation of the Self: Celebrity as Marker of Presentational Media." *Celebrity Studies* 1 (1): 35–48.

Massinger, Philip. 2007. *The Roman Actor*. Edited by Martin White. Manchester: Manchester University Press.

"The Memoirs of David Garrick, Esq." 1765. *The Gentleman's and London Magazine* (July): 224–227.

Merritt, J.F. 2001. *Imagining Early Modern London: Perceptions and Portrayals of the City from Stowe to Strype, 1598–1720*. Cambridge: Cambridge University Press.

Middleton, Thomas. 1625. *A Game at Chess*. London.

Middleton, Thomas. 1995. *A Mad World, My Masters*. In *Thomas Middleton's A Mad World, My Masters and Other Plays*, edited by Michael Taylor, 1–66. Oxford: Oxford University Press.

Miles, Abraham. 1662. "A Wonder of Wonders, Being a True Relation of the Strange and Invisible Beating of a Drum." *Broadside Ballads Online from the Bodleian Libraries*. http://ballads.bodleian.ox.ac.uk/view/illustration/18714.

Mole, Tom. 2007. *Byron's Romantic Celebrity: Industrial Culture and the Hermeneutic of Intimacy*. New York: Palgrave Macmillan.

Munro, Ian. 2005. *The Figure of the Crowd in Early Modern London: The City and Its Double*. New York: Palgrave Macmillan.

Nashe, Thomas. 1592a. *Pierce Penilesse His Supplication to the Divell*. London.

Nashe, Thomas. 1592b. *Strange Newes*. London.

Nungezer, Edwin. 1929. *A Dictionary of Actors and Other Persons Associated with the Public Representation of Plays in England before 1642*. Ithaca: Cornell University Press.

OED Online. n.d.(a). "deed, n." Oxford University Press, https://www-oed-com.ric.idm.oclc.org/view/Entry/48598 (accessed March 14, 2019).

OED Online. n.d.(b). "personation, n." Oxford University Press, https://www-oed-com.ric.idm.oclc.org/view/Entry/48598 (accessed March 14, 2019).

OED Online. n.d.(c). "star, n." Oxford University Press, https://www-oed-com.ric.idm.oclc.org/view/Entry/189081 (accessed March 14, 2019).

OED Online. n.d.(d). "wonder, v." Oxford University Press, http://www.oed.com.ric.idm.oclc.org/view/Entry/229938 (accessed January 20, 2020).

"On ye Death of ye Famous Actor, R. Burbadge." 1825. *The Gentleman's Magazine* 95 (June): 497–499.

Overbury, Thomas. 1615. *New and Choise Characters*. London.

Ovid. 1986. *Metamorphoses*. Translated by A.D. Melville. Edited by E.J. Kenney. Oxford: Oxford University Press.

Peacham, Henry. 1608. *The more the merrier*. London.

Peacham, Henry. 1620. *Thalia's banquet furnished with an hundred and odde dishes of newly devised epigrammes*. London.

Piccirillo, M.S. 1986. "On the Authenticity of Televisual Experience: A Critical Exploration of Para-Social Closure." *Critical Studies in Mass Communication* 3: 337–355.

Platt, Peter G. 1997. *Reason Diminished: Shakespeare and the Marvelous*. Lincoln: University of Nebraska Press.

Preiss, Richard. 2014. *Clowning and Authorship in Early Modern Theatre*. Cambridge: Cambridge University Press.

Quinn, Michael L. 1990. "Celebrity and the Semiotics of Acting." *New Theater Quarterly* 6 (22): 154–161.

Ratseis Ghost. 1605. London.

Roach, Joseph. 2007. *It*. Ann Arbor: University of Michigan Press.

Rochester, Joanne. 2010. *Staging Spectatorship in the Plays of Philip Massinger*. Burlington: Ashgate.

Rojek, Chris. 2001. *Celebrity*. London: Reaktion.

Rojek, Chris. 2012. *Fame Attack: The Inflation of Celebrity and its Consequences*. London: Bloomsbury.

Rowley, William, Thomas Dekker and John Ford. 1658. *The Witch of Edmonton*. London.

Schechner, Richard. 1988. *Performance Theory*. New York: Routledge.

Schickel, Richard. 1973. *His Picture in the Papers: A Speculation on Celebrity in America, Based on the Life of Douglas Fairbanks, Sr*. New York: Charterhouse.

Schickel, Richard. 1985. *Intimate Strangers: The Culture of Celebrity*. New York: Doubleday.

Sessions, William A. 1999. *Henry Howard, The Poet Earl of Surrey: A Life*. Oxford: Oxford University Press.

Shakespeare, William. 2016. *Antony and Cleopatra*. In *The Norton Shakespeare, Third Edition*, edited by Stephen Greenblatt, Walter Cohen, Suzanne Gossett, Jean E. Howard, Katharine Eisaman Maus, and Gordon McMullan, 2775–2864. New York: Norton.

Shakespeare, William. 2016. *Henry V*. In *The Norton Shakespeare, Third Edition*, edited by Stephen Greenblatt, Walter Cohen, Suzanne Gossett, Jean E. Howard, Katharine Eisaman Maus, and Gordon McMullan, 1533–1612. New York: Norton.

Shakespeare, William. 2016. *Henry VI, Part 1*. In *The Norton Shakespeare, Third Edition*, edited by Stephen Greenblatt, Walter Cohen, Suzanne Gossett, Jean E. Howard, Katharine Eisaman Maus, and Gordon McMullan, 415–490. New York: Norton.

Shakespeare, William. 2016. *Henry VIII (All Is True)*. In *The Norton Shakespeare, Third Edition*, edited by Stephen Greenblatt, Walter Cohen, Suzanne Gossett, Jean E. Howard, Katharine Eisaman Maus, and Gordon McMullan, 3269–3352. New York: Norton.

Shakespeare, William. 2016. *Macbeth*. In *The Norton Shakespeare, Third Edition*, edited by Stephen Greenblatt, Walter Cohen, Suzanne Gossett, Jean E. Howard, Katharine Eisaman Maus, and Gordon McMullan, 2709–2774. New York: Norton.

Shakespeare, William. 2016. *A Midsummer Night's Dream*. In *The Norton Shakespeare, Third Edition*, edited by Stephen Greenblatt, Walter Cohen, Suzanne Gossett, Jean E.

Howard, Katharine Eisaman Maus, and Gordon McMullan, 1037–1096. New York: Norton.
Shakespeare, William. 2016. *Pericles*. In *The Norton Shakespeare, Third Edition*, edited by Stephen Greenblatt, Walter Cohen, Suzanne Gossett, Jean E. Howard, Katharine Eisaman Maus, and Gordon McMullan, 2865–2932. New York: Norton.
Shakespeare, William. 2016. *The Rape of Lucrece*. In *The Norton Shakespeare, Third Edition*, edited by Stephen Greenblatt, Walter Cohen, Suzanne Gossett, Jean E. Howard, Katharine Eisaman Maus, and Gordon McMullan, 695–744. New York: Norton.
Shakespeare, William. 2016. Sonnet 18. In *The Norton Shakespeare, Third Edition*, edited by Stephen Greenblatt, Walter Cohen, Suzanne Gossett, Jean E. Howard, Katharine Eisaman Maus, and Gordon McMullan, 2256. New York: Norton.
Shakespeare, William. 2016. *The Winter's Tale*. In *The Norton Shakespeare, Third Edition*, edited by Stephen Greenblatt, Walter Cohen, Suzanne Gossett, Jean E. Howard, Katharine Eisaman Maus, and Gordon McMullan, 3121–3204. New York: Norton.
Sharpe, Kevin. 2009. *Selling the Tudor Monarchy: Authority and Image in Sixteenth Century England*. New Haven: Yale University Press.
Steggle, Matthew. 2007. *Laughing and Weeping in Early Modern Theatres*. Burlington: Ashgate.
Stephens, John. 1615. *Essayes and Characters, Ironicall and Instructive*. London.
Stowe, John. 1615. *Stowe's Annales, continued by Edmund Howe*. London.
Tarlton, Richard. 1570. *A very lamentable and Wofull Discours of the fierce fluds whiche lately flowed in Bedfordshire*. London.
Tarltons Jests, Drawn into these three parts. 1613. London.
Taylor, James D. 2015. *Henry Grey, 3rd Marquis of Dorset, 2nd Duke of Suffolk (c.1500–1554)*. New York: Algora.
Thomson, Peter. 2011. Richard Tarlton. *The Oxford Dictionary of National Biography* (December 11), www.oxforddnb.com (accessed August 18, 2019).
Thomson, Peter. 1994. "Rogues and Rhetoricians: Acting Styles in Early English Drama." In *A New History of Early English Drama*, edited by John D. Cox and David Scott Kastan, 321–336. New York: Columbia University Press.
Tribble, Evelyn. 2017. *Early Modern Actors and Shakespeare's Theatre: Thinking with the Body*. London: Bloomsbury.
Tribble, Evelyn. 2013. "Skill." In *Early Modern Theatricality*, edited by Henry Turner, 173–188. Oxford: Oxford University Press.
Ubersfeld, Anne. 1982. "The Pleasure of the Spectator." *Modern Drama* 25 (1): 127–139.
Van Krieken, Robert. 2012. *Celebrity Society*. New York: Routledge.
Victor, Benjamin. 1761. *The History of the Theatres of London and Dublin*. London.
Walsh, Brian. 2009. *Shakespeare, the Queen's Men, and the Elizabethan Performance of History*. Cambridge: Cambridge University Press.
Weimann, Robert and Douglas Bruster. 2008. *Shakespeare and the Power of Performance: Stage and Page in the Elizabethan Theatre*. Cambridge: Cambridge University Press.
Wilde, Oscar. 1889. "The Portrait of Mr. W.H." *Blackwoods Edinburgh Magazine* CXLVI (885): 1–21.
Wiles, David. 1987. *Shakespeare's Clown: Actor and Text in the Elizabethan Playhouse*. Cambridge: Cambridge University Press.
Williams, Roger. 1590. *A Brief Discourse of Warre*. London.
Yachnin, Paul. 2001. "The House of Fame." In *The Culture of Playgoing in Shakespeare's England: A Collaborative Debate*, edited by Anthony B.Dawson and Paul Yachnin, 187–207. Cambridge: Cambridge University Press.

Yachnin, Paul. 1996. "Personations: *The Taming of the Shrew* and the Limits of Theoretical Criticism." *Early Modern Literary Studies* 2 (1): 1–31.

Zazzali, Peter. 2016. "Star-Struck!: The Phenomenological Affect of Celebrity on Broadway." *The Journal of American Drama and Theater* 28 (1): https://jadtjournal.org/2016/03/23/ star-struck-the-phenomenological-affect-of-celebrity-on-broadway.

2 A commodity of good names

In Sonnet 111, Shakespeare seems to address, and bemoan, one of the troubling consequences of high public visibility:

> O, for my sake do you with Fortune chide,
> The guilty goddess of my harmful deeds,
> That did not better for my life provide
> Than public means which public manners breeds.
> Thence comes it that my name receives a brand,
> And almost thence my nature is subdued
> To what it works in, like the dyer's hand.
> Pity me then, and wish I were renewed.
>
> (1–8)

Lamenting that his fortune had not bestowed upon him more ample means, the poet here finds himself relegated to public performance to sustain his livelihood, which he believes has, in turn, compromised his integrity as he has conformed to public expectation. Perhaps most distressing to the speaker, though, is that his "name receives a brand." In the seventeenth century, *brand* was a multivalent and loaded term, signifying at once both a "disgrace; a stigma, a mark of infamy," as well as the seared mark of ownership imprinted onto livestock (OED Online n.d.(a), *s.v.* brand, n. 4b,d). Dympna Callaghan adds that this brand might also figuratively suggest the felon's brand, through which "his name is mutilated and not his person" (Callaghan 2013, 72). Of course, *name* here, as in much of Shakespeare, signifies more than mere nomenclature, but functions as a kind of shorthand for the identity, reputation, and biography of the individual encoded therein, so the distinctions between name and person may not be so readily compartmentalizable. While his corporeal body remains here unscathed, his person as understood as a social being has become indelibly marked by external assessment. In any of its assignations, the brand here signals the poet's lost authority over the signifying powers and circulation of a publicly evaluated name.

Bookended by the topically adjacent Sonnets 110 and 112, in which the poet similarly reaches out to an adjudicating listener for compassion and

DOI: 10.4324/9780367808976-3

compensation from the public's branding, the public stain of Sonnet 111 is further unraveled in the latter as a "vulgar scandal stamped upon my brow" (2).[1] In Sonnet 110, the poet further clarifies his public ventures that may have prompted scandal: "I have gone here and there/ And made myself a motley to the view" (1–2), with the fool's motley likely isolating theatrical craft as the public means of the following sonnet. However, as Shakespeare deems himself a motley in the public view, he does not only suggest that he has publicly beclowned himself, but that he has also become, in the public eye, a sort of patchwork conglomeration. The subsuming power of the public's stain in 111 and the immovable stamp of 112 here amount to a disintegration of the authoritative self, replaced instead by the public's chimeric amalgamation. Taken together, this tripartite meditation on the powers and effects of performance and popular perception reveals a decidedly external locus of identity production for the public person, with the resultant identity a collaboratively authored composite of public assessment. The public individual tied to that popularly projected identity is then left only to beg redress from yet another external authority.

The potency of reputation, as well as its extrinsic production and circulation, provide a consistent fixation for Shakespeare and a number of early modern writers. In *Othello*, "Reputation, reputation, reputation" is what separates the human from the "bestial" (2.3.241, 243), and in *The Merry Wives of Windsor*, Master Ford likens a blemish to his reputation to a "hole made in your best coat" (3.5.120–121), such that all the world may see and scorn. Reputation is, as Richard Allestree opines in the 1667 *The Government of the Tongue,* the "opinion and estimation among others" (Allestree 1667, 88), but in all of these treatments, reputation is largely figured, as Allestree's focus on the tongue indicates, to be the work of circulating speech within a community of one's peers.[2] In the aforementioned sonnets, however, the already anxiety-laden institution of reputation is amplified through "public means," which seemingly extend beyond one's immediate social network to a broader public at large. In fact, in Sonnet 112, the poet pleads to hear "my shames and praises from your tongue" (6), suggesting a compliant acceptance of the traditional avenues of extrinsic reputation-building in place of the wholly uncontrollable stain of public dye. The stamp, the stain, the brand, and the motley all speak to an amplification of reputation as occurs in the public sphere, where the speech often cited as reputation's primary vehicle is only one form of media available for public evaluation and circulation.

If all names are encoded with values of identificatory designation and reputation, celebrity names—like the celebrity's staged presence as discussed in the previous chapter—operate through an excess of signification, a surplus of meaning accrued through evaluation and circulation among the public. As high public visibility necessitates the dispersal of names, images, and biographies in order to achieve mass dissemination, subjective agency is likewise dispersed, scattered amongst the various social and commercial networks through which celebrity narrative is both produced and consumed. Thus, celebrities are co-authored by their publics, sometimes in supplemental alliance with, and sometimes in at least partial resistance to, the aims and interests of the celebrity's self-presentation. If, as I argue in Chapter 1, star presence on the stage hinges on an absent field for audience projection, the early modern theatrical star's offstage presence, as it migrated via the vessel of celebrity name into the bookstalls, the ballad-sheets, the market, and the arenas of idle chat, likewise invited collaborative participation. Celebrity names, as Linda Charnes argues of notorious ones, "become the property of a cultural marketplace": a "simultaneous placement (the identifying name) and displacement (the lost 'signified')" (Charnes 1993, 4).

In *Celebrity Society*, Van Krieken positions celebrities as "both the subjects and the objects of power relations" (Van Krieken 2012, 8); while the celebrity subject may ride the rising tide of fame to command the economic, affective, and political perks of prominence, the celebrity is likewise subjected to the oscillating whims of public negotiation. While the poet in Sonnet 111 is, as he notes, a man of means, he is a man of public means, with his livelihood dependent upon the very forces that have branded his name. On the other side of the equation, the public, likewise, operates in both subjective and objective capacities, with the productive power to brand arising from their consumptive practices. If theatrical stars are born on the stage, their perpetuity as celebrity depends upon an active public's everyday acts of celebrity consumption-production, in which their trade and use of a celebrity's name infuse it with value. As Michel de Certeau theorizes in *The Practice of Everyday Life*,

> To [...] spectacular production corresponds *another* production, called 'consumption.' The latter is devious, it is dispersed, but it insinuates itself everywhere, silently and almost invisibly, because it does not manifest itself through its own products, but rather through its *ways of using* the products.
> (de Certeau 1984, xiii)

As de Certeau illustrates throughout his examination of the individual's role in mass culture, consumption is itself a productive, generative act, as the consumer's use of a product is precisely what makes it mean. Quite circularly, then, the celebrity consumer's use of celebrities, from purchasing their images to fantasizing about them to further publicizing them in speech or writing, is simultaneously what imbues celebrities with cultural meaning and, thereby, constructs their public presence.

In *1 Henry IV*, Falstaff muses to Hal, "I would to God thou and I knew where a commodity of good names were to be bought" (1.2.72–74), and this chapter explores just such a commodity of good names in the early modern markets of London—not good in Falstaff's sense of a positively esteemed reputational apparel, ready-made to blanket one's ill regard in refreshed repute, but good in the sense that these names served as commercial goods. As these "name-goods" of theatrical celebrities travelled from stage to page and back again, their names became branded through circulation with diverse values, from the price of print to the projected values of their consumer-producers.

Thus, as de Certeau theorizes of consumptive production, early modern consumers of commodified celebrity names co-structured the public figures they traded in; through use, they crafted the identificatory bricolage that Shakespeare deems a motley in Sonnet 110 or the branded name of Sonnet 111. Such names, then, as Shakespeare laments, became less a form of personal identification as they were what Rosemary Coombe has labeled the multifariously authored "floating signifier" of celebrity, such that, "The names and likenesses of the famous [...] resonate with meanings that exceed the intentions or the interests of those they identify or resemble" (Coombe 2006, 722). That excess of meanings accrued in a celebrity name amounts to a kind of a second self: a publicly crafted, publicly owned, branded celebrity-entity that consumer-producers embed with social value. Thus, this chapter will explore early modern celebrity names as they "floated" from stage to stage, then stage to page, then through the market of commodities exchange where they offered early modern Londoners a human and material means of negotiating the commercial activities that governed their own lives. Finally, I conclude with Shakespeare's thorough examination of the floating signifier of a commercially traded name in *The Comedy of Errors*, in which a publicly branded name assumes, as in celebrity, a human form.

The social lives of players

"A commodity," writes anthropologist Arjun Appadurai in *The Social Lives of Things*, "is a thoroughly socialized thing" (Appadurai 1986, 6). As Appadurai argues, a commodity's value arises from a complex system of social interactions that embeds objects with "cultural biographies" (34), in that through exchange, commodities travel time and space, trade hands, and accrue social histories and associations that convey significance and impart value. Further, Appadurai maintains that objects, or "things-in-motion," move in and out of the commodity state, as their values emerge, morph, fluctuate, or disappear throughout the course of their "careers" (16). Particularly apropos to the circulation of celebrity, Appadurai positions the commodity in a space "between pure desire and immediate enjoyment" (3), with the commodity's determination as such dependent upon its ability to resist acquisition.

Appadurai's process-oriented materialism has proven diversely applicable to the study of the theater, whether in "understanding how things on stage behave in performance" (Rutter 2006, 182), or, as Jonathan Gil Harris and Natasha Korda demonstrate in *Staged Properties in Early Modern English Drama* (Harris and Korda 2002), how staged things behave outside of performance as well. "Certain props disrupt the fields of representation in which they appear by disclosing larger social lives that extend beyond the stage," writes Harris (2002, 36), and in so doing, staged commodities call attention to their broader cultural biographies in the real world of market exchange to signal their histories before and potential futures after the spectacle.[3] Though Harris aims, following Appadurai's model, to examine the means by which "commodities, like persons, have social lives" (Appadurai 1986, 3), I'd like here to offer a sort of circular reversal: celebrities, as commodities, also have social lives. In their contributions to Appadurai's volume, both Igor Kopytoff and Patrick Geary extend notions of the socialized commodity to accommodate persons as well, and as Kopytoff argues, "the conceptual polarity of individualized persons and commoditized things is recent and, culturally speaking, exceptional" (Kopytoff 1986, 64). Geary likewise notes that certain commodities, under particular circumstances, "might be the objects of commerce, but under other circumstances they more closely resemble persons" (Geary 1986, 188), as both critics suggest that the state of personhood is as fluid as that of commodity, with people similarly moving in and out of the commodity state throughout their careers. Therefore, in their purchasable availability, whether in print or performance, celebrities, like objects, move into the commodity state through their ability to arouse desire while resisting acquisition; they accrue cultural biographies quite distinct from their personal ones through their mediated circulation; and they regularly signal their availability and salability outside of their variously defined performances.[4] Early modern theatrical celebrities were, as Bristol has asserted, "living commodities" (Bristol 1996, 35).[5]

Like the commodity-object, the commoditized early modern celebrity player participated in a complex social life, his commercial appeal informed by a cultural biography that included his past performances, offstage social interactions, and appearances in other media. Further, as Harris argues of staged props, onstage, players can likewise disrupt the dramatic diegesis in which they appear in order to reveal their existence beyond the momentary spectacle. For example, Cleopatra's lament in *Antony and Cleopatra* that "Some squeaking Cleopatra" will one day "boy [her] greatness" in performance of her person (5.2.219), punctures the fabric of the play-world as it directs the audience to contemplate the presence of the boy actor currently embodying the role of Cleopatra. This kind of rupture also publicizes the actor's cultural biography, figuring the targeted player as a transportable entity who exists outside of the world presented on the stage and triggering what Jacky Bratton has theorized as the audience's intertheatric associations—that "whole web of mutual understanding between potential audiences and their players," or the theatrical "knowingness" that audiences bring with them to the theater (Bratton 2003, 37). In her parodically veiled announcement of herself as a boy actor, the staged Cleopatra demands that her audience not only consult their understanding of theatrical convention, but of the very boy who has made the declaration.

If metatheater invites attention to itself as theater, then intertheater, the theatrical analogue to intertextuality, directs attention to the connections between performances.[6] Moments of intertheatricality call upon the actors' and the audience's memories of other performances—including conventions, props, actions, and actors—to create a shared language of experience and association amongst them. Intertheatrical references then provide a potent means of publicizing the staged actor's cultural biography as such cues compel audiences to search outside the current theatrical event for a relevant set of contexts across a network of interlinked performances. But parody, in particular, such as that found within Cleopatra's lament, offers an especially effective means of generating intertheatric recall. Linda Hutcheon defines parody by "its inscribing as well as undermining of that which it parodies" (Hutcheon 1989, 101), as parody simultaneously legitimizes as cultural referent what it playfully deflates. Its self-conscious and intertheatrical referentiality requires an audience savvy to theatrical conventions and contexts as it pierces the performance with external considerations, and audiences who desire to be in on the in-joke must scan the catalogue of their theatrical experience to forge the requisite connections. Parody's generally good-spirited mockery further coalesces the audience into a collective, with their communal laughter signaling their authoritative prowess over the figure ridiculed. When centered on an individual actor, parody has the capacity to brand the player with the extra-dramatic excesses of his social history.

The Admiral's Men certainly capitalized on the publicizing potential of intertheatrical parody, especially disguise parody, as Gurr documents in *Shakespeare's Opposites* (Gurr 2009). Through disguise parody, a small company was able to maximize the stage-time of its hottest commodity, Alleyn, as he could thereby appear in multiple roles within the same play. Gurr cites specifically George Chapman's *The Blind Beggar of Alexandria* (Chapman 1598), in which Alleyn performed more than one-third of its lines in three different guises, two of which intertheatrically suggested Alleyn's most famous roles of Tamburlaine and Barrabas (Gurr 2009, 22, 24). As audiences must locate and recognize the external referent in order to respond such parodic interplay, Alleyn's disguise roles promoted his cultural biography by directing attention to the actor's availability in other performances. Further, as disguise roles alienate audiences through the defamiliarization of disguise just as they refamiliarize through intertheatrical recognition, Alleyn's embodied references to Tamburlaine and Barrabas in Chapman's play bolster the celebrity's commodity state through the delicate dance of desire and thwarted satiation that maintains value.

While this emphasis on disguise-parody was a unique feature of the Admiral's Men, similarly parodic rhetorical references to the offstage identities of actors feature in several seventeenth-century plays across companies. Jonson, for example, made regular employ of the practice of theatrical name-dropping, or direct references to the offstage identities of the onstage players-in-part. In *Christmas, His Masque* (1640, Sig. B2v), performed in 1616, Venus calls out "Master Burbage" and "Master Hemmings"; also first performed in 1616, *The Devil Is an Ass* (1640) features a sustained parodic reference to King's Man Richard Robinson. The effect of this kind of theatrical name-dropping is similar to the effect achieved through disguise-roles, in that in such moments, the celebrity-player is offered up as a floating signifier capable of attaching to and detaching from role. Through the pronouncement of the celebrity's offstage name, the play-world momentarily dissolves to highlight the player's transportability and alternate identity outside its bounds—an identity that is in the moment of performance further accruing a social history that will supplement its value. But because such moments of name-dropping remain only brief and sporadic, unlike the sustained disguise roles employed by the Admiral's Men, such utterances quickly suture the fabric of the dramatic worlds they disrupt, allowing only the most attentive audiences a fleeting peek behind the veil of character.

A brief moment of parodic name-dropping in Jonson's *Bartholomew Fair* calls special attention to the transportability of the socialized, celebrity player as well as the inverse dynamics of elevation and deflation at the heart of parody. Set amidst the bustling commercial and theatrical activity of the annual late-August Smithfield fair, the "hobby-horse seller" Leatherhead prepares to perform his puppet-show adaptation of *Hero and Leander*, when the country esquire Cokes approaches him and inquires of his basket of puppets:

COKES: Do you call these players?
LEATHERHEAD: They are actors sir, and as good as any, none dispraised, for
    dumb shows. Indeed, I am the mouth of 'em all!
    [...]
COKES: Which is your Burbage now?
LEATHERHEAD: What mean you by that, sir?
COKES: Your best actor. Your Field?
LITTLEWIT: Good, I'faith! You are even with me, sir.

(5.3.87–91, 98–101)

Reminiscent of Greene's charge in his *Groats-worth of Witte* that actors are "beautified by [poets'] feathers" (Greene 1592, Sig. C4), here, Jonson levels an intertheatric swipe at players, likening them to inanimate, wooden conduits for the voice of the dramatist, whose words provide "the mouth of 'em all." Of course, the intertheatric punchline works only so long as the audience recognizes Nathan Field—a leading player of Lady Elizabeth's Men in 1614 when the play was performed—on the stage, presumably in the part of Littlewit, as he informs the potential customer that the man Cokes seeks is standing right in front of him.[7] Like all instances of name-dropping, Cokes' question, "Your Field?", punctures the narrative to alert playgoers not only to Field's corporeal presence on the stage, but also to his theatrical history, his popular reception and fame as the "best actor," and his reputation as a leading man in a number of performances. This moment of parodic intertheater likewise reveals Field as a vendible commodity on the stage by not only pairing, but conflating, his name with a prop: as the puppet show functions as a play-within-a-play, the puppets then occupy a unique position as performers, props, and Leatherhead's vendible wares, blurring the distinction between human subject and commercial object altogether. The exchange simultaneously anthropomorphizes the puppet while reducing the actor, confronted by his puppet doppelganger, to a commoditized good. The puppet is, quite literally, a commoditized player, a purchasable performer. When Leatherhead displays his "best actor" as the puppet in the part of Leander, he collapses the distinction between the actor and the object that shares his transportable name; standing before the actor Nathan Field, he produces his "Field": a saleable product, a stage property that, by play's end, Cokes asks to take home as personal property.[8]

In a similar, though slightly more extended, episode of parodic name-dropping, John Cooke's *The Cittie Gallant* (Cooke 1614), later known as *Greene's Tu Quoque*, promotes the presence of Queen Anne's Men's star player, the clown Thomas Greene. According to Edwin Nungezer, "Greene was [...] to Queen Anne's company what Burbage was to the King's Men. His excellence as a clown made him known to all Londoners as the best comedian since Tarlton and Kempe" (Nungezer 1929, 162). First performed in 1611, *The Cittie Gallant* dramatizes among its intertwined narratives the story of the servant Bubble's sudden rise to an unexpected fortune that allows him temporarily to become his master's master. As Bubble, played by Greene, discusses plans for the evening's entertainment, he parodically reveals the actor's presence beneath the guise of character:

SCATTERGOOD: Yes, fayth, brother: if it please you, let's goe see a Play at the Gloabe.
BUBBLE: I care not, any whither, so the Clowne have a part; For ifayth I am no body without a Foole.
GERALDINE: Why then wee'l goe to the Red Bull: they say Greene's a good Clowne.
BUBBLE: Greene? Greene's an ass.
SCATTERGOOD: Wherefore doe you say so?
BUBBLE: Indeed I ha no reason: for they say hee is like mee as ever hee can look.

(Sig. G2v)

Once again, the intertheatric joke requires a savvy audience that recognizes Greene in the role of Bubble as it promotes the play's star by pronouncing his cultural biography while enticing the unfamiliar to seek out the referent should they want to participate in the collective response to parody. As parody, the dialogue here both mocks and elevates: Greene, in the part of Bubble, calls himself an ass while Geraldine relays that Greene is a good clown—or rather, that "*they* say Greene's a good Clowne," thereby reiterating Greene's laudatory reviews to the very public who produced them.

As Geraldine notes, *they* have singled out Greene as the Red Bull's star performer, as apparently did the play's audiences. Throughout the play, the newly enriched Bubble, who has deemed Latin a suitable rhetorical turn for a man of his newfound stature, repeats the only Latin phrase he knows: "*Tu quoque*," or "you also." The repeated motto must have delighted audiences, as E.K. Chambers reports that by 1612, less than a year after its debut, *The Cittie Gallant* became known simply as *Greene's Tu Quoque* (Chambers 1923, 78). In an interesting deployment of star name-dropping, the name promoted on stage grew to overshadow both the playwright and the play's title, and when Greene died in 1612, the play was not performed again for more than a decade as it had become too thoroughly intertwined with his name to continue without him. Richard Brathwaite's 1618 collection of epigrams demonstrates the clown's posthumous enmeshment with his signature catchphrase in both "Upon an actor now of late deceased: and upon his action Tu Quoque" and "Upon [Greene's] fellow actors," which includes the lines, "What can you crave of your poore fellow more?/ He does but what *Tu quoque* did before" (Sig. G5v). But if the show could not go on, the marketers of print continued to capitalize on Greene's name after his death; the title page of the 1614 quarto edition of the play boldly features Greene's name in large letters above an image of him speaking the words "*Tu quoque.*" Branded by his signature role's catchphrase, Greene's celebrity name continued to circulate the market in the absence of the person it once signified.

Tarlton and the social network

Greene's Tu Quoque offers a potent demonstration of the means by which the social lives of players were not confined to the platform of the stage. As the early modern celebrity actor's name and its attached cultural biography migrated from play to play and theater to theater, it likewise travelled through transmedial networks of performance, print, and the popular imagination, and its journey was rarely a straight line. Greene's celebrity, already adequately enough established by the staging of *The Cittie Gallant* to serve as the target of intertheatrical parody, swelled in scope through performance to achieve a popularly recognized association with his character's catchphrase, which then retitled the play in his name both informally in public chatter then formally in print, before it formed the basis of posthumous tribute and haunted subsequent performance with his still-attached name more than a decade later. The complex intertheatrical network of Greene's cultural biography is hardly aberrant, as a number of early modern actors would likewise see their branded names travel similarly tangled commercial pathways.

The exceptional celebrity of Tarlton provides the most pertinent example of such a complex commercial and affective matrix, as, like Greene, Tarlton's name, narrative, and image would continue to grace the pages of print and inflect performances well after his death, but to much more expansive distribution. As noted in Chapter 1, no actor of the era was as widely written or spoken about as Tarlton, and while the vast array of extant print references does little to demystify his life and craft, the print record paints an undeniable portrait of his massive appeal and social circulation. As noted in the previous chapter, Tarlton's name appeared in print at least three times, though somewhat dubiously, as the reporter of news (of floods, snow, and an earthquake, respectively) as well as in ballads and collections of anecdotes, and his name would continue to proliferate in print treatments for at least a century after his death. The diarist John Manningham and the Thames water-poet John Taylor, for example, recorded some of Tarlton's specific jokes (Manningham 1976 [1603]; Taylor 1629); many eulogized; and others overtly fictionalized, including several reported encounters with Tarlton's ghost. The most popular account of his life was undoubtedly *Tarltons Jests* (1613), a collection of anecdotes and witticisms composed in parts over the course of more than two decades following his death and reprinted in multiple editions. Each of these disparate accounts demonstrate the co-authorial status Tarlton and his public shared in the establishment of his celebrity. Tarlton's was a name branded by the public, bought and sold in performance and print, and wielded as communal property.

One particularly salient demonstration of the social network through which Tarlton's name and narrative were both established and traded as a transportable brand can be found in Robert Wilson's *The Three Lords and Three Ladies of London* (Wilson 1590). In this Queen's Men production, performed just two years after Tarlton's death, a ballad-selling clown named Simplicity appears onstage to display his wares before three young pages. "This is Tarltons picture" (Sig. C1v), Simplicity informs an illiterate page and, by extension, the larger theatrical audience. "Didst thou never know Tarlton?" When the page responds that he never knew the recently deceased stage clown, Simplicity takes the page's ignorance as an opportunity to eulogize: he provides a brief biography, highlights the departed clown's wit, and contrasts Tarlton's "plaine" appearance with the "fineness [that] was within" (Sig. C1v). In short, he summarizes,

> O, it was a fine fellow, as ere was borne:
> There will never come his like while the earth can corne
> O, passing fine Tarlton! I would thou hadst lived yet.
> (Sig. C1v)

Of course, Simplicity's heartfelt reverence for Tarlton mingles with his own commercial interests, as demonstrated by one page's response: "Because of thy praise, what's the price of the picture," the page Wealth immediately asks (Sig. C1v). As Simplicity quite literally establishes Tarlton's commodity value when he charges a groat for the ballad, he also imbues the commodity with complex affective value at the same time, branding the name and image at hand through his own recollection of the exceptional performance history of the "merriest fellow" to have ever graced the stage (Sig. C1v).

The staging of "Tarltons picture" has generated a number of critical speculations, both in terms of the image's materiality and its signifying capacity. Richard Levin has noted that neither the dialogue nor the stage directions ("*Shew Tarltons picture*") ever explicitly identify whether the picture is a ballad, a small woodcut taken from a book's title page, or a folio-length picture more easily seen by audience members (Levin 2000, 436); however, John Astington argues that, in line with Simplicity's profession, the picture is most likely a ballad that was "probably for sale outside the playhouse after the performance" or, more simply, "the real thing" (Astington 1997, 163), meaning, a stage property not created for the performance but one already available and saleable. Embracing Astington's reasoning, Munro then observes that "such a mass-market image of Tarlton provides an especially legible illustration of the commercial matrix that stands behind the prop" (Munro 2009, 118–119).

Tarlton's picture exemplifies Harris's appropriation of Appadurai's socialized commodity as regards the prop: here, a ballad likely available for sale outside the theater walls appears onstage to entice the audience's would-be buyers, whose consumptive desires are mirrored in the onstage customers. But this particular prop enjoys a rather more complex social life, as the picture Simplicity aims to sell on stage points not only to a vendible good, but a marketable name, already attached to and fueling the sale of other print goods on the market. In contrast to the more utilitarian or artisanal wares that Harris takes as his focus, Tarlton's picture points less to the skilled work of craftsmen than to the intangible force of a famous name and the complex matrix of memory, affect, and desire that such a name signifies or arouses. In fact, the page Wealth tells Simplicity, "There is no such fineness in the picture, that I see" (Sig. C1v), and Simplicity's sales pitch notably offers nothing of the good's artisanal value in terms of the quality of the likeness; instead, the ballad-seller waxes on in tribute to Tarlton and focuses solely on the skill of the man represented—a skill he pointedly remarks was "passing fine," meaning both exceptional and ephemeral, as he reminds his potential customers that though the man is dead, his name and image are still for sale. What Simplicity offers, then, is the tantalizing opportunity to hold on to a beloved, though departed, celebrity of the London stage, to own his name and image, to transform him, by means of a stage property, into personal property.

The staging of Tarlton's picture reveals the means by which "the real thing" for sale and in circulation is less the material picture than the immaterial force of a celebrity's name—a name that the ballad-seller infuses with additional value when he ties knowledge of this famous name to the buyer's personal worth by taunting, "if thou knewest not him, thou knewest no body" (Sig. C1v, 267). Here, Simplicity cunningly equates consumption of the image to an elevation of the consumer's value by way of cultural savvy. To buy Tarlton's image, in this exchange, is to know him; to know Tarlton, the ballad-seller instructs, is to be somebody.[9] Thus, in Tarlton, the ballad-object, Tarlton's stage history, and the consumer's self-interest all converge to generate new and enhanced value in the celebrity name for sale. This process of collaborative production is further affirmed and, in fact, amplified when the same image resurfaced on the London stage again in 1600 in Robert Armin's *Quips Upon Questions* (Armin 1600). In this scripted adaptation of extemporal practices, in which the audience shouts questions toward the stage for improvisational response, the question posed is, "Wher's Tarlton" (Sig. E3). The response recounts the story of a collier who refuses to accept word of Tarlton's recent death and so seeks him out at the theater to prove the news a falsehood. There, he encounters Tarlton's image upon the stage:

> Within the Play past, was his picture usd,
> Which when the fellow saw, he laught aloud:

> A ha, quoth he, I knew we were abusde,
> That he was kept away from all this croude.
> The simple man was quiet, and departed,
> And hauing seene his Picture, was glad harted.
>
> (Sig. E4)

As Levin convincingly argues, the "Play past" is almost certainly Wilson's *The Three Lords and Three Ladies of London* (Levin 2000, 435), and thus, the collier takes Simplicity's ballad as "the real thing"—not a vendible good, nor even a name and image, but the man himself—and leaves the playhouse contented to discover Tarlton yet living and that news of Tarlton's death "was but rumour'd prate" (Sig. E4). Levin argues that "Armin's point is that the collier was right after all because, even though Tarlton is dead, his fame lives on" (2000, 435), but if the collier accepts the man's circulating fame, as emblematized in the staged image, as a surrogate for the man himself, then the collier stubbornly refuses to accept circulating report in favor of a highly personal exchange with mediatized representation. Despite others' insistence that "he is dead" (Sig. E4), the collier remains determined from the onset to discover Tarlton alive as "he sayd that he would see him" (Sig. E4); thus, when the collier finally concludes from the picture that the actor "yet [...] lives" (Sig. E4), he has seen in the picture exactly what he vowed he would see, and the reanimate Tarlton that the collier proclaims is a personal fantasy facilitated through the availability, and salability, of Tarlton's name and image.

Taken together, the staging of and reference to Tarlton's picture in both Wilson's and Armin's plays offer a fascinating, albeit limited, glimpse into the social network of commercial circulation and affective purchase of early modern celebrity names and narratives. Here, in an almost dizzying interflow of intertheatrical and transmedial referentiality, it is not only the picture, but Tarlton-as-commodity who enjoys a vital social life through these plays. Despite his corporeal absence, the public continues to participate in a pattern of complex social and commercial interactions, if not with him, then with his brand. As in de Certeau's model, the Tarlton social network demonstrates how consumers' use of Tarlton—that is, their buying, selling, self-promoting, memorializing, and fantasizing—is the same set of processes that imbues Tarlton with meaning. Here, acts of consumption thereby become acts of value- and meaning-production. In both these plays, what Tarlton means is a motley assemblage of multifarious contributions: he is the merriest fellow of the sixteenth-century stage and a man of exceptional wit, a vendible ware, the collier's reanimated memories, and a projection of personal value and cultural acumen. Thus, Tarlton's branded name reflects as much if not more upon the public who consumes-produces him as it does upon the man himself.

Texts and the city

As both *The Three Lords and Three Ladies of London* and *Greenes Tu Quoque* demonstrate, players' cultural biographies were promulgated transmedially across the platforms of both stage and page, and while stage-players' prominence within early modern London originated and flourished in the mass forum of the theater, their names and narratives circulated to even greater penetration through a burgeoning market of theatrically inspired print. The market of theatrical print constitutes a broad spectrum of discourse, encompassing the commendatory verse noted in Chapter 1 as well as print plays, anti-theatrical polemics, theatrical apologia, jestbooks, anecdote collections and other print ephemera, as well as advertorial playbills and print-play title-pages, which were regularly posted across London. Like intertheatric parody, such print could prove disruptive, too; as Tiffany Stern observes in *Documents of Performance in Early Modern England*, "the city was textual, not in a new historical sense so much as in a literal one: it was covered in texts," as prominently posted "playbills and playbook title-pages were a major way in which the playhouse intruded into the city" (Stern 2009, 62).[10]

While these variant print forms served myriad different aims, all could be said to heighten the city's awareness of theatrical places, processes, and persons. As the market for theatrical print expanded over the final decades of the sixteenth century and the early decades of the seventeenth century, so, too, swelled the visibility of actors and companies on and in those texts. "Plays were always products to which names were attached" (Taylor 2007, 35), and print-plays provided one potent avenue for the promotion of players, especially in the seventeenth century as playbooks assumed more of a souvenir function in their orientation and thus promised to capture some portion of the theatrical spectacle, including the bodies that populated it, "as it hath been played." As a number of critical examinations of extant playbooks demonstrates, printed plays have, since their inception, contained information related to their staging, but as the turn of the seventeenth century approached, that information shifted from a primarily instructional to a memorial format, or as Matteo Pangallo notes, "from a market comprised largely of potential amateur playmakers to one comprised almost exclusively of readers: that is, from a market of mostly producers to a market of mostly consumers" (Pangallo 2015, 89). Instead of offering staging instruction, the ubiquitous title-page blurb of the early decades of the seventeenth century referenced production as a means of assigning value to the play-text by virtue of its past life, or its cultural biography, as performance. As a prefatory epistle to Shakespeare's First Folio explains, "these Playes have had their triall alreadie, and stood out all Appeales; and do now come forth quitted rather by a Decree of Court, then any purchas'd Letters of commendation" (Sig. A3); similarly, the declaration that a play has been "sundry" or "divers" times acted indicates its validity and worth, having withstood its "triall" by performance to proceed to print.

But in announcing their relationship to the performance event, printed play-texts participate in a similar disruption as do the onstage actors who signal their availability beyond the spectacle—that is, play-texts alert the reader to a commercial experience available outside the confines of the page on the city's stages, though one that now exists only in souvenir substitution.[11] As souvenir, the printed play sustains the tensions between desire and satiation, offering a material record of a spectacle that it pointedly professes as no longer available through the past-tense finality of "As it hath been played," even as the distancing "as" transforms the text into simile: the thing of the playbook, title pages tease, is not the playing of the play, but *as* it. Thus, the play-text does not only establish its own value by way of the performance it promises to preserve, but the value of the ephemeral performance event that it likewise assures can never be adequately captured in its pages—only something *as* it. The playbook's regular references to the actors' bodies that performed in the now lost spectacle—whether directly named, invoked through character or dialogue, or hinted at in the record of the applause he received—promises a tangible, possessable trace of the performing body in action as it simultaneously signals his wider, though unprintable, cultural biography.

Players' offstage identities emerged through multiple means in printed play-texts and were regularly exploited as marketing tools. Considering that early modern printers operated under no legal obligations to credit, cite, or compensate the writers, producers, or performers of plays, any acknowledgment of the playbook's prior history in performance occurred only at the discretion of the printer, who most likely included such information only when considered useful for marketing purposes.[12] "The name of an unknown author, might, after all, do a play no good service," Stern writes. "If an author's name will sell a book, it starts to feature: Shakespeare, not named on any title page before 1598, is, by 1605, featuring even on plays he had not written" (Stern 2009, 59). Though there is little uniformity to the information included on playbook title-pages, and thus little to suggest a comprehensive marketing strategy for printed plays, the widespread, though not invariable practice of announcing its past history as performance offers some suggestion as to the playbook's appeal. References both oblique and direct to actors in print-plays further suggest that actors held market appeal. Though the 1594 title-page of *A Knack to Know a Knave*, which boldly proclaims that "it hath sundrie tymes bene played by Ed. Allen and his companie, With Kemps applauded merrimentes," stands out as perhaps the most overtly and commercially explicit title-page reference to any early modern actors, actors did feature fairly regularly within playbook pages, primarily through cast lists.

As Tamara Atkin and Emma Smith's meticulous examination of early modern cast lists demonstrates, the term *actor* in playbooks is an ambiguous conflation, sometimes referring to the professional actors who performed in a play but often used to signify their dramatic roles and, in some cases, both simultaneously (Atkin and Smith 2014, 659–660). As Atkin and Smith note, the term's multivalence suggests some "ambiguity—perhaps deliberate—around the ontology of 'acting'" (659), as person who plays and part played become indecipherably intertwined, such that even the unnamed professional actor's presence haunts the printed record of his character. But several plays, including Webster's *The Duchess of Malfi* (1623), Massinger's *The Renegado* (1630) and *The Roman Actor* (1629), James Shirley's *The Wedding* (1629), and John Ford's *The Lovers Melancholy* (1629) do include the names of the actors who performed in them, while a handful single out specific actors for praise. The 1652 edition of Beaumont and Fletcher's *The Wild Goose Chase* (Beaumont and Fletcher 1652), for example, includes not only a list of characters and the actors who performed them, but a few lines of verse celebrating "two actors" (Sig. A2), John Lowin and Joseph Taylor, who are respectively cited as having acted "Most naturally" and "Incomparably" (Sig. A3). The 1612 edition of Webster's *The White Devil* includes neither a list of actors nor characters, but does append a note in praise of Worcester's Man Richard Perkins:

> For the action of the play, twas generally well, and I dare affirme, with the joint testimony of some of their owne quality, for the true imitation of life, without striving to make nature a monster, the best that ever became them. Whereof as I make a generall acknowledgment, so in particular I must remember the well approved industry of my friend Maister Perkins, and confesse the worth of his action did crowne both the beginning and end.
> (Webster 1612, Sig. M3)

As Webster's adulatory addendum links his printed play to its successful "triall" in performance, it also specifically links the play to a particular performer and, like cast lists in general, aligns the script with the stars of the stage.

The highly visible names of actors and companies certainly fulfilled a cross-promotional function as well, drawing enhanced consumer attention to the actors themselves, magnifying their visibility and redirecting attention to the players' corporeal availability on the stage, especially in the case of playbills which, like title-pages, were posted prominently throughout the city. Though no playbill dating from before 1687 has survived, Stern hypothesizes, based on anecdotal evidence and the smattering of other forms of extant advertising bills, that playbills and title pages included quite similar information, including the venue and acting company (Stern 2009, 37). In an anecdote published in his *Wit and Mirth*, the Thames ferryman and poet John Taylor suggests that playbills were rather conspicuous features in the city:

> Master Field the Player riding up Fleetstreet a great pace, a Gentleman called him, and asked him what Play was played that day. Hee (being angry to be stayd upon so frivolous a demand) answered, that he might see what Play was to be playd upon every Poste. I cry you mercy (said the Gentleman) I tooke you for a Poste, you road so fast.
> (Taylor 1629, Sig. B7)

Thus, with playbills and title-pages "upon every Poste," the names of playhouses and acting companies enjoyed substantial representation throughout London, potentially facilitating citywide familiarity.

Taylor's account also demonstrates that printed plays and advertising materials account for only a portion of the texts that circulated the names of famous players throughout London, and this brief story, while establishing Field as a recognizable celebrity who is interrupted and irritated by the demands of his public, is, interestingly, one of only five of *Wit and Mirth*'s one hundred anecdotes to label its subject by name.[13] Two of the others, Tarlton and Lady Elizabeth's man William Barkstead, are also players, suggesting that Taylor not only banked upon readers' familiarity with their names, but deemed all three to be subjects of public interest. But printed anecdotal accounts such as Taylor's offer a glimpse not only into the circulation, but the appropriation, of celebrity names in the print market, as players regularly feature simultaneously as both recognizable cultural points of reference and the butt of public jokes, not unlike the parodic interplay of the stage. Consider, for example, the following story involving Barkstead:

> *Will Backstead* the Plaier cast his Chamber-lye out of his window in the night, which chanced to light upoon the heads of the watch passing by, who angrily said, Who is it that offers us this abuse? Why, quoth *Will*, who is there? Who is here, said one of the pickled watchmen, we are the Watch. The Watch, quoth *William*, why my friends, you know, *Harme watch, harme catch*.
>
> (Taylor 1629, Sigs. A8–B1)

Both the Field and Barkstead anecdotes similarly elevate, then ridicule, their subjects, singling each man out for his recognized fame and even physically elevating him—Field upon horse, Barkstead up in his window—before gently deflating him, allowing Field's interpellator to get the last word and positioning Barkstead with his chamber pot. Another account in *Taylor's Feast* involving John Singer, who grew ill upon being served a beverage to which he had a strong aversion (Taylor 1629, 67), likewise playfully humiliates its player-subject, at once singling him out as a famous actor and then ridiculing him as he falls into "a foolish traunce" (67). Each of these anecdotes, along with a number of posthumously published anecdotes revolving around Tarlton, follows a similar narrative pattern in which theatrical celebrities' names are wielded for their popular cachet and exploited to comic effect, which points to the unique kind of fame enjoyed by celebrities who have achieved, through various avenues of circulation, the prominence to function as cultural references, though they elicit little reverence. Instead, celebrities' appearances in pamphlets consistently reiterate their base humanity, which also reaffirms the public's narrative authority over the otherwise larger-than-life celebrities of the stage.

Of course, as discussed in Chapter 1, actors were also held in high regard as the frequent subjects of printed commendatory verses, but the playful derision and mockery of stage-players evident in pamphlets extended to popular ballads as well. As the staging of Tarlton's picture suggests, players also featured in early modern ballads; Tarlton and his successor Will Kempe were especially popular subjects of the form. A ballad entitled *A Sonnett upon the pittiful burning of the Globe playhowse in London* (ctd. in Chambers 1923, II. 420–422) paints a number of prominent King's Men as bumbling fools in its comical account of the 1613 fire:

> Out runne the knightes, out runne the lordes,
> And there was great adoe;
> Some lost their hattes and some their swordes;
> Then out runne Burbidge too;
> The reprobates, though druncke on Munday,
> Prayd for the Foole and Henry Condye.
> Oh sorrow, &c.
> […]
> Then with swolne eyes, like druncken Flemminges,
> Distressed stood old stuttering Heminges.
> (22–28, 33–34)

Just as playwrights held little control over the publication of their plays, actors, as Shakespeare laments, possessed little control over the circulation of their name and image in ballad.

Perhaps nowhere is the early modern celebrity's struggle to reconcile himself to the uncontrollable manipulability of his famous name more pointedly illustrated than in Kemp's *Nine Daies Wonder*. In early 1600, after having parted ways with the Lord Chamberlain's Men (frequently speculated as due to creative differences with Shakespeare), Kemp staged an elaborate publicity stunt in which he Morris-danced from London to Norwich, a distance of approximately one hundred miles. Later that year, in an apparent bid to correct the erroneous record disseminated in popular ballads, Kemp published his *Nine Daies Wonder* (1600). While these competing ballads no longer exist, Kemp's pleas to an "impudent generation of ballad-makers" suggest a fairly extensive network of circulation (Sig. D3). As Kemp recounts his famous journey and the clamoring crowds that cheered him on, he decries the numerous unauthorized accounts of his stunt currently in print:

> I am forst to desire your protection, else every Ballad-singer will proclaime me bankrupt of honesty, A sort of mad fellows seeing me merrily dispos'd in a Morrice, have so bepainted mee in print since my gambols began from London to Norwich, that (having but an ill face before) I shall appear to the world without a face, if your fayre hand wipe not away their foule colours. One hath written Kemps farewell to the tune of Kery, merym Buffe: another his desperate daungers in his late travaile: the third his entertainement to New-Market; which towne I came never neere by the length of halfe the heath. Some sweare in a Trenchmore I have trode a good way to winne the world: others that guesse righter, affirme, I have without good help daunst myselfe out of the world: many say things that were never thought, But in a word your poor servant offers the truth of his progresse and profit to your honorable view.
> (Sigs. A3–A4)

Such pleas also suggest the tensions that the targets of such print accounts may have experienced as they lost agency over their names' circulation in the print market, with the "foule colours" with which he has been "bepainted" reminiscent of the "dyer's hand" in Sonnet 111. Kemp's branded name has, too, become stained by circulating report, with Kemp's own intervention into the record amounting to a compensatory strategy to reclaim the reins of a reputation that had spiraled outside his control. Kemp concludes with the "humble request" that balladeers "not fill the country with lyes of his never done actes, as they did in his late Morrice to Norwiche" (Sig. D3). His struggle exemplifies the often tenuous relationship between branded name and person for those whose famous names have become commodities to be bought and sold in the open market.

The second self of celebrity

Kemp likewise makes a notable appearance in what was undoubtedly a work of fannish enterprise, the anonymously penned *The Second Part of the Return from Parnassus*. Performed between 1598 and 1602 by Cambridge students, the Parnassus trilogy allegorically dramatizes the exploits of two students, Philomusus and Studioso, as they complete their university educations and attempt to secure a livelihood. Clearly fans of the theater, the plays' anonymous authors pepper the play with numerous references to playwrights like Shakespeare, Marlowe, and Jonson as well as to popular players. It is in the trilogy's third installment, however, that the plays' intertheatric referentiality reaches its apex as the young graduates attempt to secure work as actors and audition for Burbage and Kemp.[14]

When "Kempe" appears onstage, he brags about both his and Burbage's fame and their theatrical appeal, informing the would-be thespians that people travel "from North and South" to see both men perform (4.3.48), and that all the country talk of them. When Philomusus responds to Kemp, "Indeed, Master Kemp, you are very famous; but that is as well from workes in print as your part in cue" (50–52), we might say that Kemp's branded celebrity name has come full-circle. Here, a man made famous on the stage, whose name has circulated through the public sphere in print and speech, returns to the stage, but as a re-embodied projection of his fannish collaborators. This "Kempe"—a loquacious, dim-witted, and swaggering braggart—is made flesh from the stuff of his circulation; he is a parodic pastiche of the "workes in print" and "part[s] in cue" that have made him a celebrity, and the public who consumes him as product has here re-produced him. Not unlike the collier of *Quips Upon Questions* who reanimates Tarlton from his staged picture, *The Second Part of the Return from Parnassus* animates both Kemp and Burbage anew upon the stage, but here as material bodies labeled with the celebrities' names.

The characters of Burbage and Kemp on stage in the final Parnassus play put a material face on an otherwise ethereal process, through which publics generate a celebrity body—a multifariously authored assemblage of value-laden name, narrative, and image to which acts of public consumption and use continually contribute. What Shakespeare alternately calls a motley, a vulgar stamp, and a brand suggests a reputational body of extrinsic production magnified through the extremes of commodity circulation. This second self is, as film theorist James Monaco observes of celebrities, "not what they are [...] but what we think they are" (Monaco 1978, 14), and what we think they are, as the values projected upon Tarlton's picture or Kemp's fictionalized character demonstrate, can involve a convoluted maze of sometimes competing values, but primarily those of the celebrity's audiences rather than the celebrity's own. Further, as Shakespeare's sonnets and Kemp's desperate pleas in his *Nine Daies Wonder* attest, individuals' attempts to steer the course of their publicly understood selves can meet frustrating resistance in the alternate selves the public projects upon them. Thus, the public face of celebrity is most often less one individual's carefully crafted, conscious self-fashioning than a publicly generated screen.

This is not to say, however, that celebrities do not actively contribute to their public personas. Emilia Di Martino has explored the ways that celebrities "constantly negotiate their personal stories and meanings with their public" (Di Martino 2019, 14), and Lorraine York pushes against the so-called "manipulation theory" of celebrity to reconsider the role of "celebrity agency" (York 2013, 1332). As York argues, celebrity-formation is "piecemeal rather than monolithic" (1341), as the star's publicly understood person is always an active dialogue. The second self of celebrity is a recombinant amalgam of various public projections and fixations; individual performances, both of the scripted and unscripted, self-presentational varieties; market values; and circulating names, images, and narratives. But the second celebrity self always maintains at least a tenuous connection to a material person, thus resulting in the friction expressed in Sonnet 111, in which living persons struggle to reconcile themselves to, or emerge beyond, a largely uncontrollable specter of celebrity. Rather than a completely severed signifier, celebrity functions instead as a sort of tenuously attached, ethereal double: a second, popularly traded self of multifarious authorship that may or may not align with an individual's self-assessment or desires.

Because publics use celebrities in service to a complex array of affective and economic impulses, the publicly traded celebrity self is, by necessity, an equally as complex process of signification. As Morin observes in *The Stars*, the twentieth-century fan industry arose in response to audiences who demanded greater access to the film stars with whom they had grown attached in the cinema, to perpetuate their feelings of intimacy through artifacts that bore their favorites' name and likeness or seemed to offer enhanced off screen access (Morin 1960, 27). Celebrity-inspired media offers a vehicle for the perpetuation of intimate feeling, regardless of the projective quality of that feeling, and it is this same phenomenon that Armin toys with in *Quips Upon Questions*, as the image of Tarlton comes to stand in Tarlton himself, allowing one fan to leave the theater convinced he has interacted with a man dead for more than a decade. But audiences can further parlay that intimate contact into a mode of self-identification, and Grossberg suggests that celebrities provide a means of stabilizing one's own identity through external surrogacy: "The fan gives authority to that which he or she invests in, letting the object of such investments speak for and as him or herself. Fans let them organize their emotional and narrative lives and identities" (Grossberg 2006, 587). Celebrity consumption is thereby a site of intertwined economic and identificatory investment. For as much as the compulsion to purchase and possess some portion of the celebrity via material artifact speaks to the desire to know the celebrity and satiate through projection the curiosity that unfulfilled narratives arouse, commodity consumption can also operate as a bid for self-understanding, an attempt to supply the missing strands of one's own narrative as well as the celebrity's. In this way, the celebrity marketplace functions as yet another site suspended in the tensions between the subject and object of desire and between the production and consumption of celebrity. Publics thereby make both commercial and affective investments in their celebrities, and as with any investment, expect returns—whether through the celebrity's potential to designate personal value, satiate a hunger for intimacy, or provide a more stable sense of identity.

For early modern Londoners, this complex matrix of celebrity circulation—rooted as it is in both commercial and affective dynamics—may have held special resonance, given the emerging economic and social relations of the market economy. The enhanced social mobility of early modern England has been well documented, and Lawrence Stone (1966) has demonstrated how wealth and material accumulation played an increasingly important role in social status. The earliest theatrical celebrities may have appeared to embody such mobility in their social and economic ascensions and declines, while likewise providing the public a substantial means of participation in the process; by investing their resources in a highly visible, fluid commodity, the consumer-producers of celebrity could negotiate the status of public figures, whose rises and falls would then reflect back unto the investors. As co-authors of the celebrity second self, the public became complicit in the allocation of social status, and celebrity may have provided a vehicle for the demystification and negotiation of such social forces.

Celebrity, credit, and *The Comedy of Errors*

"The greatness of the celebrity is something that can be shared, celebrated loudly and with a touch of vulgar pride," writes Marshall in *Celebrity and Power*. "It is the ideal representation of the triumph of the masses" (Marshall 1997, 6). In Marshall's effusive model, the celebrity emerges "from the twinned discourses of modernity: democracy and capitalism" (4), and thus, operates as a bottom-up form of power, narrating the cultural landscape through a semiotics of democratically selected, freely traded famous persons. Indeed, a substantial part of the celebrity's appeal, and the zeal with which the public consumes and trades him, lies not in his exceptionality, but, as Taylor's humbling anecdotes and parodic play demonstrate, his ordinariness, his position as a highly visible figure to emerge from the masses. Thus, *Us Weekly* revels in its regular "Stars—They're Just Like Us!" photo features, and tabloids thrive in the decidedly human arenas of interpersonal conflict and sexual scandal. The celebrity magnifies and reflects the tensions of everyday life—particularly, as a living commodity, the otherwise abstract conditions of quotidian capitalist consumerism. "Much of what makes [stars] interesting," writes Dyer, "is how they articulate [...] the nature of work in capitalist society" (Dyer 2004, 7). As Rojek argues, "Celebrities humanize the process of commodity consumption" (Rojek 2001, 14), assigning a human face to the ebb and flow of market demand and providing a collective forum for the negotiation of market exchange and its social implications.

One way that early modern players could likewise demystify emerging market forces was through emblematizing the enhanced social mobility of their era. Early theatrical celebrities like Tarlton may have appeared to embody such mobility in their social and economic ascensions and declines. The player's "extraordinary plasticity offered a living lesson in the mechanics of social mobility and assimilation," writes Jean-Christophe Agnew in *Worlds Apart*; "the social talents of the player earned him a living, if not, as in Shakespeare's case, the insignia of a gentleman" (Agnew 1986, 122). Players provided not only an inspirational exemplar, but a substantial means of participation in the process as well. As collaborators in the construction of celebrity, the public became complicit in the allocation of social status, and celebrity may have provided a vehicle for the negotiation of such social forces.

The emergent celebrities of early modern London may have likewise provided a particularly potent symbol of the increasingly pervasive credit culture that governed nearly all market exchanges. As in a celebrity culture, the culture of credit likewise commoditized individuals by assigning them both commercial and affective value, and the parallels between credit and celebrity are further apparent in the sometimes tenuous attachment between person and credit; in fact, in many ways, credit, like celebrity, functioned as a publicly negotiated and traded name over which an individual wielded only partial control. As Craig Muldrew demonstrates in *The Economy of Obligation*, an increase in commodity exchange in early modern England, coupled with a shortage of currency, created a transaction pattern in which "almost all buying and selling involved credit of one form of another" (Muldrew 1998, 95). As Muldrew has argued, credit then took on a somewhat equalizing function in society because of the universal reliance upon it (124), and with such emphasis placed on credit, the term took on a host of meanings, ranging from trustworthiness, favorable esteem, and honor to "trust or confidence in a buyer's ability and intention to pay at some future time" (OED Online n.d.(b), *s.v.* credit, n. II, 9a).

Like celebrity, one's credit signified a conflation of personal performance and public perception, and celebrities provided an apt vessel for the negotiation of credit, with their own highly visible reputations and exchange values elevated to public display, hyperbolically mirroring the everyday social and economic

80 *A commodity of good names*

realities of the public who consumed and co-produced them. The public's active trade in celebrity media and performance may have provided some sense of restored agency in the market concerns that governed their daily lives. To this end, Agnew posits his formulation of early modern "Artificial Persons," or the means by which individuals, compelled by the demands of a credit culture, adopted modes of theatricality to preserve their ability to participate in market affairs (Agnew 1986). The theater, in Agnew's model, proved both reflective and prescriptive, demonstrating,

> how precarious social identity was, how vulnerable to unexpected disruptions and disclosure it was, and therefore how deeply theatrical it was. Everyone, dramatists seemed to say, was a player-king embroiled in a ceaseless struggle to preserve his legitimacy.
>
> (112)

As Agnew argues, the players that achieved the greatest prominence were also the most visibly fungible, adaptable to the unpredictable fluctuations of both the market and the theater. Echoing the ceaseless tensions of both theatrical performance and commodities exchange, Agnew argues of the player, "To become a luminary, he had first to become, in anthropological terms, a *liminary*—a transitional self permanently stationed at the threshold of otherhood" (115). The liminary actor, he wrote, was "a figure situated 'betwixt and between' the conventional boundaries of social identity in early modern England" (122).

Tarlton offers one example of both a luminary and a liminary. His status as a luminary star of the stage is indisputable; his popularity in the entwined institutions of the theater and the market attest to his widespread prominence. As the wonder of his time, he occupied a liminal position that elided multiple divisions at once: between subject and object, intimacy and estrangement, and actor and role. His was a presence always precariously positioned in the "betwixt and between," and as such, he might be said to have particularly embodied the tensions of both theater and market, serving for his public as a corporeal manifestation of the changing social relations and enhanced social mobility in his contemporary London. In fact, the iconic image of Tarlton with tabor and pipe that would feature so prominently for a century after his death—and the same one, presumably, on display in *The Three Lords and Three Ladies of London*—offers a potent example of Tarlton's liminary position.[15] Depicted in the country homespun of a clown, his clothing, perhaps, signifies more than a character's apparel, but perpetually fixes Tarlton as the juxtaposition between his status by birthright and, as evidenced by the purse at his hip and by sheer virtue of his iconography, the enhanced position he achieved through the tools he carried. As such, he could demonstrate both the meritorious rise of the professional theatrical performer as well as the rise in economic status possible through the everyday theatrics required of a credit culture. As a theatrical celebrity, he offered his fellow Londoners a highly visible, accessible commodity whose consumption enfranchised the public to participate meaningfully in the economic forces that governed their daily lives and, perhaps, an inspirational exemplar of upward advancement.

The theater, Agnew argues, "bestowed a human shape on the very *form*lessness that money values were introducing into exchange" (Agnew 1986, xi), much in the same way that Dyer (2004), Marshall (1997), and Rojek (2001) figure the contemporary celebrity as a human embodiment of capitalist culture. Agnew cites specifically the early modern misidentification play as particularly attuned to and emblematic of the social relations of a credit culture. As "Self [confronts] Rival Self" in staged misrecognition (Agnew 1986, 113), attempts to self-fashion meet the socially projected identities co-crafted through credit circulation, and the theater offers "a laboratory of and for the new social relations" (xi): a space in which audience and player united in a mutual exploration of social identity in the market economy. The trope of misidentification as achieved through the employment of doubling provides a potent site of inquiry into the existence of the second, publicly projected selves endemic to both credit and celebrity cultures. Such is certainly the case in Shakespeare's audacious employment of the tropes of doubling and misidentification in *The Comedy of Errors*—a play that appropriates its Plautine origins to probe "contemporary anxieties about the commercialization of social bonds" (Perry 2003, 48). In fact, this remarkable, extended episode of misidentification allegorizes a number of the processes that meet in both the everyday world of credit and its amplified extension in celebrity, including the gradual distanciation of name and person in commodities exchange, the social life a famous name accrues as it trades hands on the market, and the confrontation of self and second, publicly generated self. Visiting with greater scrutiny the theme touched upon in Sonnet 111, in *The Comedy of Errors*, Shakespeare explores to absurdist proportions the divergence of an individual's "nature" and "brand" in the figures of the twin Antipholi, identical men with identical names who experience both the rewards and restraints of their publicly misrecognized alternate selves.

Twinship divides one entity into two visually identical, though significantly divergent, forms; staged doppelgangers provide a visible and stageable means of dividing a single human agent into duality. Thus, twins, doppelgangers, and alter-egos provide an apt vessel for the interrogation of both credit and the divided selves of celebrity, demonstrating the existential split between material personhood and the passive imprint of a publicly projected double. As Balthasar warns Antipholus of Ephesus in Act 3 of the play, "slander lives upon succession,/ For ever housed where once it gets possession. (3.1.106–107); public assessment, he advises, survives and perpetuates independent of individual participation, as it circulates freely in the public sphere and ceaselessly haunts its fleshy analogue. Unbeknownst to Antipholus of Ephesus, his twin, Antipholus of Syracuse, is doing precisely what Balthasar cautions him about—circulating like slander through the Ephesian market, bearing Antipholus of Ephesus's face and name, and disrupting the social and commercial relations of the Ephesian twin, who is then forced to bear the brunt of an uncontrollable alternate

82 *A commodity of good names*

identity's interactions with the public. As Gail Kern Paster notes, in *The Comedy of Errors*, we are presented with an idealized and sustained "tidiness about debt, credit, and reputation" that "only the extraordinary duplication of the Antipholuses can disrupt" (Paster 1985, 192). Thus, the staged twins divide the wealthy merchant, Antipholus of Ephesus, from an identical self bearing his name and wielding his credit in the figure of Antipholus of Syracuse, who functions, like celebrity, as an amalgam of his twin's social and commercial history and the public's various projections onto and investments in him.

Antipholus of Ephesus begins the play a man of considerable wealth and social standing. He is, as the goldsmith Angelo informs a merchant,

> Of very reverend reputation, sir,
> Of credit infinite, highly beloved,
> Second to none that lives here in the city.
> His word might bear my wealth at any time.
> (5.1.5–8)

As Angelo extols the name of Antipholus, he demonstrates the public's commercial and affective investments in the Ephesian Antipholus: they revere and love him, which implies a level of intimate feeling, and have extended him endless credit, meaning that the public, like Angelo, places absolute faith in the cultural biography he has amassed through market exchange. He is considered by all a sound investment that promises rewards. As Antipholus relies upon his credit to participate in commerce, his good name has become a highly valued commodity that Angelo's hearty praise only enhances. Angelo is both a consumer and producer of Antipholus's valuable, commoditized name.

However, after what Emilia labels a "sympathizèd one day's error" (5.1.399), this rich, famous, and beloved Ephesian merchant finds himself bound in a chair, facing exorcism by a quack. This rapid devolution of status is partially unraveled by the sympathy Emilia attributes the day's errors: the misidentification that propels the plot remains one error, shared between twins, much as the twins might be thought to function as one being, divided into two bodies. As Kent Cartwright points out, "sympathy," in medieval and early modern England, denoted a kind of magic, particularly apropos to this drama, through which "effects could be created on a remote being by performing them on another object representative of that being" (Cartwright 2007, 332), such as a wax effigy or voodoo doll (333). Thus, the sympathized error is the result of a kind of sympathized magic, by which Antipholus of Ephesus suffers the pangs of the public's disgruntlement with his unwitting twin's activities. The parallels between sympathized magic and the day's sympathized errors are rendered further apparent by Antipholus of Syracuse's description of the Ephesian mart upon arriving there:

> They say this town is full of cozenage,
> As nimble jugglers that deceive the eye,

Dark-working sorcerers that change the mind,
Soul-killing witches that deform the body,
Disguisèd cheaters, prating mountebanks,
And many suchlike libertines of sin [...]
I greatly fear my money is not safe.
                    (1.2.97–102, 105)

Of course, the magic Antipholus of Syracuse fears is revealed, perhaps even more frighteningly, as rooted in the very real-world phenomena of theatricality and market exchange. The true magic here lies in the cunning ability of vendors and performers to part a man from his money, and as Antipholus of Syracuse assigns both commerce and performance to the realm of the magical, he blurs the boundaries between the theater and the market that overlap in the bustling port city of Ephesus. His apprehensive description of the Ephesian mart echoes early modern criticisms leveled at both institutions, particularly the "subtle craft" employed by idle persons—including players—in the Vagrancy Act of 1572, and several published accounts of marketplace deception, like Miles Mosse's 1595 warning: "Some, to cover their sinne, and to upholde their credite, have devised faire cloakes to shroud their ragged garments, and have begotten a more cunning and subtile kinde of trafficke" (58). However, the rational explanation behind Antipholus of Syracuse's fears does not mean that those fears will go unrealized. Antipholus of Syracuse's appearance on Ephesian shores signals the emergence of his twin's "representative" being in the arena of commodities exchange: a second body that, like a voodoo doll, transfers its interactions with the public onto the body of Antipholus of Ephesus. Indeed, the Syracusian's circulation in the market will, as he feared, deceive eyes, change minds, and de-form bodies—particularly, in the eyes of Ephesians who project upon him the credit they have extended to his brother.

As opposed to his accomplished and highly regarded brother, Antipholus of Syracuse emerges in Ephesus as a lost wanderer who admits to feelings of incompleteness: "I to the world am like a drop of water/ That in the ocean seeks another drop" (1.2.35–36). Here, Antipholus of Syracuse notably frames his self-assessment from an external perspective of public projection, defining himself in incomplete, liquid fluidity by how "the world" shapes him.[16] The divided nature of the Antipholi is further referenced in Antipholus of Syracuse's temporary dwelling in Ephesus: the Centaur, a being that, like the twins, is composed of two distinct halves. Also within this introductory scene, in the space of ten lines, Antipholus of Syracuse repeats his intention to "lose myself" in this foreign mart (1.2.30, 40), as he prepares to wander the frightening market that he believes may swallow up his autonomy and his money. Lost in circulation through the Ephesian mart, the second Antipholus becomes a floating signifier of his brother's "credit infinite."

As famous names accrue value as they circulate in the marketplace, the Syracusian twin's transactions imbue him with increasingly enhanced economic value. He is first greeted by Angelo, who mistakenly provides him with a gold chain commissioned by his brother, thereby demonstrating the tenuous relationship between a person and his credit. "Master Antipholus" (3.2.163), Angelo greets him. "Ay, that's my name" (3.2.164), Antipholus of Syracuse responds. "I see a man here needs not live by shifts" (3.2.180), the cluelessly fortunate Antihpholus surmises as he accepts the chain while acknowledging his baseless claim to it. As he proceeds onward through the mart, he continues to savor the perks of his brother's established credit:

> There's not a man I meet but doth salute me
> As if I were their well-acquainted friend.
> And everyone doth call me by my name.
> Some tender money to me, some invite me,
> Some other give me thanks for kindness.
> Some offer me commodities to buy.
> Even now a tailor called me in his shop,
> And showed me his silks that he had bought for me,
> And therewithal took measure of my body.
> Sure, these are but imaginary wiles
> And Lapland sorcerers inhabit here.
>
> (4.3.1–12)

Once again, Antipholus of Syracuse attributes to magic what Shakespeare and his audiences may have recognized as congruous to their quotidian experiences in both the credit culture and the culture of celebrity—that is, the gradual estrangement between person and name in the realm of commodities exchange. As Antipholus of Syracuse wanders further into the mart, he further transforms into a projective screen of his brother's fame, name, and credit. With no verifiable ties to this community, nor any history of reliable exchange, Antipholus of Syracuse yet functions as a site of both commercial and affective investment, accepting praise, thanks, currency, and goods from a public that has placed its absolute faith in his Ephesian twin's name and, undoubtedly, expects returns that this twin has no means of producing. Thus, as with the celebrity sign, the Ephesian townsfolk here collaboratively author this second self, assigning him credit and favorable esteem while enriching his status and dressing his body in luxurious fabrics. Seemingly in response to a question that Antipholus of Syracuse had previously asked of Luciana, "Would you create me new?" (3.2.39), the people of Ephesus collaboratively mold the incomplete, wandering stranger into the embodiment of their perceptions and projections of their prized Ephesian merchant.

With self severed from second self, Antipholus of Ephesus then finds himself, to use Agnew's words, "in a ceaseless struggle to preserve his legitimacy" (Agnew 1986, 112). Denied access to his home, accosted by a vendor, accused by his wife, arrested, and, ultimately, bound in preparation of Doctor Pinch's exorcism, the Ephesian twin, and rightful claimant of the benefits enjoyed by the other Antipholus, demonstrates the kind of friction Shakespeare and Kemp reveal respectively in Sonnet 111 and *Nine Daies Wonder*: he is left to beg redress from the very public that has misrecognized him for his uncontrollable alternate self. That he is guilty of none of the charges leveled against him, yet suffers for all of them, speaks to the sliver of attachment he shares with his second self. The misdeeds attributed him exist solely in the arena of public perception, yet as Antipholus of Ephesus continues to share a name and face with the embodiment of such perception, he suffers their consequences as his words and deeds prove impotent in the face of oscillating public sentiment. Reminiscent of Cassio's desperate wailing in *Othello* that without his reputation, "what remains is bestial," Antipholus of Ephesus finds himself materially intact, though reduced in the eyes of others to a baser form, as his wife questions his sanity, deems him "wretched" (4.4.110), and instructs Pinch to bind him as if he were an unruly animal. If Antipholus of Syracuse functions as the embodiment of the second self, then Antipholus of Ephesus is relegated to the position of personhood only in the strictly material sense. He has been made a motley—dyed, bepainted, stamped, and branded through public assessment.

As the day's sympathized error escalates, both twins are eventually united before the Duke, who marvels,

> One of these men is *genius* to the other:
> And so of these, which is the natural man,
> And which the spirit?
> (5.1.333–335)

Invoking the classical conception of the *genius*, or the divine, attendant spirit attached to the mortal individual, the Duke's assessment proves both astute and layered. As the twins function as two embodied forms signifying "the natural man" and his intangible double, the Duke assigns, as does Balthasar, an immortal quality to the second body substantiated through public perception. But as the *OED* notes, *genius* also denoted "the quasi-mythologic personification of something immaterial (e.g. of a virtue, a custom, an institution) [...] a person or thing fit to be taken as an embodied type of some abstract idea" (OED Online n.d.(c), *s.v.* genius, n.1e).[17] Thus, the Duke recognizes that one of the twins before him likewise functions as an embodiment of abstraction—specifically, here, the second, collaboratively authored self as emerges in cultures of credit and celebrity. The Duke then follows his initial question with, perhaps, an even more compelling one: "Who deciphers them?" (5.1.335). What he demands is a measure of authenticity, a way to isolate the man from the publicly authored double, while he admits his inability to distinguish the two; both stand before him as real, substantial bodies in whom the public has made real investments and, in the end, the Duke concludes, "I know not which is which" (5.1.365).

A commodity of good names

The Duke's sustained confusion at play's end speaks to the unrecoverable conflation of self and second self in both theatrical and market exchanges—the same kind of misrecognition that Shakespeare and Kemp aim to avert in their pleas to readers to disentangle public projection from what they assert to be their authentic persons. This difficulty in discernment is likewise what Falstaff banks upon in his desire to secure "a commodity of good names," as he aims to shield his misadventures beneath the cloak of an illegitimately procured, though publicly indistinguishable, alternate projection of self. In *The Comedy of Errors*, Shakespeare offers the realization of Falstaff's dream when the Syracusan Antipholus chances upon just such a commodity of a good name. As the Syracusan Antipholus observes that "a man here need not live by shifts," or rather, need not secure his own livelihood through individual enterprise since his name and face will suffice, he materially inhabits the invisible body of his twin's circulating esteem. He wanders the Ephesian streets branded and stamped by the external, though misplaced, assessments of the city; he becomes a motley assemblage of self and second self. As the twin Antipholi visibly externalize a set of processes that remains otherwise unseen in the world of commodities exchange, they assign human faces to the estrangements of a marketplace that trades in names as readily as it trades in gold and fabrics. Arthur F. Kinney observes that the characters of the Ephesian mart could easily have been found "on the streets outside the theater" of Shakespeare's London (Kinney 1996, 184), and thus, the misrecognitions of this bustling world of "nimble jugglers" and "disguisèd cheaters" likely resonated in quite real ways for the play's initial audiences. Theirs, too, was a world of intertwined commerce and theatrical performance that necessitated the establishment of a public name but could offer no safeguards as to what that name might signify in the disembodied exchanges of the market. Thus, like Shakespeare, like Kemp, like the Antipholi, early modern Londoners ceaselessly negotiated their social identities amidst the projections and perceptions of the city's inhabitants. In many ways, *The Comedy of Errors* offered its early modern audiences much of what the culture of theatrical celebrity likewise provided—a material distillation of the market and theatrical forces governing their daily lives.

Notes

1 E.A.J. Honigmann provocatively suggests that the scandal referenced here may suggest the scandal initiated in Greene's *Groats-worth of Witte*, especially as line 4 asks the listener to "o'er-green my bad." As Honigmann notes, this is the first appearance of the word "overgreen" in English and may work as a "punning allusion" (Honigmann 1982, 6–7). Both the Introduction and Chapter 4 of this book explore the intersections of Greene's *Groats-worth* and Shakespeare's celebrity.
2 For more early modern English treatments of reputation and circulating speech, see Thomas Hoby's translation of Castiglione's *The Book of the Courtier* (Castiglione 1561); James Cleland, *Hero-paideia, or The Institution of a Young Nobleman* (Cleland 1607); and George Web, *The Arraignment of an Unruly Tongue* (Web 1619). For critical accounts of what Lawrence Stone labels the early modern "cult of reputation," see Stone, *The Crisis of the Aristocracy* (Stone 1967, 25); and M. Lindsay Kaplan, *The Culture of Slander in Early Modern England* (Kaplan 1997).
3 For more on props, their transportability, and how they mean in performance, see Andrew Sofer, *The Stage Life of Props* (Sofer 2003).

4 Marshall similarly theorizes in *Celebrity and Power* that, "the celebrity sign is pure exchange value cleaved from use value. It articulates the individual as commodity" (Marshall 1997, xi)
5 Cerasano likewise asserts that early modern actors "became commodities to be marketed and capitalized on by playhouse owners and theatrical companies" (Cerasano 2005, 48).
6 See also William N. West's theorization of intertheatricality as distinct from metatheatricality in *Early Modern Theatricality*. As West proposes, intertheatricality "describes how theatrical performance thinks about itself, within its own medium [...]. To look for intertheatricality [...] is to seek shared memories of actions that can be called up to thicken present performances" (West 2013, 155).
7 Though numerous accounts assume Field in the part of Littlewit, Nora Johnson argues that Field more likely played Cokes; thus, Littlewit's response that "You are even with me, sir" becomes, in Johnson's interpretation, "You, Nathan Field, are standing right in front of me" (Johnson 2003, 62). Keith Sturgess likewise supports this interpretation, noting, "the jokes here work better" with Field as Cokes (Sturgess 1987, 177).
8 A number of early modern plays, as Nathalie Rivere de Carles explores, include similar moments where "actor and prop are fused" on the stage (Rivere de Carles 2013, 65). For a theoretical analysis of the fluidity between actor and prop in theater more generally, see Jiri Veltrusky, "Man and Object in the Theater" (Veltrusky 1964).
9 Scott McMillin and Sally-Beth MacLean further discuss Tarlton's image as a proclamation of personal value by suggesting that the image functions as the balladseller's counterpart to the lords' shields and becomes Simplicity's impresa (McMillin and MacLean 2006, 125).
10 For more on early modern theatrical documents, including play-bills and title-pages, see *Thomas Middleton and Early Modern Textual Culture*, edited by Gary Taylor and John Lavagnino (2007); and Matthew Steggle, *Digital Humanities and the Lost Drama of Early Modern England: Ten Case Studies* (2015).
11 For more on the souvenir's capacity to simultaneously record yet signal the unrecoverable absence of an event, see Chapter 5 of Susan Stewart's *On Longing* (1993).
12 For variant perspectives on the collaboration, or lack thereof, between playhouses and printers, see Stern (2009); Gurr (1992); and Brooks (2000).
13 With nearly every story beginning with such anonymous openers as "A nobleman of France" (Sig. B8), or "A gallant in his youth" (Sig. A8), only the stories centered around Field, Tarlton, William Barkstead, James I, and a Signeur Valdrino in King Alphonsus' service name their subjects.
14 Chapter 4 discusses the second installment of the Parnassus trilogy to more depth, especially in its dramatization of an impassioned Shakespeare fan. Katherine Duncan-Jones offers an analysis of these plays as the "enthusiastic tribute" to the stage by "university men" in *Shakespeare: Upstart Crow to Sweet Swan, 1592–1623* (Duncan-Jones 2011, 233–236).
15 This image is likely the same one referred to in a marginal note in Stowe's *Annales*: "Tarlton so beloved that men use his picture for their signs" (Stowe 1615, 697). Alexandra Halasz, in a compelling exploration of Tarlton's posthumous celebrity, convincingly argues that the signs referenced here are most likely tavern signs (Halasz 1995).
16 For more on credit, *The Comedy of Errors*, and the image of liquidity, see Collette Gordon, "Crediting Errors: Credit, Liquidity, Performance and *The Comedy of Errors*" (Gordon 2010, 165–184) and John R. Ford, "'Methinks you are my glass': Looking for *The Comedy of Errors* in Performance" (Ford 2006, 11–28).
17 Shakespeare invokes this type of *genius* in *1 Henry IV* when Falstaff labels the thin Justice Shallow "the very genius of famine" (3.2.285).

References

Agnew, Jean-Christophe. 1986. *Worlds Apart: The Market and the Theater in Anglo-American Thought, 1550–1750*. Cambridge: Cambridge University Press.
Allestree, Richard. 1667. *The Government of the Tongue*. Oxford.
Appadurai, Arjun, ed. 1986. *The Social Life of Things: Commodities in Cultural Perspective*. Cambridge: Cambridge University Press.
Armin, Robert. 1600. *Quips upon Questions*. London.
Astington, John H. 1997. "Rereading Illustrations of the English Stage." *Shakespeare Survey* 50:151–170.
Atkin, Tamara and Emma Smith. 2014. "The Form and Function of Character Lists in Plays Printed Before the Closing of the Theatres." *The Review of English Studies* 65 (271): 647–672.
Beaumont, Francis and John Fletcher. 1652. *The Wild Goose Chase*. London.
Brathwaite, Richard. 1618. *The Good Wife: or, A Rare One amongst Women*. London.
Bratton, Jacky. 2003. *New Readings in Theatre History*. Cambridge: Cambridge University Press.
Bristol, Michael D. 1996. *Big-Time Shakespeare*. London: Routledge.
Brooks, Douglas A. 2000. *From the Playhouse to the Printing House: Drama and Authorship in Early Modern England*. Cambridge: Cambridge University Press.
Callaghan, Dympna. 2013. *Who Was William Shakespeare? An Introduction to the Life and Works*. Malden: Wiley-Blackwell.
Cartwright, Kent. 2007. "Language, Magic, the Dromios, and The Comedy of Errors." *Studies in English Literature* 47: 331–354.
Castiglione, Baldassare. (1561) 1900. *The Book of the Courtier*. Translated by SirThomasHoby. London.
Cerasano, S.P. 2005. "Edward Alleyn, the New Model Actor, and the Rise of Celebrity in the 1590s." *Medieval and Renaissance Drama in England* 18: 47–58.
Chambers, E.K. 1923. *The Elizabethan Stage*. Vol. 4. Oxford: Clarendon.
"A Sonnet upon the Pittiful Burneing of the Globe Playhowse in London." 1923. In *The Elizabethan Stage* by E.K. Chambers. Oxford: Clarendon. 420–422.
Chapman, George. 1598. *The blinde beggar of Alexandria*. London.
Charnes, Linda. 1993. *Notorious Identity: Materializing the Subject in Shakespeare*. Cambridge: Harvard University Press.
Cleland, James. 1607. *Hero-paideia, or The institution of a young noble man*. Oxford.
Cooke, John. 1614. *Greene's Tu Quoque, or The Cittie Gallant*. London.
Coombe, Rosemary. 2006. "*Author(iz)ing the Celebrity: Engendering Alternative Identities*." In *The Celebrity Culture Reader*, edited by P. David Marshall, 721–769. New York: Routledge.
De Certeau, Michel. 1984. *The Practice of Everyday Life*. Translated by Steven Rendall. Berkeley: University of California Press.
Di Martino, Emilia. 2019. *Celebrity Accents and Public Identity Construction: Analyzing Geordie Stylizations*. New York: Routledge.
Duncan-Jones, Katherine. 2011. *Shakespeare: Upstart Crow to Sweet Swan, 1592–1623*. London: Arden.
Dyer, Richard. 2004. *Heavenly Bodies: Film Stars and Society*, 2nd ed. London: Routledge.
Ford, John R. 2006. "'Methinks you are my glass': Looking for The Comedy of Errors in Performance." *Shakespeare Bulletin* 24 (1): 11–28.

Geary, Patrick. 1986. "*Sacred Commodities: The Circulation of Medieval Relics.*" In *The Social Life of Things: Commodities in Cultural Perspective*, edited by Arjun Appadurai, 169–194. Cambridge: Cambridge University Press.

Gordon, Colette. 2010. "Crediting Errors: Credit, Liquidity, Performance and The Comedy of Errors."*Shakespeare* 6 (2): 165–184.

Greene, Robert. 1592. *Greenes, Groats-worth of Witte, bought with a million of Repentance*. London.

Grossberg, Lawrence. 2006. "Is There a Fan in the House? The Affective Sensibility of Fandom." In *The Celebrity Culture Reader*, edited by P. David Marshall, 581–590. New York: Routledge.

Gurr, Andrew. 1992. *The Shakespearean Stage 1574–1642*. Cambridge: Cambridge University Press.

Gurr, Andrew. 2009. *Shakespeare's Opposites: The Admiral's Company, 1594–1625*. Cambridge: Cambridge University Press.

Halasz, Alexandra. 1995. "'So beloved that men use his picture for their signs': Richard Tarlton and the Uses of Sixteenth-Century Celebrity."*Shakespeare Studies* 23: 19–38.

Harris, Jonathan Gil. 2002. "Properties of Skill: Product Placement in Early English Artisanal Drama." In *Staged Properties in Early Modern English Drama*, edited by Jonathan Gil Harris and Natasha Korda, 35–66. Cambridge: Cambridge University Press.

Honigmann, E.A.J. 1982. *Shakespeare's Impact on His Contemporaries*. London: Macmillan.

Hutcheon, Linda. 1989. *The Politics of Postmodernism*. New York: Routledge.

Johnson, Nora. 2003. *The Actor as Playwright in Early Modern Drama*. Cambridge: Cambridge University Press.

Jonson, Ben. 2002. *Bartholomew Fair*. In *Renaissance Drama*, edited by Arthur F.Kinney, 481–556. Malden: Blackwell.

Jonson, Ben. 1640a. *Christmas, His Masque. The Workes of Benjamin Jonson, the Second Volume*. London.

Jonson, Ben. 1640b. *The Devil Is an Ass. The Workes of Benjamin Jonson, Second Volume*. London.

Kaplan, M. Lindsay. 1997. *The Culture of Slander in Early Modern England*. Cambridge: Cambridge University Press.

Kemp, Will. 1600. *Kemps nine daies wonder Performed in a daunce from London to Norwich*. London.

Kinney, Arthur F. 1996. "*The Comedy of Errors*: A Modern Perspective." In *The Comedy of Errors* (Folger Shakespeare Library edition) by William Shakespeare, edited by Barbara A. Mowat and Paul Werstine, 179–198. New York: Washington Square Press.

Kopytoff, Igor. 1986. "The Cultural Life of Things: Commoditization as Process." In *The Social Life of Things: Commodities in Cultural Perspective*, edited by Arjun Appadurai, 69–94. Cambridge: Cambridge University Press.

Levin, Richard. 2000. "Tarlton's Picture on the Elizabethan Stage." *Notes and Queries* 47 (4): 435–36.

Manningham, John. 1976 [1603]. *Diary*. Edited by Robert Parker Sorlien. Hanover: New England University Press.

Marshall, P. David. 1997. *Celebrity and Power: Fame in Contemporary Culture*. Minneapolis: Minnesota University Press.

McMillin, Scott and MacLean, Sally-Beth. 2006. *The Queen's Men and their Plays*. Cambridge: Cambridge University Press.

Monaco, James. 1978. *Celebrity: The Media as Image Makers*. New York: Dell.

Morin, Edgar. 2005 [1960]. *The Stars*. Translated by Richard Howard. Minneapolis: University of Minnesota Press.

Mosse, Miles. 1595. *The Arraignment and Conviction of Usury*. London.

Muldrew, Craig. 1998. *The Economy of Obligation: The Culture of Credit and Social Relations in Early Modern England*. New York: St. Martin's.

Munro, Ian. 2009. "Page Wit and Puppet-like Wealth: Orality and Print in Three Lords and Three Ladies of London." In *Locating the Queen's Men, 1583–1603: Material Practices and Conditions of Playing*, edited by Helen Ostovich, Holger Schott Syme, and Andrew Griffin, 109–122. Burlington: Ashgate.

Nungezer, Edwin. 1929. *A Dictionary of Actors and Other Persons Associated with the Public Representation of Plays in England Before 1642*. New Haven: Yale University Press.

OED Online. n.d.(a). "brand, n." Oxford University Press, https://www-oed-com.ric.idm.oclc.org/view/Entry/22627 (accessed June 28, 2020).

OED Online. n.d.(b). "credit, n." Oxford University Press, https://www-oed-com.ric.idm.oclc.org/view/Entry/44113 (accessed July 2, 2020).

OED Online. n.d.(c). "genius, n." Oxford University Press, https://www-oed-com.ric.idm.oclc.org/view/Entry/77607 (accessed July 2, 2020).

Pangallo, Matteo. 2015. "'I will keep and character that name': Dramatis Personae Lists in Early Modern Manuscript Plays." *Early Theater* 18 (2): 87–118.

Paster, Gail Kern. 1985. *The Idea of the City in the Age of Shakespeare*. Athens: University of Georgia Press.

Perry, Curtis. 2003. "Commerce, Community and Nostalgia in *Money and the Age of Shakespeare: Essays in New Economic Criticism*, edited by Linda Woodbridge, 39–52. New York: Palgrave Macmillan.

The Return from Parnassus. 1886. In *The Pilgrimmage to Parnassus: With the Two Parts of the Return from Parnassus*, edited by William Dunn Macray. Oxford: Clarendon.

Rivere de Carles, Nathalie. 2013. "Performing Materiality: Curtains on the Early Modern Stage." In *Shakespeare's Theatre and the Effects of Performance*, edited by Farah Karim-Cooper and Tiffany Stern, 51–72. London: Bloomsbury.

Rojek, Chris. 2001. *Celebrity*. London: Reaktion.

Rutter, Carol Chillington. 2006. "'Her first remembrance from the Moor': Actors and the Materials of Memory." In *Shakespeare, Memory, and Performance*, edited by Peter Holland, 168–206. Cambridge: Cambridge University Press.

Shakespeare, William. 2016. *Antony and Cleopatra*. In *The Norton Shakespeare, Third Edition*, edited by Stephen Greenblatt, Walter Cohen, Suzanne Gossett, Jean E. Howard, Katharine Eisaman Maus, and Gordon McMullan, 2775–2864. New York: Norton.

Shakespeare, William. 2016. *The Comedy of Errors*. In *The Norton Shakespeare, Third Edition*, edited by Stephen Greenblatt, Walter Cohen, Suzanne Gossett, Jean E. Howard, Katharine Eisaman Maus, and Gordon McMullan, 1685–1750. New York: Norton.

Shakespeare, William. 2016. *Henry VI, Part I*. In *The Norton Shakespeare, Third Edition*, edited by Stephen Greenblatt, Walter Cohen, Suzanne Gossett, Jean E. Howard, Katharine Eisaman Maus, and Gordon McMullan, 1165–1244. New York: Norton.

Shakespeare, William. 2016. *The Merry Wives of Windsor*. In *The Norton Shakespeare, Third Edition*, edited by Stephen Greenblatt, Walter Cohen, Suzanne Gossett, Jean E. Howard, Katharine Eisaman Maus, and Gordon McMullan, 1463–1532. New York: Norton.

Shakespeare, William. 2016. *Othello*. In *The Norton Shakespeare, Third Edition*, edited by Stephen Greenblatt, Walter Cohen, Suzanne Gossett, Jean E. Howard, Katharine Eisaman Maus, and Gordon McMullan, 2073–2158. New York: Norton.

Shakespeare, William. 2016. Sonnet 110. In *The Norton Shakespeare, Third Edition*, edited by Stephen Greenblatt, Walter Cohen, Suzanne Gossett, Jean E. Howard, Katharine Eisaman Maus, and Gordon McMullan, 2287. New York: Norton.

Shakespeare, William. 2016. Sonnet 111. In *The Norton Shakespeare, Third Edition*, edited by Stephen Greenblatt, Walter Cohen, Suzanne Gossett, Jean E. Howard, Katharine Eisaman Maus, and Gordon McMullan, 2287. New York: Norton.

Shakespeare, William. 2016. Sonnet 112. In *The Norton Shakespeare, Third Edition*, edited by Stephen Greenblatt, Walter Cohen, Suzanne Gossett, Jean E. Howard, Katharine Eisaman Maus, and Gordon McMullan, 2288. New York: Norton.

Sofer, Andrew. 2003. *The Stage Life of Props*. Ann Arbor: Michigan University Press.

Steggle, Matthew. 2015. *Digital Humanities and the Lost Drama of Early Modern England: Ten Case Studies*. London: Routledge.

Stern, Tiffany. 2009. *Documents of Performance in Early Modern England*. Cambridge: Cambridge University Press.

Stewart, Susan. 1993. *On Longing: Narratives of the Miniature, the Gigantic, the Souvenir, the Collection*. Durham and London: Duke University Press.

Stone, Lawrence. 1966. "Social Mobility in England, 1500–1700." *Past and Present* 33: 16–55.

Stone, Lawrence. 1967. *The Crisis of the Aristocracy, 1558–1641*. Oxford: Oxford University Press.

Stowe, John. 1615. *Stowe's Annales, continued by Edmund Howe*. London.

Sturgess, Keith. 1987. *Jacobean Private Theater*. London: Routledge.

Tarltons Jests, Drawn into these three parts. 1613. London.

Taylor, Gary (assisted by Celia R. Daileader and Alexandra G. Bennett). 2007. "The Order of Persons." In *Thomas Middleton and Early Modern Texture Culture*, edited by Gary Taylor and John Lavagnino, 31–79. Oxford: Oxford University Press.

Taylor, John. 1629. *Wit and mirth*. London.

Taylor, John. 1638. *Taylors feast*. London.

Van Krieken, Robert. 2012. *Celebrity Society*. New York: Routledge.

Veltrusky, Jiri. 1964. "Man and Object in the Theater." In *A Prague School Reader on Esthetics, Literary Structure and Style*, edited by Paul R.Garvin, 83–91. Washington, D.C.: Georgetown University Press.

Web, George. 1619. *The Arraignment of an Unruly Tongue*. London.

Webster, John. 1612. *The white diuel, or, The tragedy of Paulo Giordano Vrsini*. London.

West, William N. 2013. "Intertheatricality." In *Early Modern Theatricality*, edited by Henry S. Turner, 151–172. Oxford: Oxford University Press.

Wilson, Robert. 1590. *The three Lords and Three Ladies of London*. London.

York, Lorraine. 2013. "Star Turn: The Challenges of Theorizing Celebrity Agency." *The Journal of Popular Culture* 46 (6): 1330–1347.

3 The celebrity's two bodies

INT. DRESSING ROOM – BENEATH AREA – NIGHT
Another stylish room, with every comfort for the visiting celebrity. Sofas and side-tables with nibbles, drinks, newspapers and massive floral displays. RICHARD paces dangerously. [1]

In Richard Loncraine's 1995 film adaptation of *Richard III*, Sir Ian McKellen's Richard, in his bid to secure the crown, hurries to a flower-filled dressing room before a carefully planned public appearance (act three, scene seven in the play). Seating himself before a large, brightly lit dressing room mirror, his attendants place a drape over his shoulders before a hairdresser and make-up artist arrive to carefully inspect and prepare the face he will soon present to his public. When Richard finally emerges from the dressing room door, he is transformed into the image of avuncular benevolence, his face softened and bespectacled, his arm clutching a prayer book, as the film audience, unlike Richard's, has been invited behind the scenes to witness his transformation. As detailed in the excerpted description above from Loncraine and McKellen's screenplay, Richard is a "celebrity," with the dressing room scene invoking an iconic image of the Hollywood star, framed by the flowers left by hangers-on and the white glow of the mirror's globe lights. As the film is set in an alternate version of the 1930s, the scene alludes to the early days of the film industry and its accompanying star system, through which film actors were carefully molded and promoted as idealized types through sustained performances of self that transcended the actor's scripted roles. As we are granted behind-the-scenes access into the collaborative construction of Richard-as-star, we see that Richard, likewise, is here fashioned into a type—specifically, the reluctant-yet-rising star whose ensuing aw-shucks performance of faux-humility is designed to stimulate his public's desire. The scene further points to the expanding role media and publicity came to play in the early twentieth-century political sphere, to a time when King George VI reached out to his country on the brink of war via radio address and Franklin Roosevelt adeptly harnessed the power of film to promote an assured public image through newsreels. With a strategy that owes equal parts to Hollywood glamour and calculated political scheming, Richard in the Loncraine adaptation is reimagined as an early twentieth-century political celebrity.

DOI: 10.4324/9780367808976-4

Figuring Richard as a political star of the early film era provides a particularly apt modernization of Shakespeare's play as the film and media savvy of Loncraine's Richard fittingly corresponds to the theatrical acumen of Richard in the play-text, just as Loncraine's backdrop of an emerging film industry echoes Shakespeare's own revivification of Richard within an early modern theatrical culture. Both play and film reflect meaningfully upon their respective industries and the place of those industries in the political sphere, and both highlight the extent to which Richard owes his ascent to a forked political strategy that involves both eliminating rightful claimants who thwart his path to power and convincingly performing according to the demands of medium. The theatrically astute Richard of the play-text understands from the beginning that the brutalities of war have now given way to the "fair well-spoken days" of slick oratory and pleasing façades (1.1.29), and so he quickly locates himself as the villain of an unfolding stage show. Loncraine's Richard trades theatrical prowess for cunning mass-media awareness, which is rendered apparent through scenes of Richard at microphones and his persistent direct-to-camera addresses, but perhaps most acutely when a freshly crowned Richard, along with his obsequious retinue, watch his coronation at a private film screening, thus solidifying Richard not only as king, but a verifiable film star as well. As a demonstration of "power mongers' fascination with directing and controlling the media, staging and then witnessing their triumphs" (Wilson 1998, 40), Richard is barely capable of averting his eyes from the glowing projection of his own celluloid image even as he plots the murders of his queen and nephews. Despite his weighty conversations, he smiles at his own filmed crowning; he laughs when he hears his public's recorded cheers. When he explains to Buckingham that only by his loyal confidante's advice and assistance "is King Richard seated" (4.2.5), Richard points to the screen as the evidence of their successful venture. When Richard further hints that he aims to secure his new position through murdering potential rivals, saying, "I say I would be king" (4.2.13), Buckingham responds in kind: "Why so you are" (4.2.14), he says and likewise points to the screen as proof. King Richard, both men gesturally affirm, is the man on the screen, the star of the film.

As Peter Donaldson argues, in Loncraine's adaptation, "political leadership is difficult to distinguish from media celebrity" (Donaldson 2002, 245). But as the film insistently demonstrates, this indecipherability is less a reflection of a naïve public's failure at discernment than it is an acknowledgment of the inherent congruities between two modes of power that share an easy, if disturbing, conversance. Where Alberoni once described celebrities as "the powerless elite" (Alberoni 2006 [1962]), or elevated cultural figures who possess no verifiable authority, Richard, to the contrary, demonstrates how easily media celebrity can translate to governing authority and, in turn, how readily medial formats welcome those of elevated status to amplify and reproduce their images and narratives. Celebrity and sovereignty are revealed in the film as not only similar, but symbiotic, as popular assent and political ascent mutually propel each other. Thus, when Richard and Buckingham defer to Richard's onscreen image as proof of his kingship, it becomes difficult to decipher which act confers the greater power—the solemn crowning of a new king or its flickering presentation upon the silver screen. While the former ceremonializes the transfer of power, the latter, at least to Richard and Buckingham, seems to solidify it, as king and star collapse into one celluloid image.

The screening scene, like the scene of Richard in front of his dressing room mirror, participates in a visual motif throughout the film that consistently pairs Richard with his mediatized double—whether it be his cosmetically enhanced face in the mirror, his filmed coronation, his larger-than-life portrait that hangs behind his desk, or a black-and-white photo of the victorious Yorks that marks the "glorious summer" of their rule (1.1.2). As such, the film's repetitive depiction of a doubled Richard offers a particularly legible illustration of the twin selves of celebrity: both the authoritative subject commanding the villainous plot and the collaboratively crafted object as presented through intermediaries. Such scenes also illustrate what Roach has labeled as the most salient point of convergence between monarchs and celebrities: "Celebrities, like kings, have two bodies," argues Roach (2005, 24). Alluding to Ernst Kantorowicz's influential work on the dual nature of the sovereign's body (Kantorowicz 1957)—the one corporeal and finite and the other symbolic, unbounded, and re-inhabited by successors—Roach likens the king's second "body politic" to the celebrity's "immortal body of the 'image'," which, as he notes, remains preserved whether on film or in audience memories (24). But while Roach locates the convergence between these second selves in immortality, perhaps the more compelling overlap lies in the ways that both of these invisible, second bodies condense the many into one: God, king, and country in the body politic and the public's collaborative narrative authority of the celebrity body.

Of course, the Richard of either play or film adaptation could hardly be said to embody the *character angelicus* theorized by fifteenth-century legal scholar John Fortescue, from whom Kantorowicz draws in his elucidation of the two-bodies doctrine. The second body of the king, according to Fortescue, knows neither fault nor age and, "like the angels," remains "Immutable within Time" (Kantorowicz 1957, 8). The body politic of Fortescue is incapable of sin and operates as an intercessory between the human and the divine. The scheming, bloodthirsty Richard, however, is certainly no angel, as the Loncraine film makes clear when Richard meets his death by descending into a blazing inferno like a demon cast back into the pits of Hell. Yet immediately upon his death, his successor—the soon-to-be-named Henry VII—finds for the first time the camera that had been Richard's steady companion throughout the film and seizes Richard's privilege of direct address to smile directly into it. In a twist on the transferrable body politic as enunciated in "The king is dead! Long live the king!", here, the undying body that transfers from king to king is not the *character angelicus* but the power to command the media, the filmic body, the second self of celebrity.

Throughout the film, Richard's double-bodiedness points to a second, mediatized body of celebrity rather than a king's body politic—a *character populāris*, rather than a *character angelicus*, as this second body emerges from decidedly human and collaborative, rather than divine, appointment. As is the case with all celebrities, this second, immaterial body is an aggregated repository of images, media, fantasies, speculations, and narratives co-crafted amongst Richard and his public, a conglomerated body generated from his own enterprise and performance as much as the contributions of countless others, from his makeup artist to his portrait-painter to the gathered citizens he manipulates into begging for his rule. With its repetitive emphasis on both medial formats and doubled images, Loncraine's film isolates and amplifies a dynamics at work in Shakespeare's play in which, to paraphrase Donaldson, celebrity is difficult to distinguish from monarchy, as the ability to command attention looks a lot like the ability to command. The film also materializes through visual media a doubling that the play achieves rhetorically, perhaps best encapsulated by Richard's proclamation, "Richard loves Richard: that is I and I" (5.3.181).

It is in the histories where Shakespeare offers his most thorough examinations of the substance of celebrity, as kings provide a ready-made vehicle for the interrogation of an emergent theatrical phenomenon likewise rooted not only in double-bodiedness, but in performance, fame, and the hierarchical structures that elevate a select few to privilege and power. In the figure of the staged king, monarchy and celebrity meet in much the same way they do in Richard's celluloid image, as king and star collapse into a single image in the person of the performer. But the convergence of monarchy and celebrity only intensifies in staged kings, like Richard, who cannot claim the crown by way of birthright and must instead climb popular acclaim to a position of power. As a substantial body of scholarship attests, Shakespeare's kings borrow strategies from the stage to boost their claims to power, casting light on "the necessity for the modern king constantly and publicly to perform kingship," as Jean Howard asserts (Howard 1994, 145). But if Shakespeare's celebrity-kings testify to the theatricality of the monarchy, they likewise demonstrate the ways that theatrical celebrity is structured on a model of elevated status and performance appropriated from hierarchies of birthright. As a popularly constructed, alternative form of the two-bodies doctrine, celebrity offers a demotic re-articulation of the royal *We* through the cultivation of a body popular. Shakespeare's celebrity-kings, then, can probe the similitudes and symbioses between royalty and its distorted reflection in celebrity.

Chris Fitter has recently advanced the provocative argument that, despite decades of criticism investigating Shakespeare's engagement with the two-bodies doctrine, that "nowhere, I would argue, does Shakespeare state the doctrine of the king's two bodies" (Fitter 2020, 93), as he problematizes Kantorowicz's famous dissection of *Richard II* by pointing out how, as similarly appears in *Richard III*, "monarchic succession [is] manifestly engineered by unscrupulous human scheming" rather than "providential installation" (93). In this chapter, I argue that there is room for both human scheming and a doctrine of two bodies when kings are re-invigorated upon the stage through an ethos of celebrity rather than an aura of divinity—that is, when the second body of the king is understood as a *character populāris*, collaboratively constructed in the public sphere, rather than a *character angelicus*. Shakespeare's celebrity-kings cultivate this second celebrity body in two central ways, both of which appear counterintuitive to the establishment of monarchical power: one, by loosening their association with the role of king, such that their distinctive persons peek through the veneer of role to stimulate their audience's desire for them as individuals, and two, by performing celebrity absence as opposed to royal presence, or by strategically withholding their presence in order to invite the public's collaboration. With no real claims to the divine right of kingship, this chapter argues, Richard III, Henry IV, and Prince Hal opt to establish their authority through the power of celebrity instead, as each endeavors to cultivate a discernible presence that transcends royal role and to carve out a vacant space for their public's projection and wonder. In so doing, *Richard III* and *1 Henry IV* present celebrity as popularly buttressed, alternative pathway to power and royalty's distorted, demotic double.

Celebrity, hierarchy, and the demotic turn

In *Understanding Celebrity*, Graeme Turner coined the phrase "the demotic turn" to describe the increasing visibility of ordinary people and ordinariness more generally in celebrity media (Turner 2014). Referring most specifically to reality TV and social-media stars, Turner observes that celebrity in the late twentieth and early twenty-first centuries has undergone something of a shift, as expanded opportunities for and accessible platforms of celebrity have transformed the phenomenon "from being an elite and magical condition to being an almost reasonable expectation from everyday life" (2014, 94). Turner uses the word *demotic* to capture this development in conscious resistance to the farther-reaching notions of democratization often ascribed to celebrity, which, as he states elsewhere, is "a step too far" in describing celebrity's powers of enfranchisement (Turner 2010, 2); even as celebrity may grant greater access to an increasingly diverse range of identities, Turner reminds that celebrity remains both "hierarchical and exclusive [...], no matter how much it proliferates" (2014, 93).

The demotic turn that Turner observes in the past half-century is, I would suggest, only a recent iteration of a phenomenon that has informed celebrity's long and varied histories that slides toward a realization of Andy Warhol's prediction of a universal allotment of fifteen minutes of fame. As the art historian Benjamin H. D. Buchloh notes, Warhol's projection imagines that "the hierarchy of subjects worthy to be represented will someday be abolished" (Buchloh 2001, 28), and while celebrity remains a patently hierarchical taxonomy of distinction legible in classifications like A-list or D-list, those subjects deemed "worthy to be represented" have certainly expanded in scope. However, the spectacularized ordinariness of celebrity is not a contemporary development, as evidenced by the earliest celebrity theorists' condemnations of celebrities as lacking the exceptional achievements or remarkable distinctions of the deserving famous. Rather, the demotic qualities of celebrity are fundamental to a phenomenon so staked upon the shared authority and identificatory engagement of audiences. As Marshall has argued, celebrity offers a "debunking of the customary divisions of traditional society" and a shared sense of "vulgar pride" in its elevation of the ordinary (Marshall 1997, 8), and in many ways, celebrity itself *is* a demotic turn of the rigid social stratifications born of bloodline—a kind of vernacular aristocracy, still heavily invested in the concepts of distinction and hierarchical entitlement, yet appointed through popular acclaim rather than birthright designation. But in keeping with Turner's model, a vernacular aristocracy may demystify, but does not democratize, access to power. Celebrity remains, however much access to public platforms has expanded, an exclusive club—open to those outside the direct claims of bloodline, certainly, but reliant upon the privileges of public visibility and the contributions of willing collaborators and restricted to those who can benefit their patrons and project a narrative compatible to the public's desires. "The very logic of celebrity," write Alison Hearn and Stephanie Schoenhoff, "is that only a select few can achieve success within it" (Hearn and Schoenhoff 2016, 208).

Given its exclusivity and hierarchical designs, celebrity does not so much debunk traditional social divisions as distort them into a vernacular re-articulation of the very structures it is often thought to dismantle. Thus, celebrity actually affirms the divisional stratification of the peerage, perhaps because, as Van Krieken has suggested, the social relations of celebrity find their roots in court society, even as celebrity has morphed from its courtly forebears to accommodate a broader swath of the population and to disperse the authority of favoritism to a larger, adjudicating public. Van Krieken, who describes celebrities as "democratized aristocrats" (Van Krieken 2012, 8), isolates within the royal court a "a core of a nascent 'celebrity rationality'":

> Court society established a particular psychological disposition, a certain *habitus*, organized around a constitutive theatricality and heightened visibility both upwards, to one's superiors, and downwards, to one's inferiors. The court self was perpetually performative and subject to intense and constant competition according to ever-shifting rules and norms, leading to a blurring of the boundary between public and private life.
>
> (22)

In short, Van Krieken does not see celebrity so much as a shift away from aristocratic structures as a "migration" in which that core "celebrity rationality jumped the walls of court society" to proliferate in society at large (24). In a similar vein, Lenard Berlanstein argues that celebrity "trickled down" from bourgeois culture and has "more united than divided the upper classes and the masses" through a shared interest in celebrating distinction (Berlanstein 2004, 82).

In *Symptoms of Culture*, Marjorie Garber posits that both the aristocracy and celebrity converge in a mutual insistence on the notion of greatness. As Garber argues, the idea of greatness, once a designator of noble birth, has evolved to encompass a "new ideology of the natural aristocrat" (Garber 1998, 20), in which greatness lies in both achievement and popular pronouncement (18–20).

"The modern cultural fantasy about heroes and greatness," under which Garber counts celebrity, reflects "a desire for identifiable and objective standards, and a nostalgia for hierarchy" (18). Even as celebrity expands the boundaries of what can be deemed great, it mimes the aristocracy's insistence that only a select few can embody greatness, and that these individuals, these stars, outshine their counterparts and reside amongst the heavens, elevated above their gazers.

But achievable greatness, as opposed to the greatness of noble birth, is not a strictly backwards-looking phenomenon built in the wake of a diminished aristocracy, but an alternative, demotic pathway to prominence that co-existed alongside the institutionalized hierarchies it emulated. The promise of achievable greatness fuels the power struggles and wicked machinations of Shakespeare's histories, and it is a concept *Twelfth Night* toys with in spectacular fashion when the intoxicating bait of greatness provides the most effective lure in the elaborate prank that ensnares Malvolio. "Some are born great, some achieve greatness, and some have greatness thrust upon 'em" (2.5.126–128), Malvolio reads from a planted letter designed precisely to mock him. "Be not afraid of greatness" (2.5.126). Greatness here, as in much of Shakespeare, refers to noble status, and for Malvolio, who was not born great, achieving greatness means marrying above his rank. But marrying up and into greatness, he is told, requires the successful performance of a highly detailed script. "Go to, thou art made" (2.5.135), he is instructed, and with the promise of greatness dangled before him, he predictably embarks upon a ludicrous theatrical display in attempt to achieve it. While the scene offers a farcical take-down of a pretentious, puritan busybody, it also satirizes the social-climbing impulses of those who would be great, and it submits theatrical performance as a means of bypassing the structures of birthright to greatness. Of course, Malvolio does not achieve greatness; he is rigorously humiliated instead, illustrating the potentially high risks of a theatrical strategy that simultaneously dangles high rewards. Viola, on the other hand, as the play's more successful performer, does end up marrying into the nobility, thereby affirming that some do, in fact, achieve greatness through theatrical enterprise.

The metatheatrical implications of Malvolio's fruitless attempts to perform his way into a countess's heart and noble rank are rendered unmistakable when a spectator, Fabian, comments upon his performance, "If this were played upon a stage now, I would condemn it as an improbable fiction" (3.4.115–116). This moment of theatrical self-referentiality invites us to consider the similarly fraught pathways to prominence available to the on-stage players who likewise risk public humiliation—or as Shakespeare puts it in Sonnet 110, being made "a motley to the view"[2]—for the rewards of celebrity. In many cases, as detailed in this book's second chapter, the results included both the privileges of visibility, wealth, and favor along with the indignity of public ridicule, and Shakespeare could certainly count himself a member of this exclusive yet simultaneously discomfiting club. In 1596, Shakespeare's London theatrical successes allowed him to procure a coat of arms for his father, John Shakespeare, which conferred gentleman status upon him and his descendants. The Shakespeare coat of arms, which depicts a shield, spear, and falcon, displays the motto "Non sanz droict," or "Not without merit," perhaps asserting somewhat defensively through its negative construction the validity of theatrical achievement as an alternate route to the gentry. But Shakespeare's social aspirations encountered resistance from authorities as well as his fellow theatricals. In 1602, his name was included in a list of twenty-three heraldic awardees who had been deemed by the York Herald as unworthy recipients. The appended note, "Shakespeare the Player by Garter,"[3] referencing the Garter King of Arms accused of too liberally granting applications, suggests that Shakespeare's status as a player was deemed beneath the honor. Though the challenge was eventually dismissed, Shakespeare's gentrified status met further, and more public, indignity in Ben Jonson's 1599 *Every Man out of his Humour* in the character of a country bumpkin named Sogliardo who is "so enamour'd of the name of a Gentleman that he will have it though he buyes it" (Jonson 1600, Sig. A4). Sogliardo, who has long been taken as a jab at Shakespeare, recoils at the suggestion that his freshly purchased coat of arms should be adorned with the unsubtly allusive motto, "Not without mustard" (Sig. Iv).

Shakespeare was hardly alone as a playmaker who achieved both greatness and its accompanying derision from theatrical enterprise. In addition to his gentleman status, Shakespeare accrued significant wealth; he was a sharer in the Globe and purchased the second-largest home in Stratford. Tarlton, the queen's favorite, was able upon his death to enlist the aid of royal advisor Sir Francis Walsingham to care for his son, but Tarlton, as discussed in Chapter 1, was also ridiculed for his appearance. Alleyn, likely London's wealthiest and most landed actor, purchased the manor of Dulwich for 10,000 pounds, founded a school and hospital there, and achieved the clout to marry the daughter of John Donne, Dean of St. Paul's (Gurr 1992, 91). But as the anonymous pamphleteer of *Ratseis Ghost* derisively wrote in 1605, some players had become "so wel favored" and "growne so wealthy, that they have expected to be knighted" (Sig. B1). The contempt expressed here echoes a significant body of similarly deflating treatments of actors' social elevations. John Cocke's 1615 "A Common Player," for example, reminds readers that despite pretenses that might suggest otherwise, the player remains but "the servant of the people" (Stephens 1615, 295).

The contempt that the social and financial elevations of early modern theatrical celebrities aroused is indicative of the distortive relationship achieved greatness shares with born greatness, but especially of the specifically theatrical means of achievement. While the wealth, courtly connections, and gentrified titles of theatrical success may position the early modern star in a social sphere more compatible with companies' noble patrons than with the common player, theatrical celebrity makes particularly clear what Shakespeare calls in Sonnet 111 the "public means" of its distinction—that is, that stars savor the perks of a privilege granted by their audience's applause and acclaim. The public's recognition of their own collaborative authority in the ascent of celebrities entitles them to arbitration in a way that the authority vested in birthright does not. As Turner notes of the demotic turn, celebrity offers up in place of the "elite and magical condition" of noble birth the substitution of a "reasonable expectation" of enhanced visibility and social privilege as a consequence of public performance. And while celebrity is more a funhouse-mirror reflection of hierarchical social divisions than the abolishment Warhol may have imagined, celebrity does enfranchise the public, if not to power or even to fifteen minutes of fame, with the deliberative authority of selective elevation and deflation.

Dual bodies/dueling bodies

In a 2019 essay, Rojek, like Roach before him, invokes Kantorowicz to argue that, just as the two-bodies doctrine migrated from the realm of medieval theology to that of early modern legal structures, the doctrine further transferred to the cultural arena during the Restoration where it survived as a foundational principle of celebrity (Rojek 2019, 41, 46). In Rojek's formulation, as in Roach's, celebrities, too, are gifted with immortality through the metaphysical transcendence of the second, undying body, such that Elvis and Marilyn, "despite being physically dead [...] are palpably present in culture" (53). In short, Rojek proposes, the celebrity, like a king, possesses both "a corrigible biological body and an incorrigible, mediated body" (53). However, as is the case with the concept of achievable greatness more generally, there is no reason to assume that the second celebrity body evolved only as an epilogue to a since-abandoned royal two-bodies doctrine. As an alternate pathway to privilege and visibility, celebrity existed concurrently with and mimicked both the hierarchical structures of the aristocracy and the sacred second body of the king, and just as celebrity affirmed, though distorted, the nobility's insistence on embodied greatness, it likewise upheld, though modified, the concept of a second, immaterial body.

What I have called a *character populāris* is, too, a demotic reconfiguration of birthright status, but unlike the undying, transferrable *character angelicus*—and, in contradistinction to Roach's and Rojek's formulations—I would suggest that the second self of celebrity is not immortal but, to the contrary, remarkably fragile and even volatile. While celebrity images do remain preserved, the immaterial body born of the public's desires and discourse can easily dissolve into obsolescence, and it is a common-sense adage that stars flicker in and out of the spotlight. But where these second bodies meet more securely is in their mutual convergences of the many into one, with the sanctity of the monarchy and the collective of the nation coalescing in the body politic while the public's projections, fixations, and narrative speculations condense into the body popular. However, if the king's second body is likened to an angel, the celebrity's second body enjoys a more diverse panoply of figurative imagery—from the uplifting to the unsettling.

The March 15, 1604 coronation procession of King James I offers one of the more ennobling displays of the celebrity's second self, as well as its vernacularizing reflection of the king's second body, when London's most celebrated star, Alleyn, welcomed James to the capitol city. Preserved in four different contemporary print accounts—by the playwrights Dekker and Jonson respectively, who composed most of the pageants; the architect Stephen Harrison, who designed the triumphal arches through which the king would pass on his journey from the Tower to Temple Bar; and a witness, Gilbert Dugdale—the procession provided one of the "greatest spectacles of early seventeenth-century England" (Smuts 2007, 219). James's procession marks the first coronation celebration after the establishment of London's commercial theater industry, and thus, the theater played a particularly palpable role in the festivities: not only did Dekker and Jonson (with a small contribution from Middleton) provide most of the day's oratory, but twenty-eight players, including Shakespeare and eight of his fellow King's Men, were each issued 4 ½ yards of red cloth from the Great Wardrobe, presumably for the creation of liveries to be worn in the procession.[4]

Of the seven triumphal arches erected to usher James to the throne, it was the first that officially welcomed the king into London. Inscribed *Londinium* and adorned on top with a miniature model of the city, Alleyn here played the role of *Genius Urbis,* the spirit of the entire city made flesh.[5] Alleyn was undoubtedly selected for this role both for his oft-recognized gift for oratory— Dekker reports that he performed his role "with excellent Action, and a well tun'de audible voyce" (Dekker 1604, Sig. B2v)—as well as for what Cerasano has called "his status as a celebrity" (Cerasano 2005, 53). Braudy muses upon this meeting of king and player-king, "What an instructive contrast that must have been" (Braudy 1986, 331), as he speculates as to the crowd's reception, and perception, of "the dumpy, somewhat unattractive king" and the tall, attractive, wealthy celebrity player (331), before turning his attention to the dangers inherent in such confrontations, especially "for the ruler who could not measure up [...] to the actor's physical presence" (332). But while Braudy locates the "instructive contrast" between James and Alleyn in their human, corporeal bodies, perhaps the more crucial contrast lay in their second, intangible bodies: the body politic versus its demotic double in the celebrity body.

To be certain, both men possessed commonalties on display that day: both were undeniably famous figures who drew clamoring crowds, both were positioned as simultaneous spectacle and spectator to the other's role in the pageantry, and both were understood to contain the multitudes in their persons. As Alleyn welcomed the king, he said, in verse composed by Jonson, that as *genius* he spoke on behalf of "The Councell, Commoners, and Multitude" (Jonson 1616, 850), before personalizing his oration with, "I tender thee the heartiest welcome" (851). In Alleyn, the "Multitude" becomes "I," rhetorically demonstrating his double-bodiedness and his position as both individual and collective, man and *genius,* as converge in celebrity. But there were likewise significant and striking differences apparent as well. While one was on this day celebrated before his eventual crowning, the other, as evidenced by Harrison's published illustrations, was crowned with a laurel (Harrison 1604, Sig. C1)—an achieved, not entitled, mark of distinction that asserted Alleyn's alternate pathway to this privileged place of prominence. Further, as Alleyn spoke from his elevated platform upon the arch, Dekker reports that, "Too short a time (in their opinions that were glewed there together so many hours, to behold him) did his Majestie dwell upon this first place" (Dekker 1604, Sig. C1). Even positioned, like Alleyn, as both spectacle and spectator, and even as the crowds swarmed "with such hurly burly" (Dugdale 1604, Sig. B1v), the king yet possessed the privilege to move in and out of the performance spaces prepared for him, unconfined by platform. James's platform—bestowed by God and country and a lifelong appointment—was a guaranteed accessory to his person.

Demonstrating even further distinction between the two men gathered at the Londinium arch, even as the citizenry coalesced in the person of Alleyn, the star player remained, unlike the king, a singular individual capable of detaching from any one role and moving into another. The king's guaranteed, mobile platform renders him at all times king, as the role that confines him likewise defines him; however, Alleyn's role as *Genius Urbis,* or as Tamburlaine or Faustus, are momentary embodiments, with Alleyn's tall, striking body providing the constant, veiled presence of the individual behind roles. The "code of individuality that is central to the meaning of any celebrity" (Marshall 1997, 246), offers a markedly drastic shift from the transcendent, transferrable body politic enunciated in "The king is dead! Long live the king!", in which a nameless monarchical body, immediately upon the mortal body's death, inhabits a successor. The second celebrity body remains tethered always in the public consciousness to a singular name, and celebrities then assume the paradoxical functions of celebrating individuality even as they coalesce communities in the figures of their persons. As Breda Luthar argues, "Celebrity texts are discourses on individuality," but at the same time "represent the people" as a collective—a feat achieved by proposing a particular "notion of citizenship," an imposition of "one version of 'the people'" (Luthar 2006, 143).[6] Somewhat oxymoronically, Alleyn, as celebrity, occupied a role in which his stark individualism—the "unimitable" actor (Heywood 1633, Sig. A3), whose "stalking" gait and "thundering" voice (Hall 1597, 7) became a sort of trademark—contributed to his selection as the idealized voice of the entire city.

The confrontation of James I and Alleyn, provides, as Braudy has suggested, a series of instructive contrasts, but also offers in staged tableau a notable correspondence in their social positions amidst the assembled crowds, with each man's hierarchical positioning above the gathered multitudes on display. Also on display that day in many ways was the sheer force of the people's will. Dugdale actually admonishes the crowds as a "wylie Multitude" that began to "run up and down with such unreverent rashness" that the king was forced to take retreat behind some "staire dores" (Dugdale 1604, Sigs. B1v–B2). But the people's power was on display in a less literal format as well, as their acclaim had named and elevated one of their own—an actor and son of an innkeeper—to stand high and laureled upon a platform to welcome a king. Perhaps unsurprisingly, then, this same power was often held in suspicion and outright contempt as a potentially pernicious, consumptive social force that destroyed as easily as it elevated.

While Alleyn embodied the classical convention of the *genius*, or a supernatural attendant spirit, the much more fearsome figure of the many-headed multitude featured prominently in the era as the basis of popular acclaim. Shakespeare invokes this many-headed multitude in the character of Rumour in *2 Henry IV*, in whom the "surmises" of "the discordant wav'ring multitude" circulate through "the blunt monster with uncounted heads" (Ind. 15–19). Commonly referenced by both early modern antitheatricalists and playwrights alike, the many-headed crowd dissolves the theatrical audience, and the larger city population, into an undifferentiated and monstrous mob, as threatening as it is base and unrefined. As Munro argues, to be "many-headed is the same as to be headless" (Munro 2005, 109)—that is, to lack the rule and authority of a singular, sovereign head, as of the body politic. Because this monster "was composed of masterless men, those for whom nobody responsible answered" (2005, 109), the multitude was situated somewhere outside social and political order. Unorganized and crude, its tastes were deemed uncritical and fickle, its whims volatile and dangerous. The popular man, according to William Cornwallis, is held "a loft by the pleasure of others" as "his foundation is the many headed multitude, a foundation both in respect to their number and their nature uncertaine, and consequently dangerous" (Cornwallis 1600, Sig. R5).

Jonson emerged as one of the era's fiercest critics of this wild and uncontrollable kind of popular fame. Though Ian Donaldson muses that Jonson "emerged as Britain's first literary celebrity" (Donaldson 2011, 41), it is highly doubtful that Jonson himself would have willingly accepted such a label. He generally held the popular appeal so central to celebrity in contempt as a dangerous and desperate pathway to renown. In *Cynthia's Revels*, he derides those who are "not content to be generally noted in court, but will press forth on common stages and broker's stalls, to the public view of the world" (4.3.94–96). Jonson aimed instead for an orderly kind of fame, as opposed to the unruly whims of the popular audience, and by 1605, Jonson had begun his career as a prominent masque-writer for the most exclusive audiences of the Jacobean court. Modeling his career on the classical tradition of poets he so often referenced in his writing, Jonson, who was eventually appointed James's poet laureate and paid an annual pension, fashioned himself as a kind of "poet-priest" (Braudy 1986, 322), who aimed to serve his monarch through dramatized depictions of virtue, one of which was "honourable and true Fame, bred out of Virtue" (Jonson 1609, Sig. A5), as opposed to the popular fame he decries in the dedicatory epistle to *Volpone*:

> As for those that wil (by faults which charity hath rak'd up, or common honesty concealed) make themselves a name with the Multitude, or, to drawe their rude and beastly clappes, care not whose living faces they intrench with their petulant stiles, may they doe it without a rivall, for mee! I chuse rather to live grav'd in obscuritie, then share with them in so preposterous a fame.
>
> (Jonson 1607, Sigs. A4–A5)[7]

As Jonson recuses himself from his rivals' pursuit of popular acclaim, he assigns the mass audience to bestiality—a common sentiment generally expressed in the recurrent trope of a Hydra-like public. Jonson frequently noted the crowd's propensity to lift the unskilled and undeserving to troubling prominence—a recognition only allayed by the multitude's inconstant loyalty and wavering affections.

The spectacle of sovereignty

While the intermingling of celebrity and royalty was certainly not a Shakespearean invention, as the staged spectacle of Alleyn's confrontation with King James demonstrates, Shakespeare's celebrity-kings practice a decidedly more audacious courtship of the commons than can be found in Tudor-Stuart precedent. Richard III, Henry IV, and Prince Hal each embark upon the high-risk/high-reward pursuit of popular acclaim, or achievable greatness, as an alternate pathway to the power that they cannot claim by birthright. As such, they court the many-headed multitude, with all its potential dangers, in order to cultivate a celebrity built of the people's favor. The audacity of their venture is rendered particularly apparent when held in contrast to the careful control that even the most spectacularized early modern monarchs exercised over the circulation of their public image. While the Tudors had been actively cultivating certain constituent elements of celebrity, including theatrical display and promotional strategies, for much of the sixteenth century, they, like Jonson, held the reins of their renown close. The Tudors exercised significant control over the popular discourse and fused their persons too thoroughly to their office to ever surrender to the colonizing reach of celebrity's dispersed, public authority. It is fair to say, however, that the Tudors dramatically altered the ways that monarchs interacted with their subjects and, thus, offered Shakespeare's monarchs a ready template in royal performance and self-promotion. With an unsteady claim to the throne, the Tudors' position depended heavily on symbolic, mediated displays of their power that included not only the "abundance, conspicuous consumption and magnificence" that Kevin Sharpe argues the Tudors in particular excelled at demonstrating (Sharpe 2000, 204), but also the emblematizing of the majesty of their office in the figure of their person. As Sharpe argues in *Selling the Tudor Monarchy*, Henry VIII cultivated "the Tudor brand" (Sharpe 2009, 157); he fashioned his palaces as "advertising hoardings for, as well as monuments to, the virtues and powers" he wished to promulgate (148), and he projected a public image through which "his person and the institution of the monarchy [became] inseparable in the minds of his subjects" (157). Through the abolishment of competing religious iconography, Henry ushered in what Braudy calls a "secular iconography" in the image of his person (Braudy 1986, 274), as he unleashed upon the English court the notion that "imagery was power" (278).

But the power of representative majesty carries with it certain risks, as the image's effectiveness depends upon its audience's response. To mitigate the potential for dissenting reception, Henry crafted a public image that indeterminably conflated his person with his office, thereby asserting his person as an emblem of the powers of the monarchy and the nation.[8] This strategic integration acted as a disenfranchising buffer against the kind of agency publics enjoy in the proliferation of celebrity, where the tease of the distinctive individual unable to be constrained by role stokes audience speculation and desire. Henry's representational strategies promoted his self and King of England as both inseparable and indecipherable. Elizabeth embraced her father's model of representational authority and arguably even surpassed his ability to wield the power of image as a means of establishing legitimacy. Beset by greater challenges to her authority, Elizabeth, as Doty has argued, "mastered the arts of popularity" and marshalled her people's love into political power (Doty 2017, 7). Elizabeth understood that, "We princes are set on stages in the sight and view of the world" (Holinshed 1587, 4:934), and thus, she appropriated theatrical display to the promotion of her person and glory of her office. In what Greenblatt calls "privileged visibility" (Greenblatt 1988, 64) and David Scott Kastan labels "spectacular sovereignty" (Kastan 1999, 117), Elizabeth staged elaborate pageantry and grandiose spectacles from the moment she was carried on a gold-canopied litter for her 1559 coronation procession to the annual progresses she undertook for more than four decades. But while Elizabeth availed herself to her people more directly than did her father, she maintained Henry's model of monarchical representation, tying her person firmly to her office even as she solicited her subjects' more personal affections. As Inglis argues, her coronation procession of 1559 "was certainly spectacular […] but the meaning the spectacle dramatized was not celebrity but renown. Elizabeth is renowned as being the monarch; her fame is conferred by her people on behalf of God and England" (Inglis 2010, 6). Specifically, if celebrities function as "embodiments of triumphant individualism," as Dyer has stated (Dyer 1998, 91), then Inglis reads Elizabeth's coronation instead as a celebration of the monarchy's triumphs, with the interactions between the flamboyantly paraded queen and her effusive subjects demonstrative of their mutually pledged loyalties. The people clamored for their queen, not for a glimpse of the woman distinct from her office; the lavish display spectacularized the majesty of the monarchy in celebration of England's heritage and power, rather than the individual *as herself.*

While Elizabeth counted "my people's love" as her greatest treasure, Doty likewise cautions, "it would be a mistake to think that popularity was merely a culture of celebrity" (Doty 2017, 111), as the popular appeal Elizabeth and other early modern monarchs cultivated offered political, rather than personal, access. Elizabeth, like her father, promoted her person as emblematic of her nation and a conduit through which her subjects could demonstrate their devotion to God and country. But if it is a mistake to assign the sovereign's courting of personal affection toward loyalist ends to the realm of celebrity, so too is it a mistake to dismiss celebrity as "merely" a superficial cousin to the political power of popularity. Royal popularity and theatrical celebrity share substantial commonalty, with each rooted in both the privileges and the perils of magnified visibility. However, one central and abiding distinction between these modes of engagement lies in the degree of enfranchisement each offers the public: celebrity enfranchises not through the mere power of assent, but the collaborative authority of narrative invention. Elizabeth invited her people to love her and proclaim that love as a form of political expression; celebrity is not a channel for, but born of, the people's voice.

In 1563, Elizabeth issued a proclamation regulating the production of her royal likeness and, in 1596, the Privy Council ordered the destruction of unauthorized portraits that caused "great offense" to the queen.[9] The care she took to shield her image from the invasiveness of public intervention, even as she may have invited it in her skillful solicitation of the people's love, offers just one small example of a significant divide between royal and celebrity authority—namely, that monarchs wield celebrity dynamics as a complement to, and not a substitute for, the kind of codified, institutional power that allowed Elizabeth to forbid unauthorized representation by manner of royal proclamation. As Chapter 2 demonstrates, this is not a luxury that early modern theatrical celebrities enjoyed; to the contrary, they sometimes, and quite publicly, lamented their inability to control the circulation of their commoditized names and images. Such dispersed narrative authority is dangerous for a monarch—not that the cultivation of popularity or the spectacularized display of royal power are without their risks.[10] But as Greenblatt argues, "the play of authority [...] is made to seem entirely beyond the control of those whose 'imaginary forces' actually confer upon it its significance and force" (Greenblatt 1988, 65), and Kastan adds that the people's "assent is already assumed as an aspect of the royal script" (Kastan 1999, 117). The representation of royal authority thereby walks something of a tightrope, soliciting participation at the same time as eliding the true force of the people's prerogative—a careful mitigation captured in Elizabeth's declaration that, "though God hath raised me high, yet this I count the glory of my crown—that I have reigned with your loves" (Elizabeth I 2000 [1601], 340). In the same breath that Elizabeth privileges her people's love as her pinnacle achievement and deflects her glory upon those who love her, she reminds that her elevated position has been bestowed by God; she counts her popularity here not as the foundation of her authority, but as a cherished adjunct to divinely sanctioned power. Thus, as Shakespeare revivifies the monarchs of the fifteenth century upon his sixteenth-century stage, his celebrity-kings reflect more readily upon the processes that lift the players, rather than the kings they play, to power. In their audacious performance and publicity strategies, and especially in the manner by which they detach from their safeguarding royal roles and submit themselves to the potentially pernicious whims of the public, Richard, Henry, and Hal opt for a demotic reconfiguration of the sovereignty that their births have precluded them from. What Shakespeare toys with in *Twelfth Night*—that is, the concept of performing one's way to greatness, with all its devastating risks and promised rewards—these plays exercise in deadly earnest.

Richard III and the "thousand several tongues"

When, in the first scene of the play, Richard III informs us that since his deformities prevent him from being a lover, he is "determined to prove a villain" (1.1.30), he signals to the audience what will be his most sustained role throughout the play—not the villain he intends to become, and not even the actor who plays him, but the celebrity actor who scans the available parts of the unfolding spectacle and chooses the one most likely to place him in the spotlight. Certainly, he is the villain, but villain is one of his many roles, from silver-tongued wooer to pious and reluctant leader, and certainly Richard is also an actor, as Anne Righter's (1962) and Meredith Anne Skura's (1993) work has capably explored. However, he is not only an actor, but, as Urszula Kizelbach suggests, "an Elizabethan star actor" (Kizelbach 2014, 100), so attuned to his audiences' desires that he handily manipulates them into delivering him the rewards he seeks, from the Lady Anne's heart to the throne of England. As Kizelbach states, Richard "is a good actor mainly because he distances himself from his role(s), which makes it possible to don a new mask depending on the occasion" (100).

In the end, Richard owes both his successes and his eventual defeat to calculated distances—not only the distance he establishes between himself and his various roles, but the distance he carves out between himself and his audiences. As the play opens, Richard possesses no legitimate claim to the English throne; his family's successful usurpation has left him only fourth in line for the crown. Thus, he devises a forked strategy to climb his way to power by murdering those who stand in his way and manipulating those who can lift him to power; while he hires assassins to eliminate rival claimants, he wields, and even weaponizes, performance and publicity practices to coax the support of a noble entourage and the public. He opts, then, for a demotic rather than a divine articulation of his royalty; as he readily acknowledges that he is not the "royal fruit" of the "royal tree" (3.7.146), he accepts that being named king by the people is an adequate substitute for being born an heir. As central to his ascent as his deft performances of his varied roles is his savvy publicity strategy, which relies upon performative absence designed to tease his audience's desire for his person. Rightly assessing that audiences are most apt to consent to ideas they believe are their own, and most likely to desire that which is dangled out of easy reach, Richard calculatedly withholds, gifting his audience with an illusion of agency and seducing them to supply the presence that he denies them. What Richard cannot achieve through the structures of patrilineal descent, he sets out to secure through the strange intimacy of celebrity.

Before Richard brings this strategy to the national stage, he orchestrates something of a dress rehearsal with an audience of one in Lady Anne. While Anne offers Richard a politically advantageous marriage, her courtship must overcome the sizable obstacles of her dead husband and his father, the king, both of whom Richard slew in the York usurpation of the throne. With King Henry's corpse upon the stage as a visual reminder of the significant barriers Richard's performance must penetrate, Anne greets his overtures as befitting their traumatically entangled past: she refers to him as a "foul devil" (1.2.48), a "beast" (1.2.69), and a "diffused infection of a man" (1.2.76), as she accuses him of "butcheries" (1.2.52). While he attempts first to lay out a persuasive argument and, thus, "acquit myself" (1.2.75), his rhetoric meets with much the same response: she calls him a "hedgehog" and a "homicide" (1.2.120, 123). He then attempts a shift to flattery, telling her that her "beauty was the cause" of his murderous acts; she threatens to scratch her face and "rend that beauty from my cheek" (1.2.124). He woos. She spits. Finally, his persuasion and charm exhausted, he pivots to surrender and claims he is "shamed" to the point of "salt tears" (1.2.152, 151). He offers his body up to her vengeful ire:

> If thy revengeful heart cannot forgive,
> Lo, here, I lend thee this sharp-pointed sword,
> Which if thou please to hide in this true bosom
> And let the soul forth that adoreth thee,
> I lay it naked to the deadly stroke,
> And humbly beg the death upon my knee.
> (1.2.159–165)

Anne, as he assuredly had predicted, cannot muster the strength to kill even the man who had so grievously wronged her, but it surprises even Richard how quickly she then consents to his advances, even accepting the token of a ring. "Was ever woman in this humor wooed?" he gleefully boasts. "Was ever woman in this humor won?" (1.2.214–215).

From this extended episode of fraught wooing, Richard does not only gain an unlikely wife, but extracts from the exchange what will become his publicity strategy that ultimately wins him the throne: feigned surrender to the public will. As Richard discovers here, by retreating from his assertive offense into passive capitulation, his audience has likewise shifted from resistance to collaboration. Where Anne had once commanded him to Hell, she know entreats, "I would I knew thy heart" (1.2.179). Her condemnation transformed to curiosity, Richard finds he is also now transformed. Only one scene prior, he had lamented that his "deformed, unfinished" body had rendered him unable to "court an amorous looking glass" (1.1.20, 15), but he now exclaims, "I'll be at charges for a looking glass" (1.2.241). However, he acknowledges that the body he now finds in the mirror is not the one he knows as his own:

> I do mistake my person all this while!
> Upon my life, she finds, though I cannot,
> Myself to be a marvelous proper man.
> (1.2.238–240)

Deferring his newfound, double body to the external production of another, what Richard now sees in the mirror, he admits, is the body that Anne's compliance projects upon him. In fact, Skura argues that "Anne *is* 'the amorous looking glass'" that he had previously deemed himself unable to court (Skura 1993, 66), and the body that Anne provides him is one he finds a great deal more agreeable than the one he assessed in the play's opening lament. However, beyond affirmation, what Richard ultimately takes away from his successful courtship is a lesson with broader political implications: assertion, he finds, provokes contempt, but given the semblance of agency, his audience will not only consent to him, but compose him anew.

It is a lesson that Richard takes to heart, as his success here, despite Anne's considerable resistance, emboldens and inspires him to exercise the same capitulating dynamics on a larger stage. However, rather than offer up his corporeal body, as he did with Anne, he offers up his narrative body, with the hope that the citizens will similarly project upon him a "marvelous proper" narrative of kingship. He stages himself, "*with two Bishops aloft*," before the English citizenry, with the prayer book in his hand and bishops flanking him offering up a tableau vivant of the pliant penitence that his bared breast suggested to Anne. As Buckingham pleads with him from the gathered audience to seize "the throne majestical/ The sceptered office of your ancestors" (3.7.110–111), Richard demurs. "There's no need of me," he responds from his platform above them. "The royal tree hath left us royal fruit" (3.7.144, 146). Here, he rebuffs the claim of birthright and opts for a more theatrically inspired ascension that relies upon his audience's collaboration. At Buckingham's instruction, Richard will "Be not easily won"; instead, he "Play[s] the maid's part" (3.7.44–45) and shies away from his audience's advances. With his performance of coy hesitation masking his ravenous hunger for power, he withholds his intentions to the throne precisely so that his audience will provide it. He defers authority to the people in the same way that he placed a sword in Anne's hand—as a staged illusion of agency. It is only when a nameless citizen, listed only as "Another," urges, "If you deny them, all the land will rue it" (3.7.200),[11] that Richard relents. "Will you enforce me to a world of cares?" (3.7.201), he asks, suggesting his own subjugation to the audience's authority. "I am not made of stone" (3.7.214), he concedes.

As the Richard of the Loncraine adaptation adeptly wields the enhanced visibility of film and photo to the promotion of his person, the Richard of the play-text manipulates the power of the stage. In *3 Henry VI*, he "dream[ed] on sovereignty/ Like one that stands upon a promontory" (3.2.134–135), as he boasted that he could "add colors to the chameleon,/ Change shapes with Proteus" (3.2.191–192). Here, he enacts the realization of that dream, achieving sovereignty from the promontory of the stage through his deft shape-shifting, but it is not only his thespian skill that has lifted him to the crown. As Lindsey Row-Heyveld notes, in *Richard III*, "spectatorship *is* participation" (Row-Heyveld 2018, 155), but Richard's spectators, from the loyalists he plants in the audience to the citizens who ultimately beg for his rule, are more than complicit; they are vital collaborators in his narrative of ascension. While he may perform pious reticence, they provide the requisite resistance that allows him to emerge as the reluctant hero who selflessly rises, "against my conscious and my soul" (3.7.204), to his people's rescue. By resisting all intimations of his legitimacy by birthright only to accede finally to the solicitation of "Another" who stands in as a singular representative of the popular voice,

Richard does not seize power; he hesitantly accepts it on behalf of a people crying out for his leadership. Thus, he constructs his kingship upon the unstable foundation of his collaborators' dispersed authority. His kingship, like his reflection in the mirror, is the external production of Another, and there is more truth to his admission that he is "not made of stone" than he likely realizes: King Richard is, as he suggests, the fragile, pliable projection of the public will.

As the citizens project upon Richard an image of kingship, their popularly appointed sovereignty proves as flimsy as the handsome, yet insubstantial form Anne projected upon the looking glass. The fragility, and volatility, of a celebrity-sovereignty crafted of the people's desire haunts Richard on the eve of his demise almost as much do the resurrected spirits of eleven of his murdered victims. Waking up from fearful dreams, Richard frenetically asks himself,

> What do I fear? Myself? There's none else by.
> Richard loves Richard; that is, I and I.
> Is there a murderer here? No. Yes, I am.
> Then fly! What, from myself? Great reason. Why?
> Lest I revenge. Myself upon myself?
> Alack, I love myself. Wherefore? For any good
> That I myself have done unto myself?
> On no, alas, I rather hate myself
> For hateful deeds committed by myself.
> I am a villain. Yet I lie: I am not.
> Fool, of thyself speak well. – Fool, do not flatter.
> My conscience hath a thousand several tongues
> And every tongue brings in a several tale.
> (5.3.180–192)

Richard's near-pathological dissociation fittingly follows the parade of ghosts that have just tormented him in his dreams, as the ghosts—quite literally, ethereal second bodies—preview externally a force that will disintegrate him internally. As the ghosts of his eleven victims speak his misdeeds and define him as a bloodthirsty tyrant, they exemplify the unstoppable force of the many-headed multitude whose narrative had once lifted him to, but now remove him from, power.

Upon waking, Richard frenetically launches into a tangled knot of competing self-signification, notably alternating between the singular assertion that "There's none else by" and a series of dualizing doubled identifications: "Richard loves Richard," "I and I," and "Myself upon myself." The doubled rhetoric legibly asserts his double-bodiedness, but his second body, crafted through the public voice, is decidedly flimsier and significantly more volatile than the sacred, immortal doctrine of the *character angelicus*. As he hears the voices of "a thousand several tongues," he invokes simultaneously images of the Hydra-like multitude, the multi-tongued *Fama*, and the multiple voices of the public upon whom his ascension depended. But the voices that once lifted him to power now destabilize his collaboratively crafted narrative into a splintered "several tale." Amidst the disharmonious fragmentation of his second celebrity self, he alternates between the three different descriptors of "I," "myself," and "Richard," positioning himself simultaneously as subject, object, and distant third-person. His confused and rapid alternations, combined with his intense self-questioning, suggest a desperate probe to isolate an identifiable self that he had already offered up to the public for construction. The answer to all his questions—whom he fears, from whom should he flee, upon whom shall he seek revenge—is always the same dissociated and objective "myself," a second self, but severed, distanced, and fragmented now that the fickle voices of the multitude have abandoned him.

In Loncraine's film adaptation, upon Richard's battlefield demise, his successor Richmond finds the frame and offers a direct-to-camera smile, suggesting in a twist on the transferrable body politic that the celebrity body instead has moved on to the new king. The play-text, however, asserts quite the opposite when the victorious Richmond announces that "We will unite the white rose and the red" and then questions, "What traitor hears me and says not 'Amen'?" (5.5.19, 22). As the soon-to-be-named Henry VII makes clear in the first seconds of his rule, there is no room in his kingship for the kind of public speculation or narrative invention that lifted the "long-usurped royalty" of Richard to power (5.5.4). As king, he establishes the narrative framework of his sovereignty and commands a singular, uniform, and affirming response that renders all other voices treasonous. Declaring Richard's rule to be illegitimate, King Henry surveys the noble dead and commands his followers to "Inter their bodies as becomes their births" (5.5.15), suggesting a return to the traditional hierarchical structures of birthright authority that the nation's momentary intoxication with the seductive lure of celebrity had temporarily displaced.

Henry IV: a public wonder

Upon rising from his feigned battlefield death near the close of *1 Henry IV*, Falstaff informs an incredulous Hal that, "I am not a double man" (5.4.134). Assuring his friend that he is indeed alive and not the ghost of his former, fallen self, Falstaff clarifies, "If I be not Jack Falstaff, then am I a jack" (5.4.134–135). Of course, Falstaff is a jack, as well as Jack Falstaff, as he mimics yet negates the kind of doubled rhetoric that signified Richard's self-fragmentation. As Falstaff claims, he is not a double man, because the two identificatory options he proposes are one in the same. For all of Falstaff's flamboyant fabrications, scheming, and carousing— that is, for all the things that make him a lower-case jack—he could not be said to be duplicitous; his mendacity and machinations are so self-consciously theatrical and performed with such abandon as to render the upper-case Jack absolutely transparent. But his assertion of singular authenticity gestures toward the duplicity around him and, specifically, to the actual double man he is addressing.

The first Henry IV play is a play about double men and doubled men. With two royal Henrys, two father figures to the prince, two Percy men rising against the king, and a climactic confrontation of "Harry to Harry" (4.1.121), *1*

Henry IV is a play saturated in what Matt Bell calls "uncanny masculine doubling" (Bell 2011, 112)—a doubling only further articulated through paired principal settings (the Boar's Head and the palace) and mirrored conflicts (Gads Hill and Shrewsbury). But the dramatized doubles here do not so much reflect as refract; they offer similitude without sameness, a bent likeness that distorts the double in much the same way that celebrity structures distort royal ones. Just as the name *Hal* offers the prince's tavern gang a familiar iteration of *Harry* Monmouth, doubles in *1 Henry IV* provide demotic re-articulations of royal persons, institutions, and pursuits that highlight commonalities even as the colloquial doubles distort their official precedents. Falstaff, for example, presides over the Boar's Head like King Henry reigns from the royal court. While the Harry known as Hal conspires to humiliate Falstaff in their planned heist, the Harry known as Hotspur conspires with rebellious factions to overthrow the King of England.

But if Henry and Hal encounter their distorted doubles throughout the play, they are also double men in and of themselves in precisely the way that Falstaff is not. While the king and his heir are likewise given to theatrics, they play with purposes other than mere survival or to indulge their extravagant excesses. King Henry and Prince Hal perform in order to cultivate a *character populāris:* a popularly generated double crafted in the substance of the people's wonder. As is the case with Richard III, Henry acknowledges that he owes his position to popular "Opinion, that did help me to the crown" (3.2.42), and both father and son solicit the public's collaboration to fortify the shaky merits of their claim with the power of celebrity. This is a process that the king began in *Richard II*, when, as the royal aspirant known as Bolingbroke, Henry IV engaged in "courtship to the common people" (1.4.24). As his royal predecessor observed, a young and not-yet-crowned Henry, upon his march into exile at the king's command,

> [...] did seem to dive into their hearts
> With humble and familiar courtesy,
> What reverence he did throw away on slaves,
> Wooing poor craftsmen with the craft of smiles
> And patient underbearing of his fortune
> As 'twere to banish their affects with him.
> Off goes his bonnet to an oysterwench.
> A brace of draymen bid God speed him well,
> And had the tribute of his supple knee.
> (1.4.25–33)

Denied the king's favor from above, Bolingbroke sought out support from the commons below. His display of humility and solidarity with the people, despite his elevated rank, provokes the king's ire who, as Doty states, views the spectacle as "an act of debasement, in which Bolingbroke acts like a player attempting to tease smiles from his audience" (Doty 2017, 45). But as the king has debased him by banishing him from his home, Bolingbroke courts the common people through ingratiating performance as an alternative to the grace his king withholds. Richard II rightly sees this demonstration as both "craft" and "wooing," and when the king bemusedly wonders if Bolingbroke aims to take "their affects with him" into exile, he correctly assesses his rival's strategies: Bolingbroke marshals the people's affections into the public opinion that will lift him to the crown.

But if popular appeal boosts Bolingbroke to the kingship, it proves in *1 Henry IV*, as it does in *Richard III*, an unstable foundation upon which to establish lasting sovereignty. As the play opens upon a "shaken" Henry (1.1.1), the king's primary concern is to devise a coalescent strategy to unify his fractured country and solidify his authority, so that England may "March all one way" (1.1.15). With his successful assumption of the crown rooted not in a birthright claim but in usurpation, he understands the fragility of his position and, thus, proposes to legitimate his uneasy kingship with the grandiose gesture of a Holy Land crusade in the model of the *Cœur-de-Lion*. But his designs are soon set aside by news of troublesome skirmishes along two of England's borders, and by Hotspur's flouting of standard military procedure in his refusal to send his noble prisoners to the king. Hotspur, the younger Percy who, along with his father, backed Bolingbroke's ascent to power, pointedly demonstrates the perils of Henry's strategic appeals for support, as Hotspur's former fealty has turned to contempt for a charismatic king who once swayed, but now shames, him. Hotspur believes that he and the other nobles who supported Henry's bid for the crown have been "fooled, discarded, and shook off" (1.3.177) by the overtures of "this vile politician Bolingbroke" (1.3.239). Like the deposed Richard, Hotspur now sees the king's ingratiating charm as a cunning, intoxicating craft—a "candy deal of courtesy" from a "fawning greyhound" (1.3.248, 249)—as he deems Henry a "king of smiles" (1.3.244).

Hotspur's ire is fueled in part by a disdain for pretense and affectation—a contempt he demonstrates when he refuses the "popinjay" who likewise "smiled and talked" (1.3.50, 41). But the rage that spurs his insurrection against the smiling king is also motivated by his recognition of the part he played in the king's elevation, that he "bowed [his] knee" to the king's flatteries and (1.3.243), like the oysterwench, succumbed in fealty to the king's dramatic overtures. This realization involves both the sting of being hoodwinked and an acute understanding of the king's power as contingent upon external support—a support Hotspur realizes he could just as easily throw behind Mortimer and wield to his own advantage. As he will note later in anticipation of battle, it was by an outward "face" that the king "did [...] win/ The hearts of all that he did angle for" (4.3.82–84), but the "golden multitudes" that supported him have now recognized their own king-making powers and, thus, have banded together to "pry/Into this title" which they find "Too indirect for long continuance" (4.3.103–105). As Hotspur here acknowledges, the king's authority is only "indirect"—not inherent to his person through bloodline, but bestowed through intermediaries. In his about-face from sworn devotion to rebellious defiance, Hotspur embodies the fickleness of popular favor and the brittle authority of a sovereignty staked on the people's good will. Recognizing their own agential authority in the king's reign, Hotspur's faction seizes upon the transferability of their "Opinion, that did help [Henry] to the crown" and organizes in support of another.

For his part, Henry recognizes fairly early in the play that the strategies that worked in his campaign are not the same ones to grant him longevity:

> My blood has been too cold and temperate,
> Unapt to stir at these indignities,
> And you have found me, for accordingly
> You tread upon my patience. But be sure
> I will from henceforth be more myself,
> Mighty and to be feared, than my condition,
> Which hath been smooth as oil, soft as young down,
> And therefore lost that proud title of respect.
>
> (1.3.1–8)

While Greenblatt argues in *Shakespearean Negotiations* that in this passage, "'To be oneself' here means to perform one's part in the scheme of power rather than to manifest one's natural disposition" (Greenblatt 1988, 46), Henry's choice of the words *my condition* to contrast to *myself* allows for a more ambiguous reading than the tidy contrast of role versus real. The parallel structure of *my* self and *my* condition suggest the kind of doubling that Falstaff personally disavows as the king divides himself into two, but his use of the circumstantial *condition* to describe his soft, smooth demeanor does not necessarily denote authenticity. To the contrary, he just as easily suggests that his softness—that is, his smiles and ingratiating gestures—were the conditionally appropriate response to the demands of his since-achieved aspirations. Elsewhere in Shakespeare, smoothness is a quality associated with theatrics and deception; *in 2 Henry VI*, "smoothing words/ Bewitch your hearts" (1.1.153–154), and Richard III laments that he cannot "smooth, deceive, and cog" with the "apish courtesy" of courtiers (1.3.48, 49). Thus, the king's condition seems as much a performance as the might he now intends to embody. This might is likely the same kind of posture he had hoped to procure in his thwarted plan to emulate the Lionheart through holy expedition, but that proposal now put aside, Henry must demonstrate his strength domestically to quell dissent.

If Henry's downy demeanor, or condition, can be put aside, then so, too, can the might of *myself* be put on, which proves here equally as conditional. But if, as Richard Dutton has argued, "Henry IV is an actor-king" (Dutton 1998, 13), he is not so much putting on a show here as he is unraveling it. Saying the quiet part out loud, Henry reveals himself in this moment as a man in transition between roles—between the charismatic politician who won the crown and the mighty king necessitated by civil strife. As he offers a peek behind the roles he plays to the man who plays, he teases his audience, like a celebrity, with a momentary glimpse of his person distinct from the various parts he embodies. In this middle space between might and softness, he then further reveals that his performance of self is not only conditional as befitting present needs, but contingent upon his audience. He has been smooth, he acknowledges, but will now "be feared," with his passive verb construction reorienting subjective power to his audience. He solicits his audience now to fear him in the way they once cheered and supported him, but to be feared echoes of the same external locus of affective production as did his campaign strategy, which was to be "wondered at."

The wayward Prince Hal, too, mirrors his father's passive syntax in his famous soliloquy, as he reveals to the audience his strategy to be "wanted," "wished for," and, likewise, "wondered at." Like his father, he understands that their usurped authority requires a firmer platform of support, and so he similarly courts the commons, but to excesses his father never fathomed in his liberal public courtesies. Given, as *Henry V* retrospectively assesses, to "open haunts and popularity" (1.1.160), Hal whiles away his days and nights in an Eastcheap tavern with a gang of thieves and drunkards. However, as he reveals, the Boar's Head miscreants are not the audience whose support he aims to galvanize, but rather, the bit players in the grand production of his calculated, star-like ascension. As he states,

> Yet herein will I imitate the sun,
> Who doth permit the base contagious clouds
> To smother up his beauty from the world,
> That when he please again to be himself,
> Being wanted he may be more wondered at
> By breaking through the foul and ugly mists
> Of vapours that did seem to strangle him.
> (1.2.175–181)

Hal's prediction that he will one day again "be himself" once he departs from the "foul and ugly" company he keeps mirrors his father's intention to "be more myself": in both instances, the self refers to the majestic role of king. As the sun commonly functioned as a symbol of the English kingship, however, Hal plans to "imitate," not be, the sun[12]; what he aims to "be" is "wanted" and "more wondered at"—the passive object of his public's desire and speculation. More star than England's sun, the prince aims for something *like* the sacred majesty of the monarchy, but he, like his father, embraces the passive syntax that prioritizes his audience's projections over inherent kingly virtue.

Throughout this private confession, Hal reveals that his extended sojourn amongst the Eastcheap reprobates is all part of an elaborate publicity strategy; by debasing himself amongst the commons, his ensuing "reformation" will "show more goodly and attract more eyes" (1.2.188–189). His planned reformation is, once again, more rooted in public perception than in his own inherent merit. By setting a precedent sullied in scandal, Garber suggests that "he will seem more virtuous and more powerful when he does emerge as himself" (Garber 2004, 330), and Doty similarly argues that, "Hal produces this bad reputation as a foil to his real self" (Doty 2017, 74). However, as is the case with his father, there is little to suggest that Hal's eventual arrival at "himself" is any more authentic than his present "loose behavior" (1.2.183). Like the king, Hal is here situated as a man in transition between two calculated performances designed to elicit specific responses from his audience. His ultimate aim is not to become the sun, but to produce an overarching personal narrative of reformation. He is not attempting to replace his former, depraved self for his predicted, "goodly" one, but cultivating a narrative trajectory that only inspires wonder when both are taken together in aggregate. Like his father, like Richard III, Hal intends to demonstrate that he can move fluidly between roles, that a discernible individual exists not tied to any one role that he might play. That Hal can be the drunken thief of Eastcheap, the valiant warrior-king of *Henry V*, and, most importantly, the singular figure who can traverse the bounds between them, is the narrative substitution for a sacred monarchy that his father's usurpation does not allow for—a spectacular story of transcendence, elevated through his audience's wonder. What he lacks in *character angelicus*, he intends to make up for with a *character populāris*.

Hal also embraces his father's strategic performance of absence as a means of stoking his public's desire for his person. As Hal theorizes of his proposed reformation,

> If all the years were playing holidays,
> To sport would be as tedious as to work;
> But when they seldom come, they wished for come.
> And nothing pleaseth but rare accidents.
> (1.2.179–182)

Without his base companionship and debauched pastimes, Hal understands that the regal authority he intends to assume would seem an unremarkable and expected feature of his office. But, as Richard III realizes, an audience denied his princely presence will pine for it. This is precisely the strategy that his father will unfold to him as the basis of his own support when he admonishes his heir for becoming "So common-hackneyed in the eyes of men,/ So stale and cheap to vulgar company" (3.2.40–41). In an extended episode of public-relations instruction, Henry, unaware of his son's planned trajectory, berates Hal for his tavern indiscretions and offers his own strategic courtship of the commons as a prescriptive exemplar:

> By being seldom seen, I could not stir
> But, like a comet, I was wondered at,
> That men would tell their children "This is he!"
> Others would say "Where, which is Bolingbroke?"
> And then I stole all courtesy from heaven

> And dressed myself in such humility
> That I did pluck allegiance from men's hearts,
> Loud shouts and salutations from their mouths,
> Even in the presence of the crowned King.
> Thus did I keep my person fresh and new,
> My presence like a robe pontifical—
> Ne'er seen but wondered at.
>
> (3.2.46–57)

To be a king, Henry claims, one must be "wondered at": another passive construction that privileges his public's active role in his elevation, and one he deems so vital to his ascension that he emphatically asserts the phrase twice within ten lines.[13] His pathway to power, as he relays, involved careful staging mitigated by premeditated scarcity in order to whet his public's desire, but never satiate it. His audience, in turn, probed and clamored, not in due devotion to God and country, but in a shared spirit of curiosity that centered only on the individual man, Bolingbroke.

Though Kastan figures Henry's preoccupation with wonder as part of a subjugating impulse that "denies that its viewing subjects are the source of his power" (Kastan 1999, 136), Henry's careful attention to his spectators, as evidenced in his recitations of their responses, suggests he understands quite well the potency of the people's power. As he availed himself to their "extraordinary gaze,/ Such as is bent on sun-like majesty" (3.2.78–79), he was looking back, cataloguing and assessing a response that embodies Hal's earlier simile: Henry was wondered at, because he imitated the sun that peeks out only sporadically. But as a demonstration of his cognizance as to where his power lies, he coaxed from the people a gaze "such as" the one that bends on majesty; like his son, Henry is not the sun, but the people look upon Henry as if they were looking at a king, not because majesty inheres to his person, but as a consequence of his rarity. As his "state/ Seldom but sumptuous, showed like a feast" (3.2.57–58), he did not subject them to his presence but withheld it, wearing it only occasionally like ceremonial vestments so that his presence, also in echo of his son's plot, became a holiday. To the English citizenry, Henry was, as Boorstin theorized of celebrity, a human event,[14] as dazzling and fleeting as a comet.

Wonder, as detailed in Chapter 1, is a complex affective interaction that lies at the heart of celebrity, and as Henry dissects the strategy by which he marshalled the people's wonder into political power, he demonstrates a keen understanding of wonder's properties. Wonder, as Greenblatt theorizes in *Marvelous Possessions*, signifies a state of attention, incredulity, excitement and, perhaps above all, "an unappeasable desire for more" (Greenblatt 1991, xi). The savvy king then seduces his audience into a state of wonder as a demotic alternative to the sacred majesty of the kingship. Rather than assert his presence, he feigns humility and opts to perform absence instead, as he anticipates that his public will fill the void of his absence with their own projected speculations and desires. He refuses to appease their appetite, and his reticence to stage himself to the public, like Richard III's reluctance to accept the crown, bestows on the public a sense, however calculated, of agency in the selection of their monarch. Thus, the public, here as well as in *Richard III*, becomes the active co-author of a narrative of royal ascent.

Making greatness familiar

When Sir Henry Wotton attended the infamous 1613 production of another history, *Henry VIII*, that razed the Globe "to the very grounds," he composed a brief review of the play in a letter to Sir Edmund Bacon:

> The Kings Players had a new Play, called *All is true*, representing some principall pieces of the raign of Henry 8, which was set forth with many extraordinary circumstances of Pomp and Majesty, even to the matting of the stage, the Knights of the Order, with their Georges and Garter, the Guards with their embroidered Coats, and the like: sufficient in truth within a while to make greatness very familiar, if not ridiculous.
> (Wotton 1672, 426)

It is in *Henry VIII* that, as detailed in this book's first chapter, a group of unnamed gentlemen labels a procession of nobles and the new queen "stars indeed," and that provocative pronouncement is part of a larger narrative strategy within the play that shines a light on the English citizenry's capacity for discernment and definition. More than any other play by Shakespeare, *Henry VIII* relies upon the circulating conversations of the public to relay its most crucial plot points: Buckingham's trial, Henry's marriage to Anne, the death of Wolsey, the birth of Elizabeth, and Anne's coronation as queen are all relayed through the gossip of unnamed gentlemen. If, as the play's given title of *All Is True* suggests, these conversations are deemed the credible conduits of English history, then the play situates truth in the narrative exchanges of the *vox populi* and allows the people to narrate and define the highborn. Perhaps it is this popular power that provoked Wotton's censure of the play's familiarizing effects; while the great parade across the stage in spectacular majesty and with all ceremonial pomp, it is ultimately the gentlemen who tell their stories and, indeed, name them stars.

In *Richard III* and *1 Henry IV*, the titular monarchs, along with Hal, likewise count upon their audiences to fashion them into stars as they ride the crest of popular celebrity to the thrones their birthrights would deny them. Theirs, too, is a familiar greatness—achieved rather than inherent and born of the people whose narrative authority they corral and harness but nonetheless rely upon as the source of their sovereignty. Their divergent trajectories exemplify the high-risk/high-reward stakes not only of celebrity-sovereignty, but of celebrity as a whole. The people's will is fickle, volatile, at times easily swayed and at others rigidly discerning, yet undeniably potent and efficacious. King-makers and king-breakers both, the public lends its voice toward the construction of the star's second celebrity body, but the many-headed multitude can just as easily consume, as Richard's disintegration demonstrates. Like the gentlemen onlookers in *Henry VIII*, Richard's and Henry's publics name them stars in a demotic revision of kingship that similarly elevates their targets to positions of privilege, power, and visibility. As these plays stage the "elite and magical" monarchy as the "reasonable expectation" of successful performance and publicity strategies, they do not only familiarize greatness as a still exclusive yet achievable reward, but in turn ennoble the familiar through celebrity's vernacular hierarchy.

Notes

1 From Scene 79 of the screenplay for *William Shakespeare's Richard III*, directed by Richard Loncraine (Loncraine 1995) and written by Ian McKellen and Richard Loncraine (McKellen and Loncraine 1995). The entire screenplay, including stills from the film and McKellen's annotations, is available on Ian McKellen's website, *Ian McKellen: Official Home Page*.
2 Chapter 2 provides a detailed analysis of Shakespeare's Sonnets 110, 111, and 112 and their elucidations of the potential risks involved in theatrical enterprise and high public visibility.
3 As detailed in "A copy of some coats and crests lately come to my hands given by William Dethick when he was York Herald," held by the Folger Shakespeare Library, Washington, D.C. (MS V.a. 350, p. 28) (1600).
4 As detailed in "Progress of James I through the city of London", held by the National Archives, Kew, UK (LC 2/4/5, pp. 77–80) (National Archives 1604). Shakespeare is listed first of nine of the king's players (78).
5 D.J. Hopkins offers a detailed examination of James's Royal Progress and of the theatrical significance of the *Londinium* arch specifically in Chapter Three of *City/Stage/Globe: Performance and Space in Shakespeare's London* (Hopkins 2008, 103–146).
6 For more on the celebrity's position as both individual and representative member of a collective, see Barry King in both "Stardom, Celebrity, and the Para-Confession" (King 2011, 7–24) and "Stardom, Celebrity, and the Moral Economy of Pretending" (King 2016, 315–332), as well as the concluding chapter in Marshall (1997, 241–247).
7 Jonson did soften his stance somewhat in the Prologue to *Epicoene*, when he mentions those writers who "will taste nothing that is popular" (6), before declaring his intentions are "not to please the cook's tastes but the guests" (9).
8 As Michael Billig demonstrates in *Talking of the Royal Family*, this strategy of conflating royal person and the perpetuity of the nation is still a central to the publicity practices of today's English royal family. Even given celebrity journalism's ravenous appetite for royal headlines, royal celebrities are, Billig argues, safeguarded against some of celebrity's most potent volatilities, as the royal family is perceived "to embody a national heritage and the future continuity of a nation" (Billig 2002, 220).
9 For more on Elizabeth's portraiture, including steps taken to suppress unauthorized depictions, see Roy C. Strong, *Gloriana: The Portraits of Queen Elizabeth I* (Strong 2003).
10 As a powerful counter-example of the dangers of celebrity-monarchy in which royal person becomes severed from royal office, a substantial body of scholarship has charted the tragic decline and ultimate demise of Marie Antoinette in relation to her celebrity. As Dorothee Polanz (2018), and Antoine Lilti (2017) have each discussed, Marie Antoinette cultivated a personal celebrity separate from, and at the expense of, her role as monarch.

11 While the Norton edition cites this character as "Another Citizen," as does the first quarto edition printed in 1597, the First Folio attributes this line to Catesby instead.
12 Alexander Leggatt similarly argues, "Hal can only promise to *imitate* [the sun]—to produce, as his father did, a good performance in the role of king" (Leggatt 1988, 90–91).
13 In a compelling examination of a possible influence on Shakespeare's *1 Henry IV*, Colin Burrow notes that "the politics of wonder" stems from a popular sixteenth-century rhetorical handbook titled *Ad Herennium* (Burrow 2018, 41), which similarly uses solar imagery to explain the wonder provoked by rare occurrences (38–40).
14 See the Introduction for more on Boorstin's theory of celebrity, in which he figures celebrities as "human pseudo-events," or embodiments of publicity stunts (Boorstin 1961).

References

Alberoni, Francesco. 2006 [1962]. "The Powerless 'Elite': Theory and Sociological Research on the Phenomenon of the Stars." Translated by Denis McQuail. In *The Celebrity Culture Reader*, edited by P. David Marshall, 108–123. New York: Routledge.
Bell, Matt. 2011. "When Harry Met Harry." In *Shakesqueer: A Queer Companion to the Complete Works of Shakespeare*, edited by Madhavi Menon, 106–113. Durham: Duke University Press.
Berlanstein, Lenard R. 2004. "Historicizing and Gendering Celebrity Culture: Famous Women in Nineteenth-Century France." *Journal of Women's History* 16 (4): 65–91.
Billig, Michael. 2002. *Talking of the Royal Family*. London and New York: Routledge.
Boorstin, Daniel. (1961) 1992. *The Image: A Guide to Pseudo-Events in America*. New York: Vintage.
Braudy, Leo. 1986. *The Frenzy of Renown: Fame and Its History*. New York: Vintage.
Buchloh, Benjamin H.D. 2001. "Andy Warhol's One-Dimensional Art." In *Andy Warhol*, edited by Annette Michelson, 1–48. Cambridge: MIT Press.
Burrow, Colin. 2018. "Shakespeare's Authorities." In *Shakespeare and Authority: Citations, Conceptions and Constructions*, edited by Katie Halsey and Angus Vine, 31–54. London: Palgrave Macmillan.
Cerasano, S.P. 2005. "Edward Alleyn, the New Model Actor, and the Rise of Celebrity in the1590s." *Medieval and Renaissance Drama in England* 18: 47–58.
"A copy of some coats and crests lately come to my hands given by William Dethick when he was York Herald." 1600. Folger Shakespeare Library, Washington, D.C. MS V.a. 350: 28.
Cornwallis, William. 1600. "Of Popularitie." In *Essayes*. London.
Dekker, Thomas. 1604. *The Magnificent Entertainment, given to King James*. London.
Donaldson, Ian. 2011. *Ben Jonson: A Life*. Oxford: Oxford University Press.
Donaldson, Peter. 2002. "Cinema and the Kingdom of Death: Loncraine's Richard III." *Shakespeare Quarterly* 53 (2): 241–259.
Doty, Jeffrey S. 2017. *Shakespeare, Popularity and the Public Sphere*. Cambridge: Cambridge University Press.
Dugdale, Gilbert. 1604. *The Time Triumphant*. London.
Dutton, Richard. 1998. "Shakespeare and Lancaster." *Shakespeare Quarterly* 49 (1): 1–21.
Dyer, Richard. 1998. *Stars*. London: British Film Institute.
Elizabeth I. 2000 [1601]. "The Golden Speech, from the Papers of Sir Thomas Egerton." In *Elizabeth I: Collected Works*, edited by Leah S.Marcus, JanelMueller, and Mary Beth Rose, 340–344. Chicago: Chicago University Press.

Fitter, Chris. 2021. *Majesty and the Masses in Shakespeare and Marlowe: Western Anti-Monarchism, the Earl of Essex Challenge, and Political Stagecraft.* New York: Routledge.
Garber, Marjorie. 1998. *Symptoms of Culture.* New York: Routledge.
Garber, Marjorie. 2004. *Shakespeare After All.* New York: Anchor.
Greenblatt, Stephen. 1988. *Shakespearean Negotiations: The Circulation of Social Energy in Renaissance England.* Los Angeles: University of California Press.
Greenblatt, Stephen. 1991. *Marvelous Possession: The Wonder of the New World.* Chicago: Chicago University Press.
Gurr, Andrew. 1992. *The Shakespearean Stage 1574–1642.* Cambridge: Cambridge University Press.
Hall, Joseph. 1597. *Virgidemiarum sixe bookes.* London.
Harrison, Stephen. 1604. *The Arches of Triumph.* London.
Hearn, Alison and Stephanie Schoenhoff. 2016. "From Celebrity to Influencer: Tracing the Diffusion of Celebrity Value across the Data Stream." In *A Companion to Celebrity*, edited by P. David Marshall and Sean Redmond, 194–212. Malden, MA: Wiley Blackwell.
Heywood, Thomas. 1633. "To My Worthy Friend, Mr. Thomas Hammon, of Grayes Inne." In *The Tragedy of the Rich Jew of Malta* by Christopher Marlowe, Sig. A3. London.
Holinshed, Raphael. (1587) 1965. *Holinshed's Chronicles of England, Ireland, and Scotland.* New York: AMS Press.
Hopkins, D.J. 2008. *City/Stage/Globe: Performance and Space in Shakespeare's London.* New York: Routledge.
Howard, Jean. 1994. *The Stage and Social Struggle in Early Modern England.* New York: Routledge.
Inglis, Fred. 2010. *A Short History of Celebrity.* Princeton: Princeton University Press.
Jonson, Ben. 1600. *Every Man out of His Humor.* London.
Jonson, Ben. 1607. *Volpone, or The Foxe.* London.
Jonson, Ben. 1609. *The Masque of Queenes.* London.
Jonson, Ben. 1616. "The Speeches of Gratulation." In *The Workes of Benjamin Jonson.* London. 850–851.
Jonson, Ben. 2001. *Epicoene.* In *Ben Jonson's Plays and Masques*, edited by Richard Harp. New York: Norton. 111–199.
Jonson, Ben. 2012. *Cynthia's Revels.* In *The Cambridge Works of Ben Jonson*, vol. 1, edited by Eric Rasmussen and Matthew Steggle. Cambridge: Cambridge University Press.
Kantorowicz, Ernst. 1957. *The King's Two Bodies: A Study in Mediaeval Political Theology.* Princeton: Princeton University Press.
Kastan, David Scott. 1999. *Shakespeare After Theory.* New York: Routledge.
King, Barry. 2011. "Stardom, Celebrity, and the Para-Confession." In *The Star and Celebrity Confessional*, edited by P. David Marshall and Sean Redmond, 7–24. New York: Routledge.
King, Barry. 2016. "Stardom, Celebrity, and the Moral Economy of Pretending." In *A Companion to Celebrity*, edited by P. David Marshall and Sean Redmond, 315–332. Malden: Wiley Blackwell.
Kizelbach, Urszula. 2014. *The Pragmatics of Early Modern Politics: Power and Kingship in Shakespeare's History Plays.* Amsterdam and New York: Rodopi.
Leggatt, Alexander. 1988. *Shakespeare's Political Drama: The History Plays and the Roman Plays.* London: Routledge.
Lilti, Antoine. 2017. *The Invention of Celebrity.* Translated by Lynn Jeffress. Cambridge: Polity.

Loncraine, Richard (dir.). 1995. *Richard III*. Directed by Richard Loncraine. Performed by Ian McKellen, Annette Bening, and Richard Broadbent. United Artists.

Luthar, Breda. 2006. "Community of Sameness: Political Celebrity and the Creation of the National Ordinary." In *Media Communities*, edited by Brigitte Hipfl and Theo Hug, 143–166. New York: Waxmann Munster.

Marshall, P. David. 1997. *Celebrity and Power: Fame in Contemporary Culture*. Minneapolis: Minnesota University Press.

McKellen, Ian and Richard Loncraine. 1995. *William Shakespeare's Richard III: A Screenplay*. Ian McKellen Official Home Page. Accessed January 15, 2020. https://mckellen.com/cinema/richard/screenplay/index.htm.

Munro, Ian. 2005. *The Figure of the Crowd in Early Modern London: The City and Its Double*. New York: Palgrave Macmillan.

National Archives. 1604."Progress of James I through the city of London." Kew, UK. LC 2/4/5: 77–80.

Polanz, Dorothee. 2018. "Portrait of the Queen as a Celebrity: Marie Antoinette on Screen, a Disappearing Act (1934–2012)." In *The Cinematic Eighteenth Century: History, Culture, and Adaptation*, edited by Srividhya Swaminathan and Steven W. Thomas, 28–43. London: Routledge.

Ratseis Ghost. 1605. London.

Righter, Anne. 1962. *Shakespeare and the Idea of the Play*. London: Chatto and Windus.

Roach, Joseph. 2005. "Public Intimacy: The Prior History of 'It'." In *Theatre and Celebrity inBritain, 1660–2000*, edited by Mary Luckhurst and Jane Moody, 15–30. New York: Palgrave Macmillan.

Rojek, Chris. 2019. "The Two Bodies of Achieved Celebrity." *Historical Social Research Supplement* 32: 39–57.

Row-Heyveld, Lindsey. 2018. *Dissembling Disability in Early Modern English Drama*. New York: Palgrave.

Shakespeare, William. 2016. *Henry IV, Part 1*. In *The Norton Shakespeare, Third Edition*, edited by Stephen Greenblatt, Walter Cohen, Suzanne Gossett, Jean E. Howard, Katharine Eisaman Maus, and Gordon McMullan, 1165–1244. New York: Norton.

Shakespeare, William. 2016. *Henry V*. In *The Norton Shakespeare, Third Edition*, edited by Stephen Greenblatt, Walter Cohen, Suzanne Gossett, Jean E. Howard, Katharine Eisaman Maus, and Gordon McMullan, 1533–1612. New York: Norton.

Shakespeare, William. 2016. *Henry VI, Part 3*. In *The Norton Shakespeare, Third Edition*, edited by Stephen Greenblatt, Walter Cohen, Suzanne Gossett, Jean E. Howard, Katharine Eisaman Maus, and Gordon McMullan, 265–342. New York: Norton.

Shakespeare, William. 2016. *Henry VIII*. In *The Norton Shakespeare, Third Edition*, edited by Stephen Greenblatt, Walter Cohen, Suzanne Gossett, Jean E. Howard, Katharine Eisaman Maus, and Gordon McMullan, 3269–3352. New York: Norton.

Shakespeare, William. 2016. *Richard II*. In *The Norton Shakespeare, Third Edition*, edited by Stephen Greenblatt, Walter Cohen, Suzanne Gossett, Jean E. Howard, Katharine Eisaman Maus, and Gordon McMullan, 885–956. New York: Norton.

Shakespeare, William. 2016. *Richard III*. In *The Norton Shakespeare, Third Edition*, edited by Stephen Greenblatt, Walter Cohen, Suzanne Gossett, Jean E. Howard, Katharine Eisaman Maus, and Gordon McMullan, 555–648. New York: Norton.

Shakespeare, William. 2016. Sonnet 110. In *The Norton Shakespeare, Third Edition*, edited by Stephen Greenblatt, Walter Cohen, Suzanne Gossett, Jean E. Howard, Katharine Eisaman Maus, and Gordon McMullan, 2287. New York: Norton.

Shakespeare, William. 2016. *Twelfth Night*. In *The Norton Shakespeare, Third Edition*, edited by Stephen Greenblatt, Walter Cohen, Suzanne Gossett, Jean E. Howard, Katharine Eisaman Maus, and Gordon McMullan, 1907–1972. New York: Norton.

Sharpe, Kevin. 2000. *Remapping Early Modern England: The Culture of Seventeenth-Century Politics*. Cambridge: Cambridge University Press.

Sharpe, Kevin. 2009. *Selling the Tudor Monarchy: Authority and Image in Sixteenth Century England*. New Haven: Yale University Press.

Skura, Meredith Anne. 1993. *Shakespeare the Actor and the Purposes of Playing*. Chicago: University of Chicago Press.

Smuts, Malcolm. 2007. "Thomas Dekker, Stephen Harrison, Ben Jonson, and Thomas Middleton, The Whole Royal and Magnificent Entertainment of King James through the City of London." In *Thomas Middleton and Textual Culture*, edited by Gary Taylor and John Lavagnino, 498–506. Oxford: Oxford University Press.

Stephens, John. 1615. *Essayes and Characters, Ironicall and Instructive*. London.

Strong, Roy C. 2003. *Gloriana: The Portraits of Queen Elizabeth I*. London: Random House.

Turner, Graeme. 2010. *Ordinary People and the Media: The Demotic Turn*. London: Sage.

Turner, Graeme. 2014. *Understanding Celebrity*, 2nd ed. Los Angeles: Sage.

Van Krieken, Robert. 2012. *Celebrity Society*. New York: Routledge.

Wilson, Robert F., Jr. 1998. "Hunchbacked Fuhrer: The Loncraine-McKellen Richard III as Postmodern Pastiche." *Shakespeare Bulletin* 16 (2): 39–41.

Wotton, Sir Henry. 1672. *Reliquiae Wottonianae, or, A collection of lives, letters, poems: with Characters of Sundry Personages*. London.

4 A Shakespeare that looks like Shakespeare

In a 2017 headline, the online sports and pop culture network *The Ringer* asked, "What's with All the Sexy Shakespeares?" (Herman 2017). The accompanying article specifically targeted the short-lived TNT series *Will* (2017a), a fictionalized account of a young Shakespeare's exploits as a London upstart, or what the article dubbed "a proudly ridiculous origin story for William Shakespeare that involves […] a suspicious amount of coiffing" (2017). As promotional images for the show centered on Laurie Davidson's smoldering, stubbled, square-jawed embodiment of a twenty-something Shakespeare, the article aptly noted that *Will* was far from the first entry in the "hot Shakespeare" catalogue, and similar articles, corresponding to the series' release, likewise probed the trend in sexy Shakespeares. A *Gizmodo* article begged in its headline, "God Save Me from Young, Sexy Shakespeare and His New TV Show" (Trendacosta 2017), while a *Vulture* article asked, "Who's the Sexiest Shakespeare Ever?" before counting down such options as *Will*'s Davidson and Colin Firth's take on the bard in *Blackadder* (Jung 2017). Shakespeare himself claimed the number-2 spot, right behind the list's definitive winner, Joseph Fiennes in *Shakespeare in Love*.

As the blogosphere greeted the debut of *Will* with a mix of condescending amusement in its "re-sexified version" of Shakespeare and dry disdain for its lack of historical accuracy (Herman 2017), online commentators generally treated the show's depiction of Shakespeare as a novel, even ludicrous, contrivance; *The Ringer* went so far as to assure readers that Shakespeare was not "actually that hot" (2017), as it attempted to demonstrate that a sexually desirable Shakespeare was not only a Hollywood fabrication, but a farcical intervention in the historical record as well.

Hollywood, however, can hardly lay claim to the sexy Shakespeare genre of representation. If *Will* brought the question of Shakespeare's sex appeal to online speculation, a few years earlier, Stanley Wells and the Shakespeare Birthplace Trust thrust a similar set of questions into the arena of academic Shakespeare study. At the 2009 news conference announcing the recently re-attributed Cobbe portrait (previously thought to depict Sir Thomas Overbury), Wells described the controversial painting as a "pin-up," while a promotional brochure for its exhibition promised, "This Shakespeare is handsome and glamorous" (quoted in Burns 2009). Online response varied little from the cynical

DOI: 10.4324/9780367808976-5

reception that would later greet *Will*. "Was Shakespeare a hottie? Was Homer a hunk?" Ron Rosenbaum taunted, tabloid-style, in a scathing *Slate* write-up, before arriving at his crucial declamation: "You would think, from recent coverage of the portrait newly claimed to be of Shakespeare [...] that these are valid literary questions rather than evidence that the culture of celebrity has irretrievably corrupted literature" (Rosenbaum 2009).

Rosenbaum's notion that the pernicious specter of celebrity had come to take possession of a sacred literary history haunts each of these online responses, whether the perceived travesty of a sexed-up Shakespeare is greeted with fluttering bemusement or stark outrage. Each of these reactions also treats the intersection of celebrity and literature as an unorthodox, even perverse departure, ignoring a long history of literary celebrity commonly acknowledged in discussions of authors ranging from Lord Byron to Salman Rushdie.[1] But what seems particularly bristling for each of these reviewers is the specifically corporeal emphasis of the cited texts; here, Shakespeare—in *Will* or to Wells—is not a body of work, but a body.

Rosenbaum equates this fleshly focus to a preoccupation with celebrity, through which, as discussed in Chapter 1, bodies are regularly scrutinized as texts that not only provide greater insight into the private lives concealed behind public faces, but are also inscribed with cultural meaning. Indeed, the promotional brochure accompanying the Cobbe portrait exhibition rendered such processes transparent. Noting this Shakespeare's handsomeness, the brochure proceeds to ask, "so how does this change the way we think about him? And do the painting and provenance tell us more about his sexuality, and possibly about the person to whom the sonnets are addressed?" (quoted in Burns 2009). In a fitting testament to the processes of celebrity, the ad attempts to extract from the blush in his cheeks and arch of his brow both Shakespeare's sexual preferences and his literary motivations. As James A. Knapp suggests, "the temptation to see the coherent mind in these images of the face is powerful" (Knapp 2016, 2).

For Shakespeare, however, the inverse is equally as true: the desire to see Shakespeare's face, and body as a whole, as a reification of what we think we know of his mind is just as strong a compulsion. Concealed within the Cobbe portrait's unveiling, and the questions that prompt its viewers to find Shakespeare's biography through iconography, is the contradictory impulse to craft a corporeal Shakespeare out of the raw material of narrative—that is, to build a Shakespeare body from his body of work. As strong as is the temptation to isolate Shakespeare's mind within the visible details of his embodiment through portraiture, there exists an equally as intoxicating counter-impulse to shape an embodied Shakespeare out of the extant traces of his mind—namely, from what the poet describes in Sonnet 74 as his "line" which "still with thee will stay" (3, 4) long after "my body being dead" (10). But if the poet deems his physical body "Too base of thee to be remembered" (12), he remains relatively alone in that opinion, as the hunt for a suitably Shakespearean body continues to remain a fervent pursuit more than 400 years after his death.

Only two images of Shakespeare, both created after his death, received the commendation of his peers as true likenesses: the Droeshout engraving accompanying the First Folio in 1623 and the bust aside Shakespeare's tomb in Holy Trinity Church. Neither option has satiated the public hunger for a Shakespeare body befitting the Shakespeare corpus, whether due to the Droeshout engraving's "disheveled appearance and encephalous forehead" (Holderness 2011, 182), or the "dull eyes and fat jowls" of the Stratford bust (Duncan-Jones 2001, 197). J. Dover Wilson, who famously likened Shakespeare's memorial bust to a "self-satisfied pork butcher," argues that both images "stand between us and the true Shakespeare" (Wilson 1960, 6), and the bust, in particular, Robert Shaughnessy notes, "has dismayed those who hoped that Shakespeare might have looked more, well, like *Shakespeare*" (Shaughnessy 2011, 71).

But what would a Shakespeare that looks like Shakespeare look like? At the unveiling of the Sanders portrait of Shakespeare in 2001, Richard Monette, then artistic director of the Stratford Shakespeare Festival, offered one possibility to *The Baltimore Sun*: "This is a very romantic picture, the way we want Shakespeare to look, like a bohemian" (Nickerson 2001). Eric Rasmussen suggests yet another likely attribute: detailing his experience of getting taken in by a forged Shakespeare portrait, Rasmussen admits that when he stared into the eyes of the painting, he thought, "Wow, those look intelligent. Yes, that *could* be him!" (Rasmussen 2011, 96). In his hopeful inference that a genuine likeness of Shakespeare would stare back with the kind of intelligence readers find in the Complete Works, Rasmussen reaffirms Monette's contention—that there is a way we want Shakespeare to look and, further, that audiences are most likely to consent to depictions in line with their own desires, fantasies, and projections than those corresponding to the unsatisfying, though peer-reviewed, early representations. But if the public's desires remain far from monolithic—romantic, bohemian, intelligent, handsome, glamorous, sexy—they do seem to share a common source, emerging from the wellspring of Shakespeare's verse rather than any preservation of his likeness. Each of the aforementioned descriptors correspond to a desire to *see* a Shakespeare that *feels* appropriately Shakespearean. As Rasmussen continues, "When you immerse yourself [...] in the world of Shakespeare's writing, you want to look into the eyes of the person who created these sublime pieces of dramatic literature" (2011, 96). But it might be more apt to say that, in Shakespeare's face, we want to look into the eyes of the literature itself: the eyes sparkling with lovers' fire in *Romeo and Juliet* (1.1.184) or projecting "hard-favour'd rage" in *Henry V* (3.1.8). Eyes, perhaps, something like the sun.

The history of Shakespeare's many embodiments—from portraiture and statuary to onscreen characterization—offers a secular, alternative model of word made flesh. This chapter explores the ceaseless, centuries-old, and highly collaborative cultural undertaking to locate a Shakespeare that looks like Shakespeare and how that search for an appropriately Shakespearean body is a function of the evolving modes of celebrity Shakespeare has participated in both during and since his lifetime. As Tamara Heaney and Sean Redmond theorize of the celebrity body,

Celebrity embodiment then is not simply about the body of the celebrity as it literally presents itself in the social and representational world, but the range of values, meanings, and affecting qualities that are attached to its skin, bones, and torso. The celebrity body is never neutral: it carries with it the discourses, concerns, and passions of the age.

(Heaney and Redmond 2016, 401)

The corporeal body of Shakespeare, despite its perceived capacity to condense a maze of swirling narrative ambiguities into a durable materiality, is an inherently unstable form, informed, like celebrity as a whole, by the "passions of the age" in which it incarnates, assuring that no single Shakespearean body can ever satisfactorily endure. As critics have demonstrated, the earliest, contemporarily approved representations of the bard's body have devolved over the centuries into sites of disappointment at best, and ridicule and revulsion at worst. Contemporary portrayals that seem to offer a potent, animated corrective to earlier lackluster physiologies enjoy flashes of amusement, even accolades, before provoking confusion and contempt. When his image is deemed too estranged from familiar depictions, it is ridiculed as too hot, too coiffed, too corrupted by a cult of celebrity. Too familiar, and Shakespeare is deemed too fat, too bald, too lifeless to have crafted such lively verse.

But the quest for Shakespeare's body is less an exercise in archaeology than in semiology–that is, we are not so much trying to sift through the rubble of centuries of depictions for one true likeness as we are actively crafting a human architecture to narrate our own experiences, desires, concerns, and fixations. In a creative inversion of the second self of celebrity as discussed in Chapter 2, Shakespeare's audiences, saturated with a Complete Works' worth of interiority but denied the exteriority of a material body with whom to interact, perpetually recreate and reproject a suitable, corporeal Shakespeare unto the work and mythos understood as Shakespeare. Thus, the question is not so much *what* Shakespeare looks like, but *which* Shakespeare looks like Shakespeare *when*? What body aptly captures not the likeness of the early modern poet, but the identificatory needs of the present audience? As this chapter argues, the collaborative crafting of Shakespeare's somatic body is an ongoing cultural project begun during the poet's own lifetime, when Shakespeare emerged as both a literary and theatrical celebrity in the closing decade of the sixteenth century and audiences sought to claim a close affinity with the poet to the point of imagined, even intimate relations with the poet's living body. One of the primary ways audiences achieved this sense of intimacy with Shakespeare was through fantasizing the poet's corporeal body into existence from the substance of his verse, and it is a practice that has continued long since Shakespeare succumbed to his mortal trappings. In the centuries following his death, audiences have crafted their Shakespeares in the bodies of other actors—Shakespearean celebrities like David Garrick, Edmund Kean, and Lawrence Olivier—who professed, and received contemporary consent, to present Shakespeare in new mortal frames capable of carrying on their thespian shoulders both Shakespeare's lost presence and the contemporary desires of their audiences. Finally, this chapter concludes with an analysis of current embodied Shakespeares-as-television-characters, specifically *Will*'s titular hero and Shakespeare as presented in "The Shakespeare Code" episode of *Doctor Who,* both of whom transport viewers to reimagined versions of Shakespeare's early modern London while representing Shakespeare as a twenty-first-century body. All of these Shakespearean bodies—molded in words in early modernity, incarnated in human hosts from the eighteenth through the twentieth centuries, and embodied through scripted portrayal in contemporary TV—participate in a similar set of dynamics that inform the hunt for a suitably Shakespearean portrait of Shakespeare: they all stress the corporeality, even the carnality, of a man known primarily as a discursive entity, and they project upon his body of work a material, mortal body capable of dialogic exchange, both with readers/spectators and the wider cultural concerns of the eras they inhabit.

Shakespeare's celebrity/Shakespearean celebrity

To begin to address the evolution of Shakespeare's corporeal celebrity body, it is first necessary to complicate the very idea of "Shakespeare's celebrity"—a phrase often casually employed by critics in discussions of Shakespeare's cultural endurance and prominence in pop culture, but often to somewhat ambiguous ends. Discussions of Shakespeare and celebrity generally travel two distinct tracks: Shakespeare's celebrity, or the celebrity status of William Shakespeare the playwright; and Shakespearean celebrity, or the famous figures, generally actors like Garrick or Olivier, whose celebrity status is inextricably linked to their associations with Shakespeare. To begin with the former category, critical explorations of Shakespeare's own celebrity took shape in earnest in 1996 with Bristol's *Big-Time Shakespeare*, which argues that Shakespeare, quite unusually, has operated as a celebrity for centuries:

> Other literary figures may achieve canonical status within the academic community [...], but Shakespeare is unusual in that he has also achieved contemporary celebrity. Such an achievement entails an aptitude for controversy that keeps Shakespeare's name above a certain threshold of public attention. [...] Shakespeare has been a celebrity for just about as long as the social state of being a celebrity has existed.
>
> (Bristol 1996, 2)

For Bristol, Shakespeare's celebrity is a function of the "big time": an institutionalized mix of widespread visibility and cultural cachet that has transformed Shakespeare's name over time into a bankable, highly commutable trademark. Bristol's formulation of Shakespeare's incorporate currency has proven highly influential in the decades since its publication; however, the flowering of celebrity studies since the book's publication has offered new complications to notions of Shakespeare's celebrity centered so squarely on appropriability and market clout. Notably, Bristol's model leaves out important questions of personal identification and the para-social relationships between star and fans in its focus on corporate concern. Celebrity is an immediate, fragile exchange that thrives on sustained tensions of desire between respondent bodies; put quite simply, the historical Shakespeare can no longer reciprocate. No matter how popularly he is appropriated to meet cultural or commercial needs, his iconic image remains indelibly situated in the English Renaissance, so much so that he vies with the most famous English queen in English history as the representative embodiment of that era. While Shakespeare as a name, a concept, and a body of work remain today both ubiquitous and ever-evolving, his putative portraiture is helplessly archaic, fixed as the starched-ruff speaker of *thee*s and *thou*s.

Consider, for example, Paul Prescott's summary of Shakespeare's celebrity: noting Shakespeare's unfixed placelessness in pop culture to the extent that "any bald-headed, bearded man need only don a ruff and grab a quill to be easily recognizable as 'Shakespeare'," Prescott argues that, "Someone this easily impersonated is a major celebrity" (Prescott 2010, 269). While Prescott's assessment of the playwright's celebrity is undoubtedly offered at least somewhat tongue-in-cheek, this formulation speaks to one of the obstacles of Shakespeare's celebrity just as it opens up discussion of the alternate model of Shakespearean celebrity. As Prescott acknowledges, Shakespeare's image remains so firmly rooted in early modern England that the only means of rendering his image knowable is metonymically through the era's signature accoutrement. Even as Shakespeare's verse may continue to speak relevantly to contemporary audiences, his body remains frozen in time, perennially affixed to the accepted portraiture of the seventeenth century, and the fact that any bald, bearded man can become him merely through the adoption of ruff and quill suggests that the same ruff and quill, without a body at all, might suffice to evoke the name Shakespeare. Shakespeare is here rendered less a celebrity than a highly transportable emblem of early modernity.

This is not to suggest that celebrity is incapable of outliving the human body. It can, for a time, and Rojek has discussed the considerable effort fans put in to maintain the "living cultural presence" of cherished and departed stars (Rojek 2001, 64). Some, he notes, go to the extent of denying the reality of a celebrity's death, as in the case of Elvis Presley or Tupac Shakur, in order to generate new narratives of the celebrity's escape from public scrutiny to enjoy a more mundane, but highly relatable, private life (2001, 63). Yet others, like the devotional fans that make regular pilgrimages to Graceland, reject the celebrity's death by bestowing an almost superhuman, if not quasi-religious, lingering presence that negates death's finality in proclamation of the celebrity's ceaseless cultural power, often figured as preternaturally capable of responding relevantly to eras far removed from the celebrity's own (2001, 64). However, these quasi-divine formulations tend to hold less in common with the interpersonal dynamics of celebrity than with the cults of hero- and legend-worship, with one-time celebrities transformed through the disfiguring lenses of nostalgia and mourning into magnified abstractions of the qualities once associated with them. Loosed from their human frames, unanchored celebrity narratives can render a deceased celebrity less a person who embodied certain ideals than the raw ideal itself, such that the name James Dean, for example, does not so much signify a person as the concepts of youthful rebellion and alienation.[2]

Such dynamics have certainly propelled a certain strand in Shakespeare's enduring legacy, but this kind of cultural endurance, I would argue, is not celebrity. Instead, the aggrandizing impulses of memorialization initiated by a Romantic-era readership that positioned Shakespeare as nearly synonymous with the abstract ideals of poetic and personal sagacity carved out a superhuman, starkly unrelatable, and mythologized genius. As Samuel Taylor Coleridge put it in 1817, Shakespeare was "the greatest genius, that perhaps human nature ever produced" (Coleridge 1817, 13). In 1840, Thomas Carlyle provided an extended meditation on Shakespeare's immortal intellectual powers when he named Shakespeare a "poet-hero." Citing the poet-hero's timelessness, he writes,

> perhaps the opinion one sometimes hears a little idolatrously expressed is, in fact, the right one [...] That Shakespeare is the chief of all Poets hitherto, the greatest intellect who, in our recorded world, has left record of himself in the way of literature. On the whole, I know not such a power of vision, such a faculty of thought, if we take all the characters of it, in any other man.
>
> (Carlyle 1840, 121)

Carlyle's formulation evokes the etymological origins of the hero, posthumously imbuing Shakespeare with a quasi-divine genius and rendering him the prescient bearer of eternal truths. This concept of the universal Bard has proven remarkably resonant, with its adherents inspiring George Bernard Shaw to coin the term *bardolatry* in 1901 to describe their profuse reverence (Shaw 1906 [1901], xxxi).

Bardolatry continues to provide one of the platforms upon which Shakespeare's legacy yet thrives; in 1998, Harold Bloom made a forceful case for the phenomenon's expansion: "Bardolatry, the worship of Shakespeare, ought to be even more a secular religion than it already is. The plays remain the outward limit of human achievement: aesthetically, cognitively, in certain ways morally, even spiritually" (Bloom 1998, xix–xx). But Shakespeare-worship, as it was often labeled before Shaw coined the term, provides a significant barrier to the fantasized, interpersonal relations integral to celebrity, as such apotheosis estranges the celebrated figure to inaccessibly elitist heights of grandiose abstraction. Yet this type of worship co-exists with a decidedly less reverent strain of the poet's enduring fame. As Bristol points out, Shakespeare's name has become a highly marketable brand, and it is one available today on a range of products from Shakesbeer to Shakespeare action figures to Wm. Shakespeare's Bard of Soap. But whether Shakespeare lives on as the quasi-religious god of human achievement or a bar(d) of soap, neither provides a platform for intimate interrelation. To the contrary, these contrasting embodiments—in the ethereal stuff of ideal or the too, too solid substance of corporate goods—paradoxically places Shakespeare at opposite extremes of the spectrum of desire simultaneously: so estranged as to defy personhood altogether, yet so familiar as to exist recognizably as kitsch.

But the somatic body provides a point of mediation between extremes, a space upon which Shakespeare has achieved celebrity, both in his own early modern London and through subsequent centuries. As Heaney and Redmond note of celebrity bodies, "We search their flesh for all sorts of desiring and desirable markers [...]. Through surveying and monitoring the celebrity body, we strip them down to size" (Heaney and Redmond 2016, 402). Bodies humanize. They cut through both the aggrandizement of nostalgia-fueled worship and the trivialization of corporatized production to assert the celebrity's human frailty as a counterbalance to their magnified status. As Prescott's ruff-and-quill formulation suggests, the celebrity we attribute to Shakespeare resides in his ability to be impersonated—that is, to take a human form, to be made person—to which a robust record of Shakespeares incarnate attest. As Shakespeare, the man from Stratford, can no longer function as a contemporary celebrity due to his mythologized, superhuman status and immobile positioning as an icon of seventeenth-century England, his celebrity survives today in the institutions of Shakespearean celebrity and onscreen Shakespeares, through which new stars seem to offer renewed access to and relationships with a human Shakespeare. But Shakespeare was most certainly a celebrity during his own lifetime, as extant records attest to his widespread visibility, his public's active collaboration in his celebrity narrative, and his capacity to provoke the intimate desires and para-social longings of his public. As a number of critics including Bristol and Johnson have noted, Shakespeare seems to have eschewed publicity in his lifetime, yet he is by far the most enduring celebrity to have emerged from the early modern theater (Bristol 1996, 2; Johnson 2003, 163). The following analyses of early modern celebrity media, from gossip to tribute to scandal, demonstrate how Shakespeare's reticence to cultivate his own fame coaxed his audiences to collaboratively craft and project upon him a celebrity narrative and, indeed, a celebrity body, much in the same way that Shakespeare's celebrity-kings, as discussed in Chapter 3, seduced their audiences to co-create their narratives of authority. Shakespeare's contemporaries participated in a series of exchanges that range from the fantastical to the visceral to the erotic to the hostile, but each singles out Shakespeare's corporeality as a means to engage familiarly with a man known primarily through verse.

Sweet Mr. Shakespeare

Though Shakespeare never received the kind of hearty print accolades for his playing as were bestowed upon his contemporaries Alleyn or Burbage, Shakespeare's celebrity emerged, as with other early modern celebrities discussed in this book, from both the stage and the booksellers' stalls. Though the stage would have provided an ideal space for audiences to survey and interact with Shakespeare's physical form, too little is known about his career as an actor to engage in such speculation. Theatrical tradition maintains that he played the ghost of Old Hamlet, but the only plays he is definitely known to have performed in are Jonson's *Every Man in His Humour* and *Sejanus*, staged in 1598 and 1603 respectively, and he is named first in the First Folio's list of twenty-six actors to have appeared in his own plays. But even if, as Johnson has argued, "Shakespeare never cultivated a star persona" as an actor in the same manner as fellow actor-turned-playwright Nathan Field (Johnson 2003, 163), the earliest extant print reference to Shakespeare, Greene's bitter *Groats-worth of Witte* (Greene 1592), singles him out as an actor, though, lamentably for the author, one recently turned playwright. Greene's *Groats-worth* does, however, establish a paradigm for print accounts of Shakespeare that a slew of others would follow in placing a particular focus on Shakespeare's body, even as it rails against his burgeoning poetic career and, as befitting a celebrity, introduces Shakespeare to the London literary scene by means of scandal.[3]

Published posthumously by Henry Chettle in 1592, Greene rails against the young actor for presuming to join the ranks of university-educated playwrights like Peele, Marlowe, and himself:

> for there is an vpstart Crow, beautified with our feathers, that with his *Tygers hart wrapt in a Players hyde,* supposes he is as well able to bombast out a blanke verse as the best of you: and being an absolute *Iohannes fac totum,* is in his owne conceit the onely Shake-scene in a country.
> (Greene 1592, Sig. F1v)

With plays on both Shakespeare's name and a line from *3 Henry VI*, the reference is as unmistakable as the contempt within which it is couched, and the fleeting attack not only testifies to Shakespeare's presence on the London theatrical scene but also suggests something of his name recognition, as Greene's rhetorical structures bank upon his reading public's ability to isolate the referent amidst his unsubtle allusions.[4] But as noted in the Introduction, Greene's invective places a peculiarly visual focus on his target, especially considering that what piques his ire is the actor's audacity in dabbling in the decidedly aural realm of dramatic verse. But Shakespeare, and his unnamed fellow usurpers, are repeatedly referenced through visible imagery: they are "beautified with our feathers," "garnisht in our colours," "painted monsters," and "buckram gentlemen" (Sigs. F1v–F2), suggesting that the player-poet's enhanced visibility, facilitated by the staged presence of his body, renders his poetic craft illegitimate, leaving these players-cum-poets only "Apes" who "imitate," fit to be seen but not to be heard in their own voices (Sig. F1v). Greene's choices of adjectives—*beautified, garnished, painted*—betray the polemicist's own chagrin at his complicity in rendering the speaking body suitably, though deceptively, attractive to audiences, as he has provided through his

A Shakespeare that looks like Shakespeare 133

playmaking the vehicles of the player-poets' visibility, to the extent that the upstart crow has now gained the ill-gotten authority to be heard as well as seen. Thus, this earliest extant reference to Shakespeare, while positioning him on both the stage and at the quill, overtly wraps him in the human stuff of a player's hide and aligns him with a body designated as obstacle to the playwright's craft.

Greene's invective appears to have stoked the fires of an emerging scandal within London's theatrical community, and in many ways, and almost certainly quite contrary to his intention, Greene's attack planted the seeds of Shakespeare's publicly crafted and circulating celebrity narrative by compelling the defenses of those caught in the scandal's crosshairs. Within months of the *Groats-worth*'s publication, two writers associated with the theater stepped forward to distance themselves from Greene's attacks. Chettle, the pamphlet's editor, submitted a public plea for forgiveness in his *Kind-Hart's Dreame*:[5]

> About three moneths since died M. Robert Greene, leaving many papers in sundry Book sellers hands, among other his Groats-worth of wit, in which a letter written to divers play-makers is offensively by one or two of them taken, and because on the dead they cannot be avenged, they willfully forge in their conceites a living author [...]. I am as sory, as if the original fault had beene my fault, because myselfe have seene his demeanour no less civill than he excelent in the quality he professes: besides divers of worship have reported his uprightness of dealing, which argues his honesty, and his facetious grace in writing, that approoves his art.
>
> (Chettle 1592, Sigs. A3v–A4)

That Shakespeare is the intended target of his compensatory flattery is suggested by Chettle's references to both his graceful writing and excellent *qualitie*, which, according to the *OED*, signified the now obsolete meaning of "Profession, occupation, business, *esp.* that of an actor" (OED Online n.d.(a), *s.v.* quality, n. 6a). Further, Chettle's hasty, public *mea culpa* offers some suggestion not only of the magnitude of the scandal but also of Shakespeare's growing popularity, considering the measures Chettle undertook to sever his name from Greene's pointed barbs. That same year, Nashe would, in his *Pierce Penilesse*, similarly refute accusations that he authored the polemic, informing his readers that,

> a scald, trivial, lying pamphlet cald *Greens groat-worth of wit* is given out as being my doing. God never have any care of my soule, but utterly renounce me, if the least word or sillable in it proceeded from my pen, or if I were any way privie to the writing or printing of it.
>
> (1592, Sigs. Pilcrow 2v)

Interestingly, in the same text wherein Nashe rebuts his supposed involvement in Greene's pamphlet, he also, like Chettle, heaps praise upon Shakespeare's drama. Of *1 Henry VI*, Nashe muses,

"How would it have joy'd brave Talbot [...] to thinke that after he had lyne two hundred yeare in his Tombe, hee should triumphe again on the Stage, and have his bones newe embalmed with the teares of ten thousand spectators at least"

(Sig. F3)

Nashe's assessment of the play's reception shines a notably favorable light on Shakespeare's burgeoning career as dramatist, testifying not only to his popular standing but to the visceral responses of his playgoers, with "ten thousand spectators at least" moved to tears by his dramatic offerings.

As Greene's *Groats-worth* expanded in significance from a singular print polemic to a three-person drama of accusation and disavowal playing out on the stage of popular print,[6] Shakespeare could be said to have emerged as the show's silent star: a newly arrived theatrical figure taking shape in the discourse of his peers. Even though he is never named, with Greene's initial "Shake-scene" coming closest to direct designation, Shakespeare takes form through references to his dual crafts in both playing and playmaking and through the precise nature of his colleagues' discourse: the media scandal. Media scandals, as David Rowe points out, while always unstable and of uncertain consequence, can provide a startlingly efficacious means of bolstering a celebrity's appeal in that scandal has a tendency to humanize its target, as "scandalous insinuations" operate as "narrative imperatives" that require counter-narratives for resolution (Rowe 1997, 205). Thus, celebrity scandals, as in the case of Greene's harsh take-down and the subsequent questions of its authorship, coax narratives of reconciliation not only out of the target but of those similarly swept into the aura of the scandal, thus creating a narrative of "alienation and reintegration" for the celebrity (205), not unlike the processes of estrangement and intimacy central to the dynamic of celebrity itself. Thus, the very invective aimed at disenfranchising Shakespeare from a career at the quill seems to have, counterproductively, solicited the public not only to defend but legitimize and further promulgate his craft, all while humanizing Shakespeare as vulnerable and magnifying his presence in the theater. In realization of the polemicist's anxieties, Jeffrey Knapp notes, "within two decades Shakespeare's purported dream of himself as the only 'Shake-scene' would in certain irrefutable respects come true" (Knapp 2009, 37), and Greene himself may ironically have laid the groundwork for this vision to grow to fruition.

Even without the impetus of invective, Shakespeare's peers would, for the next two decades, continue to rally around the player-poet in a manner similar to the one initiated by Greene, Chettle, and Nashe by tying together Shakespeare's twin trades in writing and acting and defending the poet against an ambiguous and invisible charge of illegitimacy. Thus, Greene initiated for Shakespeare a consistent celebrity narrative that invited the public's collaboration in his sustained relevance. In 1603, for example, John Davies of Hereford praises Shakespeare for the very comingling of playing and versifying that provoked Greene's ire when he muses,

> Players, I love yee, and your Qualitie,
> As ye are Men, that pass time not abus'd:
> And some I love for painting, poesie.
> (Davies 1603, 215, 15–17)

In a marginal note following the word "poesie," Davies adds the initials "W.S. R.B."; considering that Burbage, the leading actor of the King's Men, was also known as a painter, it seems likely that these initials aim to clarify which of his beloved players Davies specifically addresses: Burbage, whom Davies also admires for his painting, and Shakespeare, whom he admires for his poetry. But the poem takes a more somber turn in its conclusion, as Davies notes how "the stage doth staine pure gentle bloud/ Yet generous yee are in minde and moode" (215). Here, the poet suggests that in the popular perception, Shakespeare's work as an actor had tarnished him in a manner reminiscent to Shakespeare's own lament in his Sonnet 111 that his public occupation had stained him, "like the dyer's hand" (7). But Davies, like Chettle and Nashe before him, rises up in Shakespeare's defense by pointing to an invisible interior in mind and mood that belies false public perceptions of his exterior.

In 1611, Davies provides a much more direct commendation in his *Scourge of Folly* with the poem "To Our English Terence Mr. Will. Shake-speare." Nestled in a collection that features similar tributes to such contemporary London luminaries as Jonson and Inigo Jones, Davies's poem in praise of Shakespeare highlights both his acting and writing, while also adopting a similarly apologist tone:

> Some say (good Will) which I, in sport, do sing,
> Had'st thou not plaid some Kingly parts in sport,
> Thou hadst bin a companion for a King;
> And, beene a King among the meaner sort.
> Some others raile; but, raile as they thinke fit,
> Thou hast no railing, but a raigning Wit:
> And honesty thou sow'st, which they do reape;
> So, to increase their Stocke which they do keepe.
> (Davies 1611, 76)

As in his earlier poem, Davies acknowledges the stain playing has left on Shakespeare as one that places him "among the meaner sort." As Knapp notes of Davies' assessment, "By pretending to be a king, Shakespeare has actually rendered himself unfit for princely company" (Knapp 2009, 43), but Davies once again champions Shakespeare as a man of singular achievement to emerge from a base arena, seemingly responding in defense to an unheard indictment of his dual professions. The defense is furthered in the poem's title; in the same volume in which Davies labels King's man William Ostler a "Roscius for these times" (98), he deems Ostler's fellow Shakespeare "Our English Terence" and employs the trope discussed in Chapter 1 wherein contemporary celebrities are depicted as heirs to the players and poets of antiquity. As a celebration of the cultural present by means of displacing the past, Shakespeare is here aligned with a poet of humble origins; Terence, born a slave and a freed by the power of his verse, was one of the most popular ancient Roman playwrights in the early modern era. As "our English Terence," Shakespeare is legitimized by classical precedent just he supplants his predecessor in the contemporary imagination.[7]

The stain of playing, and the need to rally in both the trade's and Shakespeare's defense, would continue to inflect tributes to Shakespeare even after his death. In his 1643 *A Chronicle of the Kings of England*, Sir Richard Baker seems positively chagrined to include theatricals in his catalogue of Elizabethan "Men of Note," yet he carries forth anyway:

> it might be thought ridiculous to speak of Stage-players; but seeing excellency in the meanest things deserves remembering [...] For writers of Playes, and such as had been Players themselves, William Shakespear and Benjamin Johnson, have specially left their Names recommended to Posterity.
>
> (Baker 1643, 120)

As Baker's careful disclaimer demonstrates, popular perception still held stage-playing as a meaner sort of occupation, with Shakespeare and Jonson emerging here as exemplary figures amidst the rabble of their trade. But the embarrassment Baker confesses in acknowledging player-poets amongst the figures of political consequence he cites elsewhere in his tome suggests his recognition of their cultural weight, even as he feels compelled to couch their achievement in triviality. The defense Baker extends to Shakespeare and his ilk (he also mentions Burbage and Alleyn in the same passage), he likewise extends to himself; acknowledging Shakespeare and Jonson's seemingly ridiculous inclusion in his chronicle provides a means of insulating himself from similar charges of frivolity: he is aware, he makes clear, that he is including paltry celebrities in his history of great English persons, and he wields his ability to see excellency even in their feeble craft as a mark of his own merit as chronicler.

Baker's defense of select players, and his concurrent self-defense, offers an example of the kind of identificatory participation publics can engage in with celebrities, as here, Baker presents a sense of reciprocity in his compulsion to simultaneously elevate Shakespeare above the stigma attached to playing as he severs himself from that same stigma by self-consciously declaring the unorthodoxy of players' inclusion. Though Baker's identification with these star players remains both brief and subtle, many tributes to Shakespeare within his own lifetime render writers' identificatory impulses quite explicitly and to great depth. While all of the examples cited thus far speak to Shakespeare's work as both poet and player, the majority of his contemporary tributes home in on Shakespeare as poet, both dramatic and lyric, and the intimate interactions readers ascribe to their reading and hearing of his verse. In fact, while few critics designate Shakespeare as a celebrity during his own lifetime, those few who do generally place him in the category of literary celebrity as poetry seems to have provided the primary medium through which audiences felt they came to know him. Duncan-Jones, for example, deems Shakespeare already a "literary celebrity" by the time of his 1609 publication of *Shake-speares Sonnets* (Duncan-Jones 1997, 69), and James Bednarz counts Shakespeare as part of a small group of "celebrity poets" in the early seventeenth century (Bednarz 2012, 47).

Literary celebrities occupy a unique position in celebritydom, as one of the primary sites of interaction between celebrities and their publics—that is, in the celebrities' own flesh-and-bone bodies—is for the most part absent in their primary medium of contact. Thus, while in the previously cited tributes, Shakespeare's human body is always hinted at in reference to its presence on the stage, even as it is generally figured as demeaning his poetic craft through its corporeal availability to his audiences, celebrity-identification through the decidedly less material forum of verse arrives via a more complex dynamics of engagement. Mole describes how Lord Byron, commonly accepted as one of the earliest and most prominent literary celebrities of the nineteenth century, provided a pathway to identificatory bonds with his readers in his cultivation of a "hermeneutic of intimacy" in his poetry (Mole 2007). This hermeneutic of intimacy, Mole writes, "worked by suggesting that his poems could only be understood fully by referring to their author's personality, that reading them was entering a kind of relationship" (23). This intimate style transformed his readership into a select body of initiates, bestowing a sense of privileged knowledge upon readers just as it asserted the poet as a singular, humanized speaker. Byron's celebrity was also supplemented by regular and recognizable public appearances and publicized personal exploits, but the affective heart of his celebrity, despite the constellation of sites whereupon it was generated, was the cultivation of a distinct authorial personality—a person, a body, a biography—that facilitated the personalization of and imagined relationship with a figure known primarily through verse.

In early modern England, the same phenomenon occurred through what Douglas Bruster has labeled "embodied writing": a late Elizabethan rhetorical turn in which "English books became remarkably thick with the personal" and, thus, asserted both writers and their characters as markedly more human and relatable (Bruster 2000, 49). Embodied writing, according to Bruster, "tended to collapse the traditional distance between bodies and texts" and forge "a more intimate connection between person and page" (50), offering a sort of proto-hermeneutic of intimacy in its gestures toward knowable public figures and open eroticism of the human body. Influenced by both highly personal, polemical pamphleteering and theatrical development,[8] embodied writing also, Bruster argues, transformed the print trade and ushered in an era of literary best-sellers (56), as readers came to identify texts as the distinct products of certain writing bodies with whom they could engage repeatedly and claim a sense of knowing. Thus, embodied writing provided one of the keys to literary celebrity, in which "authors' lives jostle with their works" (Braun and Spiers

2016, 449), such that the bodies of authors and bodies of work become indeterminable conflations.

Bruster specifically cites Shakespeare's *Venus and Adonis* as literary best-seller and example of embodied writing, and *Venus and Adonis* factors, unsurprisingly given its popularity, in a number of contemporary references to Shakespeare. In fact, the first extant praise poem to reference Shakespeare, Richard Barnfield's 1598 "A Remembrance of Some English Poets," omits entirely his work for the stage and focuses solely on his longer poems:[9]

> And Shakespeare thou, whose hony-flowing Vaine,
> (Pleasing the World) thy praises doth obtaine.
> Whose *Venus,* and whose *Lucrece* (sweete, and chaste)
> Thy name in fames immortall Booke have plac't.
> Live ever you, at least in Fame live ever:
> Well may the Bodye dye, but Fame dies never.
> (Sig. E2, 13–18)

If *Venus and Adonis* offers an example of embodied writing, Barnfield supplies a potent example of the sense of intimacy such writing can engender in readers. It offers a remarkably personalized tribute as it calls Shakespeare by name, aligns him with his work, and calls special attention to the body of the poet, which is acknowledged here as a mortal counterpart to the abstraction of his fame. The poem also inaugurates a distinctly erotic and recurrent trope in early modern celebrations of Shakespeare in associating the poet and his craft with honey and sweetness. As an early modern trope, honey was regularly employed as an erotic agent, often figured as seductive to the point of intoxication: when Anne attempts to explain her previously inconceivable marriage to Richard in *Richard III*, she admits, "my woman's heart/ Grossly grew captive to his honeyed words" (4.1.78–79); Ophelia declares that she "sucked the honey" of Hamlet's "music vows" (3.1.155); Hamlet fixates on his mother "honeying and making love" to his uncle (3.4.83). As such, Barnfield asserts the public's distinctly erotic pleasure in reading Shakespeare.

"Sweet, honeyed, sugary, rosy, fiery-hot, charming, lust-stung, attractive, wanton, passionate, nymphish, burning in love," Michael Keevak logs, "these are the adjectives that quickly became associated with Shakespeare's poetic style" (Keevak 2001, 47). The same year that Barnfield penned his commendation to Shakespeare's sweetly seductive verse, Meres invoked the same trope in his praise of the "mellifluous & honeytongued Shakespeare" (Meres 1598, 281), where he likewise anatomizes the poet in singling out his tongue as the source of his sweetness. The first extant praise poem dedicated solely to Shakespeare, John Weever's 1599 "*Ad Gulielmum* Shakespeare," employs a similar, though highly amplified, trope:

> Honie-tong'd *Shakespeare* when I saw thine issue
> I swore *Apollo* got them and none other,

> Their rosie-tainted features cloth'd in tissue,
> Some heauen born goddesse said to be their mother:
> Rose-checkt *Adonis* with his amber tresses,
> Faire fire-hot *Venus* charming him to loue her,
> Chaste *Lucretia* virgine-like her dresses,
> Prowd lust-stung *Tarquine* seeking still to proue her:
> *Romea Richard* ; more whose names I know not,
> Their sugred tongues, and power attractiue beuty
> Say they are Saints althogh that Sts they shew not
> For thousands vowe to them subiectiue dutie:
> They burn in loue thy children *Shakespear* het them,
> Go, wo thy Muse more Nymphish brood beget them.
> (Weever 1599, Sig. E6)[10]

Once again honey-tongued, this highly eroticized Shakespeare is presented not only as seductive, but the virile father to an indefinite brood of dramatic characters (with "more whose names I know not"). Shakespeare has likewise dallied with the divine and impregnated a "goddesse" who continues to bear him children that speak, like their potent father, in "sugred tongues." Shakespeare's seductive arts are further iterated in the poem's description of the thousands who vow "subiectiue dutie" to his characters and, by extension, him as well. Weever's commendatory verse, like Barnfield's, attributes Shakespeare's rapt audience to the poet's irresistibly erotic verse and engages intimately with both the poet's and his characters' bodies, highlighting those frequently blazoned features of tongues, cheeks, and tresses while bathing the entire sonnet in the sexual imagery of procreation.

Given a vast field rife with worthy contenders, it is perhaps the anonymously penned, highly satirical *The Return from Parnassus* that most keenly renders as legible Shakespeare's seductive capacities and the intimate interrelation between Shakespeare and his readers. As the second installment of the Parnassus trilogy staged by Cambridge University students between 1598 and 1602, *Return* provides perhaps the first and most literal embodiment of Shaw's bardolatry, centuries before the term's coinage, when a wealthy and foppish courtier named Gullio vows to "worshipp sweet Mr. Shakespeare, and to honour him […] lay his Venus and Adonis under my pillowe" (4.1.101–103). Gullio, whose name singles him out as a gull, functions fairly blatantly as a mockery of Shakespeare's most ardent fans, and his employment of the "sweet" trope, which he exercises repeatedly in the play, signals a degree of awareness with the commonly invoked descriptors of Shakespeare contemporarily in circulation. Throughout the play, Gullio feebly attempts to wax Shakespearean with impromptu, half-cribbed love poetry and declares Shakespeare the superior poet to the "foole" Chaucer and the lifeless Spenser (4.1.78, 80), before announcing his intention to "have [Shakespeare's] picture in my study" (3.1.200). And while Gullio's excessive admiration could easily be interpreted as an endorsement, *The Return from Parnassus* readily distinguishes its hearty commendation from concurrent print praise in that the admiration expressed here is, as Macbeth says, "a tale/ told by an idiot" (5.5.25–26). Gullio's praise, as effusive and affectionately conveyed as that of Barnfield and Meres, is here rendered as ill-informed and tottering to absurdity. Combined with his vainglorious professions of poetic savvy and profligate patronage, and further staged in contradistinction to the university-educated poet-for-pay who easily exploits his love for Shakespeare and parts him from his money, Gullio's unrestrained lionizing can only be seen as fawning, excessive indulgence.

As Gullio renders explicit in his profuse praise, his admiration extends well beyond the realm of Shakespeare's verse to Shakespeare's person, so much so that he desires the poet's likeness in his study and hopes to absorb Shakespeare's poetic prowess through osmosis from beneath his pillow as he sleeps; his choice of adjectives, "*sweet* Mr. Shakespeare," combined with his desire to take Shakespeare to bed, demonstrate a longing for intimate interaction. But while he craves corporeal interaction, he placates himself with mediatized intervention, both through Shakespeare's picture and his book, though he claims strong identificatory bonds even through the mediation of print and portraiture. As he recites the poet's verse, he does not just imagine a relationship with Shakespeare, but imagines himself as Shakespeare, and Shakespeare becomes a primary vessel through which he proclaims himself. As such, Duncan-Jones labels the Parnassus plays "the culmination of many admiring responses from Shakespeare's Elizabethan fan club" (Duncan-Jones 2011, 235), but while the Parnassus plays are undoubtedly works of fannish enterprise, as evidenced by their thorough familiarity with Shakespeare and other early modern theatricals, the plays' derision for effusive followers suggests the plays aim as much to elevate as to deflate. Yet it is Gullio, the embodied condensation of fawning admiration, not Shakespeare, who is held up to the most pointed ridicule, which offers some suggestion of the presence of real-life Gullios in the playwrights' contemporary London.

The famous anecdote London law student John Manningham recorded in his diary in 1601 certainly seems to uphold the notion that Shakespeare, and other early modern theatricals, maintained an impassioned following who, like Gullio, craved interaction beyond that allowed on page or stage:

> Upon a time when Burbage played Richard III there was a citizen grew so far in liking with him, that before she went from the play she appointed him to come that night unto her by the name of Richard III. Shakespeare, overhearing their conclusion, went before, was entertained and at his game ere Burbage came. The message being brought that Richard III was at the door, Shakespeare caused return to be made that William the Conqueror was before Richard III.
>
> (Manningham 1976 [1601], Folio 29b)

Like Weever's poem, the anecdote figures Shakespeare as virile and seductive, this time marked not by his syrupy verse, but by a kind of roguish charm as he bests and playfully humiliates his masculine rival to seduce an amorous playgoer. The story further recounts, though highly dubiously, the exploits of a decidedly theatrical figure, and, more specifically, a distinctly Shakespearean one. The anecdote embodies its Shakespeare from his own body of work as it invokes a number of the playwright's favored tropes: disguise, the bed-trick, rival lovers, social transcendence, and a metatheatric glimpse into the offstage antics of actors. This Shakespeare is, too, "a king among the meaner sort" as he plays a sort of carnivalesque version of William I who conquers in the bedroom rather than the battlefield. Particularly remarkable about this amusing anecdote is the way in which various strains of Shakespeare's celebrity all seem to intertwine here: the rivalry between playwright and player as found in Greene, the hint of scandal, the seductive capacities of Shakespeare's play, the poet's virility, the zeal of the admirer and, perhaps most abidingly, the corporeal, even carnal focus on Shakespeare as an eroticized body.

Three centuries, three Shakespeare(an)s

Perhaps even more remarkable than the Manningham anecdote's distinctly Shakespearean flavor is that this same anecdote resurfaced in 1759 in Thomas Wilkes' *General View of the Stage*, especially considering that Manningham's diary was not discovered until the nineteenth century, which means that Manningham's account recorded a story of enough public interest to survive and circulate in gossip, if not in lost print sources, for a century and a half (Bate 1997, 24). The 1759 reappearance, which the author offers, seemingly in recognition of its prurient appeal, "without any precursory excuse" (Wilkes 1759, 220), includes a number of enhanced flourishes befitting the trend in intrigue-laden domestic comedies that characterize the era: the citizen is now a married woman whose husband is away, she sends her lady to deliver the request to Burbage, they arrange a secret three-tap knock at the door to signal his illicit arrival, and Shakespeare physically emerges at the end, popping his head out the window rather than sending word to declare his victory (220–221). The Wilkes retelling also makes sure to inform readers that Shakespeare "had wrote Romeo and Juliet" and therefore "did not want [for] wit or eloquence" in his enticement of Burbage's would-be paramour, even as "the lady was very much surprised at Shakespear's presuming to act Mr. Burbage's part" (221). Here, not only does Wilkes endow Shakespeare with the seductive capacities of his most famous dramatic wooer, but he specifically designates Shakespeare as a player in an unfolding drama, though here reversed with the playwright playing a role scripted by an actor. Even more pointedly than the Manningham account, the Wilkes revision embodies its Shakespeare from his body of work, this time signposted through direct reference: this Shakespeare, the Wilkes account instructs, is both Romeo and Romeo's author combined.

It is of little surprise that this anecdote would resurface in the middle of the eighteenth century, given the confluence of concurrent Shakespeare-centered events and developments that signal not just a resurgence in interest, but a likely as-of-yet unseen fervor for the playwright and his works. The anecdote appears roughly simultaneously with the first print use of the word *Shakespearean* in 1754 (OED Online n.d.(b), *s.v. Shakespearean,* adj. A), signaling that Shakespeare had become enshrined in language as a signifying adjective. It also follows the 1740 installation of Peter Scheemakers's Shakespeare memorial in Westminster Abbey, which designated Shakespeare, along with Chaucer, one of England's national poets. But perhaps more germane to the interest in salacious Shakespeare anecdotes is not Shakespeare's new home in Poets' Corner as it was his new home within the human architecture of the era's most celebrated stage star, Garrick, who initiated a paradigm of Shakespearean celebrity that continues to resuscitate Shakespeare in the bodies of new stars like Benedick Cumberbatch and David Tennant today. Garrick, whose London debut in the part of Richard III resonated profoundly with theatergoers, so thoroughly intertwined his public persona with Shakespeare that the two became an irretrievable, hybrid entity on London stages and pages, as well as in mass-market art and statuary. "It is hard to say whether Shakespeare owes more to Garrick, or Garrick to Shakespeare," James Granger commented in 1769 of the two actor-manager-playwrights' popular symbiosis (Granger 1769, 288).

As *Shakespearean* is a word that denotes, according to the *OED*, "having the characteristics of William Shakespeare or his dramatic or poetical productions" (adj. a), it is a term that conflates, like the Wilkes or Manningham anecdotes previously cited, person and text in a single signifier. The Shakespearean celebrity, then, could be said to embody in human form what the term *Shakespearean* signifies rhetorically, as Shakespearean celebrities like Garrick, Kean, and Olivier did not only perform Shakespeare's dramas and offer renewed access to his texts, but provided in their persons a freshly re-embodied Shakespeare as they professed to offer special access to Shakespeare the man as well. Garrick adapted Shakespeare's plays and was said by one contemporary "to restore [Shakespeare] to his genuine splendor [...] unincumbered with the unnatural additions" (T. Davies 1780, 93); thus, Garrick was figured as offering a more real, truer Shakespeare than what had come before. But his live, animate body offered on and off the stage a fleshly vessel with which audiences could interact once more, as he presented himself as not only an actor and adapter, but an impassioned fan who truly understood the target of his intense devotion. The conflation of Shakespeare and contemporary actor, along with the conflation of virtuoso performance and fawning admiration to the point of special knowledge, continue to inform the institution of Shakespearean celebrity today, thus allowing actors to embody the term *Shakespearean* in their likenesses to both text and person. The Shakespearean celebrity, according to Barnes, "appears to offer a solution (however temporary or illusory) to a desire to know what Shakespeare is 'really like'" (Barnes 2017, 7) and provides, as Blackwell notes, "an embodiment of the meanings, associations, and complexities of Shakespeare in their contemporary moment" (Blackwell 2018, 33).

Shakespearean celebrities offer through their bodies what praise poems, pamphlets, and anecdotes had previously provided: an embodied, seemingly knowable Shakespeare, but touchable, audible, and visible, crafted in flesh instead of words, but just as much a site of fantasized projection and public collaboration as the embodied text. In the four centuries since Shakespeare's death, numerous stars have risen to provide just such a living, breathing host to the specter of Shakespeare's celebrity, each one a new entry in the ever-expanding catalogue of Shakespearean bodies befitting the Shakespeare corpus. Barbara Hodgdon details over a dozen current and historical "Shakespearean stars," beginning in the seventeenth century with Richard Burbage and continuing through the twenty-first with Michael Gambon (Hodgdon 2007). Barnes has acutely examined the reigning Shakespearean star of the twentieth century, Olivier, and the "ways in which *Shakespeare* is appropriated through Olivier's star image" in filmed Shakespeare and through autobiography (Barnes 2017, 9), while Blackwell probes the Shakespearean celebrity's contemporary digital environment in her discussions of stars like Tom Hiddleston, along with their analog forebears like Garrick and Branagh (Blackwell 2018). Each, whether they emerged from the platforms of the stage or the big screen or the little ones, participates in a highly enmeshed, collaborative enterprise that, like Wilkes' anecdote, conflates Shakespeare, Shakespearean character, and popular fantasy in a single multivalent body.

Garrick was undoubtedly the first Shakespearean celebrity, dedicating the bulk of his career to establishing himself as Shakespearean in every arena he inhabited. As Vanessa Cunningham argues, "a generation of playgoers came to 'know' Shakespeare primarily through Garrick" (Cunningham 2008, 5), and though Garrick is generally credited with stoking the flames of bardolatry that quickly swept across England, then Europe, in the eighteenth century, it is more accurate to say that Garrick made opportune use of, rather than initiated, the Shakespeare craze. As the Poets' Corner installation demonstrates, the rising tide of reverence for the departed dramatist was already well underway. But in stark counterbalance to Shakespeare's apotheosis as national poet,[11] the long eighteenth century also gave rise to a distinctly humanizing, fresh batch of Shakespearean rumor, like the resurrected Manningham anecdote, which perpetuated and enlarged the intangible narrative body of Shakespeare's celebrity while filling in with wild speculations the many biographical lacunae left behind.

John Aubrey's 1679 *Brief Lives*, for example, claimed Shakespeare to be the son of a butcher, who "when he kill'd a Calfe he would doe it in a high style, and make a Speech" (Aubrey 1679, 334). Aubrey also offers the only extant physical description of the Stratford poet: "He was a handsome, well-shap't man" (Aubrey 1679, 334). Of greater intrigue, however, is his suggestion that Sir William Davenant, seventeenth-century adapter of Shakespeare's works, may have been Shakespeare's illegitimate son:

> Mr William Shakespeare was wont to goe into Warwickshire once a yeare, and did commonly in his journey lye at this house in Oxon, where he was exceedingly respected [...] Now Sir William would sometimes, when he

was pleasant over a glasse of wine with his most intimate friends—e.g. Sam Butler [...] say, that it seemed to him that he writ with the very spirit that did Shakespeare, and seemed contented enough to be thought his Son. He would tell them the story as above, in which way his mother had a very light report, whereby she was called a Whore.

(Aubrey 1679,177)

As was the case during his lifetime, Shakespeare's disembodied celebrity continued to affirm his seductive capacities and place him at the center of scandal, while likewise asserting his humble origins and the natural genius that would lift him from obscurity. Continuing in this tradition, in 1709, Nicholas Rowe prefaced his six-volume edition of Shakespeare's complete works with the biographical sketch, *Some Account of the Life &c. of Mr. William Shakespear*, in which he claimed that scandal forced the young Shakespeare to the theater after he had engaged in the "practice of deer-stealing" (1709, xlvii). Like Aubrey, Rowe offers a myth of origin to the Shakespeare narrative, birthing his reputation in scandal, as did Greene's bitter pamphlet, and stressing his common upbringing as not only the antecedent to but the driving force behind his poetic career. That accounts such as these circulated throughout eighteenth-century England suggests that while Shakespeare's somatic body succumbed to its mortality, his ethereal celebrity body, crafted through the kind of personal, embodied writing that shaped his yet living presence, continued to circulate and shape him in the stuff of words. However, Garrick's luminous rise to the heights of theatrical stardom provided an apt human vessel for the distribution of such narratives, and Garrick put considerable effort into tying not only his narrative, but his own body, to Shakespeare through performance, portraiture, and, perhaps most profoundly, statuary.

No extant artifact more aptly captures the human, corporeal conflation of Shakespeare and Garrick than Garrick's prized statue, Roubiliac's *Shakespeare*, which stood as the centerpiece of the London actor's Temple to Shakespeare at his Hampton home. The statue, a life-size marble carving, is modeled as much on Garrick as it is on Shakespeare, as it is widely held that Garrick posed for its sculpture (Dobson 1992, 179; Shapiro 2010, 30), and thus, the statue memorialized not just Shakespeare, but Shakespeare's reanimation in the body of his most ardent eighteenth-century admirer. This conflated revivification is captured in a 1758 poem by Paul Whitehead, in which Roubiliac's statue is imagined to versify his gratitude to his patron Garrick: "I rise, I breathe, I live/ In you—my Representative!" (Whitehead 1777, 19–20). As Whitehead's lines suggest, Shakespeare was thought to take material shape not just in the body of Garrick, but in representations of his body as well, and Garrick would persist in this amalgamating pursuit, as he proceeded to stamp his image upon the poet's legacy by commissioning, then mass-producing paintings that juxtaposed both men's likenesses. During his 1769 Jubilee, for example, he placed Gainsborough's *Portrait of Garrick with the Bust of Shakespeare* on permanent display in Stratford's Town Hall (McPherson 2015). The installation of his portrait, his head nestled against the immobile shoulder of the watchful bard, wove Garrick's image indelibly into the fabric of Shakespeare's legacy at its point of origin, perhaps suggesting a sort of rebirth: the reanimation of Shakespeare in the body of his most diligent spokesman.

If Garrick did not launch a cultural fixation with Shakespeare, it is fair to say that, as Celestine Woo asserts, he "tangibly enlarged Shakespeare's audiences and media of communication within society" (Woo 2008, 2). Offstage and apart from Garrick's many celebrated performances of Shakespeare's characters, Shakespeare accompanied Garrick through the celebrity media of the eighteenth century, occupying spots in periodicals and at art sales, where reproduced prints of Garrick's portraits and miniaturized statuary, often pairing if not conflating his image with Shakespeare's, were sold to a mass public. Through Garrick, Shakespeare's body became for the first time easily possessable, immediately recognizable, and endlessly reproducible, but it was a body crafted in Garrick's own likeness as much as in Shakespeare's, and as Heather McPherson argues, Garrick's intrusions into the reconstruction of the Shakespearean body were greeted as welcome interventions: given that the uninspiring likenesses offered in the Droeshout engraving and Stratford bust "failed to satisfy the public's appetite for a modern living effigy, it is not surprising that Garrick's features increasingly came to fill that void" (McPherson 2015). As Garrick domesticated Shakespeare's body and transformed him into a household good, he also transformed Shakespeare into a more appropriately Shakespearean body, as he offered up his own as a corrective to a disappointing extant record.

While Garrick was certainly the first Shakespearean celebrity, it would be Kean, the eccentric star of the nineteenth-century stage, who would become the first English actor accorded the Shakespearean label in print, when John Keats noted in 1933 [1817], "The acting of Kean is Shakespearian" (60). For Keats, *Shakespearean* was an undeniably corporeal assignation, as his anatomical reviews of Kean's performance make explicit: "The hand is agonized with death; the lip trembles with the last breath [...] The very eye-lid dies" (1933 [1817], 60). That Keats would so closely align both Kean and the label *Shakespearean* with the micro-gestures of an animate body suggests something of how Kean emerged in the early 1800s as the successive heir to Garrick's mantle[12]: the nineteenth-century Shakespearean celebrity, much like Garrick, could not only recite Shakespeare, but had to embody him as well.

Kean's visceral embodiment of Shakespeare also provided a distinctly human counterbalance to the cerebral Shakespeare concurrently promoted by Romantic thinkers. With Shakespeare already firmly established as England's national poet and his body already a mass-produced household idol, Kean's London debut as Shylock on the newly resurrected Drury Lane stage coincided with a powerful movement, led by the Romantic critics Coleridge, Hazlitt, and Lamb, to wrest Shakespeare from popular arenas and reposition him as a singular literary genius. According to Hazlitt, Shakespeare was the only poet able to deliver the "definite truth" (Hazlitt 1920 [1817], xx). As such, the fleeting theatrical event was deemed an inefficient vehicle through which to deliver the sheer magnitude of his poetic mastery and unparalleled insights. Hazlitt railed against "the exhibition of the most insupportable and hateful spectacles" of staged Shakespeare (xxii); Coleridge went so far as to assert that Shakespeare wrote for readers, not spectators, claiming, "Shakespeare, as secure of being read over and over [...] provides this for *his readers*, and leaves it to them" (Coleridge 1884, 180). As Romantic thinkers, Shelley and Keats notably excepted, appropriated Shakespeare as a symbolic embodiment of their own Romantic ethos and figured the relationship between Shakespeare and the public as an intimate encounter with extraordinary genius freed from the intermediary of actors, Kean's electric, physically compelling performances provided a distinctive counterweight.

As Kean re-asserted Shakespeare as a human body against the countering impulses of Romantic thinkers, he upheld the paradigm initiated by Garrick that promoted Shakespeare as a visceral pleasure. As a contemporary biographer noted shortly after Kean's death, critics often compared Kean to Garrick, and a select group of admirers gifted Kean with items to demonstrate such similitude, including a lace tippet that once belonged to Garrick and a portrait of Garrick enacting the part of Abel Drugger (Cornwall 1835, 133); however, as the biographer notes, Kean himself modeled his career more closely on that of the literary celebrity Lord Byron, as both men "pandered to the taste they wished to govern" (Cornwall 1835, 235). Thus, Kean demonstrates the layered accretion of meaning at work in the conflated Shakespearean celebrity: Kean's celebrity presence encompassed aspects of Shakespeare's, Garrick's, and Byron's celebrity in a single signifying body.

The reigning Shakespearean celebrity of the twentieth century, Olivier, further amalgamated the Shakespearean celebrity body within his person, as he confessed to having both studied and emulated Kean's body in his own performance, allowing that, as Barnes notes, in Olivier's cinematic portrayal of *Richard III*, "the bodies of Olivier, Kean, and Shakespeare are suffused into an overarching Shakespearean star body in performance" (Barnes 2017, 100). As was the case with Garrick, Olivier's filmed performances meant that a generation of filmgoers came to know Shakespeare primarily as presented through the body of Olivier, but Olivier's body contained multitudes, offering renewed access not only to Shakespeare, but to Shakespearean celebrities who had housed his disembodied presence in his wake. But as Olivier liberally borrowed from both past and contemporary Shakespearean actors, he asserted his special connection to Shakespeare quite overtly. By the time Olivier's *Henry V* garnered four Academy Award nominations and launched Olivier's career as a Shakespearean film star, Olivier had already and quite self-consciously established himself as a Shakespearean stage actor; as he confessed, he purposefully set out to acquire this title:

> My ambition required it. I required it of myself. I knew it wouldn't happen unless I crashed that market. [...] I just went on and on, and after about a year the Press referred to me as "that Shakespearean actor." Then I knew it had been done.
>
> (Coleman 2005, 80)

Modeling his career on that of Garrick or, more recently, the first knighted actor Sir Henry Irving, Olivier turned to Shakespeare in a bid to boost his gravitas and set out to become known as a Shakespearean. Olivier began his career as a Shakespearean at the Old Vic in London. There, intertwining his own burgeoning career with Shakespeare's well established one, he noted of his performance alongside the accomplished Gielgud, "I was the upstart" (Coleman 2005, 63), echoing the accusation that helped to define Shakespeare's own celebrity.

Though Olivier had already performed in numerous films by the time he took on *Henry V*, the film's success, followed by the success of his filmed *Hamlet* in 1948, which won Best Picture and Best Actor Oscars, allowed him to transfer his London esteem as a notable Shakespearean to worldwide celebrity. Olivier had, like his theatrical forebears, provided a new human frame in which to house the spectral body of Shakespeare's celebrity, and he not only self-consciously acknowledged, but seemed to relish his role as Shakespearean celebrity. He frequently gestured to his active collaboration with Shakespeare, claiming, for example, in a 1983 interview, "Mr. Shakespeare and I are very close, you know. We've done a lot for each other" (Lewis 1996, 164). Further promoting the special, highly enmeshed relationship the two shared, he claimed a kind of intuitive, nearly empathic understanding of Shakespeare. Of his straightforward delivery style, he mused, "I didn't have to sing it, because I spoke Shakespeare naturally. I spoke Shakespeare as if that was the way I spoke" (Coleman 2005, 63).

He furthered that empathic relationship by following a Shakespearean trajectory from upstart to a "king among the meaner sort," as he held in balance the elitism of his acclaimed thespianism and a knighthood with a penchant for popular films and television commercials. In 1974, the Shakespearean actor and newly appointed member of the House of Lords appeared in a televised ad for Polaroid. Seconds into the commercial that never calls him by name, Olivier commands his audience to "Come a bit closer," as we zoom in not upon the camera he holds in his hands, but to his face, as he offers his body up to public consumption just at the point in his career when a barony suggested an unapproachable elitism. Olivier was mocked for this move in multiple forums—popular and elite alike—but his commercially motivated streak found precedence in Shakespeare's own career and, indeed, in the careers of Shakespeareans like Garrick who introduced Shakespeare to the mass market.

TV's sexed-up Shakespeares

If Olivier ushered Shakespeare to the screen, screens—whether silver, small, or smart—have provided a comfortable home for Shakespeare ever since, allowing him ample room to stretch and transform into an ever-evolving array of re-embodied possibilities by means of the Shakespeare character. As the final form of (re)embodied, celebrity Shakespeare I take up in this chapter, Shakespeare-as-television-character provides a culmination of the rhetorically embodied Shakespeare of early modern accounts and the subsequent reincarnations of

Shakespeare via his human hosts, the Shakespearean celebrities. Fictionalized, embodied Shakespeares on TV offer a scripted and narrativized, corporeal Shakespeare in perpetuation of the centuries-old search for a suitably Shakespearean body befitting his body of work. As Courtney Lehmann argues in her analysis of Shakespeare's authorial and corporeal re-embodiment in *Shakespeare in Love*, "Cinema has always argued the ontological priority of bodies over texts" (Lehmann 2002, 102), and by extension, I would include television in this formulation as well, as both formats offer up fleshy, mobile bodies as sites of meaning and cultural negotiation. In the Shakespeare character, enacted, embodied Shakespeares explicitly invite us to scrutinize Shakespeare's body, often with direct, rhetorical cues, such as in "The Shakespeare Code" episode of *Doctor Who*, when the Doctor's assistant Martha's first comment upon seeing Shakespeare in the flesh is to note that he does not look like his portraits. Such cues ask us to investigate Shakespeare's body as presented to us for signs of familiarity and moments of departure, to consult a historical record of representation we are assumed to carry in our memories, to weigh this current incarnation against our expectations, and, perhaps, even to add this new representation to our current catalogue as part of the multifarious construction of an ongoing and ever-morphing Shakespeare body.

If Shakespearean celebrities re-present Shakespeare in new bodies to new eras, filling in the narrative gaps in Shakespeare's biographical body with a contemporary celebrity's own biography, and re-membering a lost, dis-membered body with a live and animate host, fictionalized Shakespeares participate in much the same process, but with a temporal twist. Shakespearean celebrities retrieve the estranged Shakespeare from his seventeenth-century home to resuscitate him in, and refamiliarize him to, the celebrity's contemporary cultural environment. Shakespeare-as-character typically estranges us from our own temporal landscape and transports us to a reimagined early modern London—inflected, to be sure, by our own contemporary cultural fixations, but presented as the lost author's true home, a time when Shakespeare doesn't yet know he's Shakespeare, and where, to paraphrase Ophelia, he knows what he is but not what he may be. There, whether in *Doctor Who* or *Will*, we are offered a glimpse into the flowering of a history we know is destined to unfold and the voyeuristic thrill of beholding a body in action that we know primarily as a body of work. In short, we are offered the opportunity to engage with Shakespeare as celebrity, in his own time, in his own body, through the ebb and flow of his professional highs and lows.

Of course, the fictionalized Shakespeare-as-character remains, as Emily Saidel has argued, "a fantasy Shakespeare, an imagined Shakespeare, the dream of Shakespeare" (Saidel 2012, 108), which holds true to the notion of celebrity Shakespeare and celebrity more broadly, as celebrity always carves out a vacant space for public projection. As Shakespeare's scant biography opens ample space for speculation, fantasy, and projection, fictionalized Shakespeare exploits a wide-open field of possibility, even as it can claim not to dismiss entirely an established biographical background. Further, with little by way of agreed-upon portraiture, and even less conferring verisimilitude, Shakespeare's body operates, too, as a blank screen upon which to construct a Shakespeare that looks like Shakespeare. But a Shakespeare that looks like Shakespeare is a cultural fantasy, informed by a complex matrix of contemporaneous concerns and preoccupations, which, as Lanier argues, articulate "popular notions of authorship and cultural hierarchy, collective ideas, attitudes, aspirations, desires and anxieties that have a variety of political inflections" (Lanier 2002, 112–113). For the remainder of this chapter, I will explore some of those popular notions and collective ideas as embodied in the figures of Shakespeare in *Will* and "The Shakespeare Code" episode of *Doctor Who* (Palmer 2007), especially concerning Shakespeare's eroticized body, his position between his early modern world and our own, and, indeed, his celebrity status, including the acknowledgment of his own unfinished narrative that invites perpetual revision.

John Madden's 1998 *Shakespeare in Love* might be said to have inaugurated a new visual template for onscreen representations of Shakespeare, divorced from the bald and beruffled stock-image in favor of what Lehmann calls "the full-bodied fleshiness of sexual desire" (Lehmann 2002, 102). In Joseph Fiennes's take at the bard, the smooth dome of the Droeshout engraving is dispensed for tousled brown locks, and the starched collar is dismissed in favor of a dangerously unfastened shirt baring the poet's torso almost to the navel. Scene after scene, the film solicits the spectator's desiring gaze, as Shakespeare stares back with a smoldering, nearly penetrative desire, physically embodying the intimate poetics of Shakespeare's embodied early modern writing. In Madden's Shakespeare, sexual desire and playwrighting are intertwined as an unrecoverable, conflated force propelling the poet's body into action—an enmeshment made especially legible during intercut scenes of Shakespeare's amorous bedroom overtures providing the dialogue for *Romeo and Juliet*.[13] This kind of poetsexuality has, in *Shakespeare in Love*'s wake, provided a kind of hallmark to twenty-first-century onscreen depictions of Shakespeare, where the standardized aging, ruff-and-quill Shakespeare has given way to a young, shiny-coiffed, libidinously versant Shakespeare. Examples abound, from the 2007 Spanish romantic comedy *Miguel y William*, featuring Will Kempe as a seductive, long-haired Shakespeare vying for his lover's affection against his rival Cervantes, to *Bill*, a farcical, 2015 Monty Python-reminiscent comedy in which Matthew Baynton's scruffy Bill Shakespeare gives up his gig as a Stratford lute player to pursue playwrighting in the city. It is little surprise that Shakespeare's so-called "lost years," the period between the 1585 birth of his twins and his 1592 appearance in the *Groats-worth of Witte*, provide the setting for most of these portrayals, as they offer up a blank span in which we know even less about a man that we know very little about, thus opening up the possibilities for a re-embodied Shakespeare to unbounded characterization.

Yet given *carte blanche*, the choice *du jour* trends toward the young and erotic, and Fiennes-as-Shakespeare's signature unfastened blouse and full mane have become near staples of contemporary incarnations, as has the intermingling of sexuality and poetic practice. In the cases of "The Shakespeare Code" and *Will*, that sexuality is depicted as overtly fluid, even as both Shakespeares engage in heterosexual relations. In "The Shakespeare Code," Dean Lennox Kelly's rugged, shaggy-haired Shakespeare flirts shamelessly, though unimaginatively, with the Doctor's assistant, Martha. When the Doctor, played by David Tennant (incidentally, a contemporary Shakespearean celebrity in his own right) interrupts the pair, saying that they "can all have a good flirt later," Shakespeare surveys the contours of the Doctor's lithe body before provocatively asking if that's a promise. Wide-eyed, the Doctor responds that "fifty-seven academics just punched the air," in a nod to ongoing debates regarding the historical Shakespeare's sexuality, here settled by way of time machine as bisexual. But if the academic in-joke plays tongue-in-cheek with sexual speculation, it also lifts Shakespeare's sexuality to the forefront of a contemporary audience's unanswered questions. As Lanier points out, both time travel and magic have become narrative tropes "to bring Shakespeare in contact with modernity" (Lanier 2007, 107), and such tropes regularly function as forms of critique, in which confrontation between the man and what we have made of him become revealed as either ludicrous or overly belabored. This quick acknowledgment, and even quicker dismissal, of an ongoing debate pokes at our own fixations, to the same impulses that, as discussed in this chapter's opening, attempted to divine Shakespeare's sexuality from his portraiture. In "The Shakespeare Code," the answer proves inconsequential to the remainder of the episode, other than to humorously illuminate, then playfully satiate, the viewer's desire for a sexually unambiguous Shakespearean body.

If sexuality provides a running joke in "The Shakespeare Code," from Shakespeare's smirking come-on to the Doctor to the pathetically cliched pick-up lines he attempts with Martha, sexuality provides the narrative and atmospheric backbone to *Will*, which offers perhaps the most audaciously sexual Shakespeare to emerge in recent years. Spanning one ten-episode season in 2017, *Will* charts the adventures of a highly ambitious, 25-year-old Shakespeare freshly arrived to a Baz Luhrmann-esque 1589 London: a city of dirty streets and Tudor architecture populated by colorfully clad citizens ambling to a score of indie and punk rock. The theater is depicted as the freewheeling sexual funhouse of London: Burbage is paid to have sex with a noblewoman while her husband watches from a distance; Kit Marlowe escorts Will to an orgy at Francis Bacon's home; Will has sex with Alice Burbage beneath the stage trapdoor. Davidson's Will, apropos of this distinctly libidinous theatrical environment, is depicted as young, virile, and handsome, ever stubbled and luxuriously coiffed, almost always in a blue doublet or shirt to magnify his large, striking blue eyes. His ready companion and sometime-rival, Kit, is a tortured, emo, openly queer, androgynous artist. Though Will and Kit never engage in a sexual relationship, the series provides a steady stream of sidelong glances, nearly nose-to-nose encounters, soft whispers, and physical hostilities between the two. Though Lisa S. Starks finds a distinctly straight Shakespeare in *Will*, despite "a range of sexualities in the theatre world" of the series (Starks 2019, 224), it is fair to say that queer longing bubbles just beneath the surface of Will's blue doublet throughout the entire series. While Starks correctly points out that during the one instance when Kit sneaks a kiss from Will, the titular character recoils (2019, 224), she omits the way he lingers beforehand, face-to-face and lying atop Marlowe, his face betraying his astonishment, perhaps confusion, with a strange new erotics with which he is unfamiliar. Even if, as Starks points out, Will offers only a "queer lite" Shakespeare (220), Shakespeare's sexuality emerges in *Will* as far from settled—a sexuality in process, perhaps, in line with the unsettled Shakespeares made possible by Shakespeare-as-character.

If sexuality and poetic prowess become intertwined in contemporary depictions of Shakespeare, Shakespeare's poetic abilities, too, are often presented as far from established, negating to some extent the myth of Shakespeare's genius in favor of an often struggling, frequently borrowing, and even at times outright incompetent Shakespeare. As Lois Potter astutely notes, "a surprising number of writers have created a fictional Shakespeare who is virtually inarticulate" (Potter 2012, 433), perhaps nowhere more forcefully than in Roland Emmerich's 2011 *Anonymous*, an anti-Stratfordian take on Shakespeare that paints, in this case, the imposter poet as what Roger Ebert deemed "a notch or two above the village idiot" (Emmerich 2011). But even in less extreme cases, such as in both *Doctor Who* and *Will*, Shakespeare is sometimes depicted as less eloquent than gilded anthologies might lead one to believe. In "The Shakespeare Code," for instance, when the Doctor and his assistant Martha first see Shakespeare on the Globe stage, the Doctor can hardly contain his anticipation to hear the "genius, the most human human" poet speak his "beautiful, brilliant words." When Shakespeare then informs his cheering audience to "shut [their] big fat mouths," the Doctor sinks in deflation. "You should never meet your heroes," his assistant offers. Interestingly, though Shakespeare's inelegant call to the crowd proves understandably dispiriting for the Doctor, it paradoxically proves the Doctor's assessment correct: Shakespeare is undeniably human, as capable of penning *Love's Labour's Lost*, which had just concluded, as of spouting infelicitously. Shakespeare is, in his opening scene in the episode, transformed from legend to man, preceding our hour-long journey with this Shakespeare who is not yet Shakespeare.

This scene foreshadows several moments throughout the episode in which Shakespeare is shown to poach lines he hears in passing for as-of-yet unwritten plays. When the Doctor muses, "All the world's a stage," Shakespeare suggests that he will store that line for later use. Of course, we as spectators know that he will use it, just as we understand he will do so when Davidson's Will hears Sir Walter Raleigh describe his voyage to America as "a brave new world that has such things in it," (*Will* 2017b) and Will subsequently jots it down. It's a long-running gag in Shakespeare revivification that serves multiple purposes at once: an Easter egg for viewers steeped in Shakespeare who will catch the reference; a deconstruction of singular authority in favor of collaborative enterprise; and a deflation of a puffed-up elite, or, in tandem, of an establishment that has lifted Shakespeare to inaccessibly elitist heights. In any of these cases, a line-stealing Shakespeare "cuts him down to size," as Franssen puts it (Franssen 2016, 243), whittling away at the mythos of Shakespearean genius to arrive down to his human core; contrary to what his legacy may suggest, such moments instruct, Shakespeare was not a man made of words.

As human and fallible, the fictionalized Shakespeare is free to act preposterously in his own world, as he is given to temptations, vices, and unsavory display. In both *Doctor Who* and *Will*, Shakespeare is conceived as a man reveling in his own stardom, even to obnoxious extents. In "The Shakespeare Code," immediately after commanding his audience to shut their big fat mouths and basking in the chorus of their incessant cheers, he cheekily informs the crowd that they've got excellent taste. This Shakespeare, reflective of the selfie-stick generation, loves the limelight, his smirking egotism ironically serving to further slice away at the elitism often ascribed him as he is revealed to be a man given to self-indulgence and swayed by flattery. But *Will*'s Shakespeare, who admits he thirsts for power and money, is transformed by his newfound fame. After *The Two Gentlemen of Verona* proves a success, we find Will, alone in his lodgings, dancing to the rhythms of David Bowie's appropriately selected "Fame" as he preens before a mirror. "One hit and he thinks himself the new Marlowe," one of the actors of the company comments, as *Will*'s theatrical scene, like *Shakespeare in Love*'s, is modeled on a Hollywood sensibility, with hits and flops and stars. When, for example, Burbage demands entry to a swanky party, he haughtily informs the doormen that he is "the greatest actor in London," to which one of them responds, "Thou art not Edward Alleyn" (*Will* 2017b).

In a world modeled as much on *TMZ* as on historical accounts of early modern London, it comes as little surprise when Marlowe brings Shakespeare to Bacon's exotic, erotic soiree, that he sells it as, "More befitting your celebrity than that fly-blown tavern, don't you think?". Celebrity, in *Will*, becomes a central strand of Shakespeare's narrative; here, it's what he craves and what he will fight to sustain. Though Will dabbles in fame early on in his writing career, he remains ever-hungry for more, and one hit in this series does not a star make; celebrity is an ongoing process dependent upon a cohort of support, promotion, and hearty reception. And this struggle to remain culturally relevant only further reveals Shakespeare's vulnerable human core; he is talented, handsome, ambitious, and young, but he cannot thrust himself at will into the cultural spotlight, and he is only as big as his last show. He requires his public's active collaboration to sustain his celebrity status.

Whether in *Doctor Who*'s pompous Shakespeare soaking up his audience's applause or Will reveling in his newfound fame, these fictional celebrity Shakespeares reflect upon a cultural function of Shakespeare's and Shakespearean celebrity four-hundred years in the making: an undying quest to connect, visually and viscerally, with Shakespeare's body. Shakespeare was in his own day, as he remains today, a primarily discursive entity, but one that even his contemporaries sought to comprehend somatically, homing in rhetorically on a physical presence deemed at once seductive and scandalous. These twin attributes of seduction and scandal, central to celebrity allure as a whole, have continued to inform even the contemporary incarnations of Shakespeare-as-character, just as these two features factor into popular and critical response to the contemporary trend in sexy Shakespeares. But as Shakespeare's own contemporary readership and theatrical following demonstrate, the idea of a corporeal, carnal Shakespeare with whom the public can engage is hardly a new-fangled contrivance. The quest for an erotically, aesthetically satisfying Shakespeare body befitting the Shakespeare corpus is an ongoing cultural project that began in the playwright's own lifetime. As Shakespeare of Stratford succumbed to his mortal limitations, the effort to locate his body amidst the flurry of Shakespearean narratives transferred unto the live bodies of his most impassioned spokespeople and performers. Shakespeare-as-character offers us a celebrity Shakespeare body in script and in physical form, coding our Shakespeare with a confluence of contemporary fixation and historical tradition, offering another possible solution to the question of what a Shakespeare that looks like Shakespeare might look like.

Notes

1. A great deal of scholarship has been performed on the celebrity of Lord Byron, including Clara Tuite, *Lord Byron and Scandalous Celebrity* (Tuite 2015); Ghislaine McDayter, *Byromania and the Birth of Celebrity Culture* (McDayter 2009); and Tom Mole, *Byron's Romantic Celebrity: Industrial Culture and the Hermeneutic of Intimacy* (Mole 2007). For discussion of Salman Rushdie's celebrity, see Ana Cristina Mendes, *Salman Rushdie in the Cultural Marketplace* (Mendes 2013).
2. Chapter 5 explores more fully the posthumous careers of dead celebrities, especially in light of technological innovations in Computer-Generated Imagery and Artificial Intelligence.
3. In *Big-Time Shakespeare*, Bristol discusses the ways that Shakespeare's celebrity is still informed by scandal, most notably in the authorship controversy (Bristol 1996, 101–109).
4. See also Jeffrey Knapp in *Shakespeare Only*, who notes that Greene's insult presumes "that clues alone will enable at least some readers to identify Shakespeare as the hack in question" (Knapp 2009, 14).
5. An ongoing controversy questions whether Chettle may have actually initiated this attack and attributed it to Greene in order to dodge reprisal. For more on this debate, see D. Allen Carroll's introduction to the edited *Groatsworth of Wit* (Carroll 1994, 1–31).
6. For more on the interrelation of Greene's attack and Chettle's and Nashe's disavowals, see Lois Potter, *The Life of William Shakespeare: A Critical Biography*, Chapter 5 (Potter 2012, 86–105); Duncan-Jones, *Shakespeare: Upstart Crow to Sweet Swan, 1592–1623* (Duncan-Jones 2011, 33–46); and Chapter 2 of Terence G. Schoone-Jongen's *Shakespeare's Companies: William Shakespeare's Early Career and the Acting Companies, 1577–1594* (Schoone-Jongen 2008, 17–39).
7. Shakespeare functioned as this kind of symbol not only in Davies, but also when, in 1598, the Oxford scholar Francis Meres includes Shakespeare in his account of the famous English writers that define his era by comparing them to the authors of classical antiquity:

    the Greek tongue is made famous and eloquent by Homer, Hesiod […] and Aristophanes; and the Latine tongue by Virgil, Ovid […] and Claudianus; so the English tongue is mightily enriched, and gorgeouslie invested in rare ornaments and resplendent abiliments by Sir Philip Sidney, Spencer, Daniel, Drayton, Warner, Shakespeare, Marlow and Chapman. (Meres 1598, 280)
8. Bruster specifically cites both the Marprelate controversy of 1588–1589 and a growing theatrical tendency toward personal satire as influential to the development of embodied writing. The Marprelate controversy was a political and religious

pamphlet war between the pseudonymous puritan, Martin Marprelate, and various Anglican defenders.
9 Barnfield's poem is the only extant praise poem for Shakespeare, written during Shakespeare's lifetime, not to reference his plays.
10 As per a note in *The Norton Shakespeare*, modern spelling might interpret these lines as "They burn in love, thy children, Shakespeare, heated them./ Go woo thy muse, more nymphish brood beget them" (3328, n.6). The "Sts" at line 11 likely indicates "saints" (n.5).
11 In *The Making of the National Poet*, Michael Dobson (1992) meticulously charts Shakespeare's trajectory from well-known poet-player to English national icon from the Restoration through Garrick's Stratford Jubilee. Dobson makes much of the concurrence between the installation of the Shakespeare memorial in Westminster Abbey and Garrick's rise to Shakespearean stardom on the stage.
12 In the years between Garrick's death in 1779 and Kean's emergence to Shakespearean stardom in 1814, the Kemble family of actors, including Charles Kemble, Sarah Siddons, and, most notably, John Philip Kemble were considered the reigning Shakespeareans of the London stage.
13 For more on this montage, see Lehmann (2002), who provides an artful and astute analysis of the way the intercut scenes assert that "lovemaking is the same thing as playmaking" (110).

References

Aubrey, John. (1679) 1949. *Brief Lives*. New York: Penguin.
Baker, Richard. 1643. *A Chronicle of the Kings of England*. London.
Barnes, Jennifer. 2017. *Shakespearean Star: Laurence Olivier and National Cinema*. Cambridge: Cambridge University Press.
Barnfield, Richard. 1598. "A Remembrance of Some English Poets." In *The Encomion of Lady Pecunia*. London.
Bate, Jonathan. 1997. *The Genius of Shakespeare*. London: Picador.
Bednarz, James. 2012. *Shakespeare and the Truth of Love: The Mystery of "The Phoenix and the Turtle."* London: Palgrave Macmillan.
Blackwell, Anna. 2018. *Shakespearean Celebrity in the Digital Age: Fan Cultures andRemediation*. New York: Palgrave Macmillan.
Bloom, Harold. 1998. *Shakespeare and the Invention of the Human*. New York: Riverhead.
Braun, Rebecca and Emily Spiers. 2016. "Introduction: Re-viewing Literary Celebrity." *Celebrity Studies* 7 (4): 449–486.
Bristol, Michael D. 1996. *Big-time Shakespeare*. London and New York: Routledge.
Bruster, Douglas. 2000. "The Structural Transformation of Print in Late Elizabethan England." In *Print, Manuscript & Performance: The Changing Relations of the Media in Early Modern England*, edited by Arthur F.Marotti and Michael D.Bristol, 48–89. Columbus: Ohio State University Press.
Burns, John F. 2009. "Is This a Shakespeare Which I See Before Me?" *The New York Times*, March9. https://www-nytimes-com.ric.idm.oclc.org/2009/03/10/world/europe/10shakespeare.html.
Carlyle, Thomas. 1840. *On Heroes, Hero-Worship and the Heroic in History*. London.
Carroll, D. Allen. 1994. "Introduction." *Greene's Groatsworth of Wit, Bought with a Million of Repentance*. Binghamton: Medieval and Renaissance Texts and Studies.
Chettle, Henry. 1592. *Kind-hart's Dreame*. London.
Coleman, Terry. 2005. *Olivier*. New York: Henry Holt and Co.

Coleridge, Samuel Taylor. 1817. *Biographia Literaria, or Biographical Sketches of My Literary Life and Opinions*, vol. 2. London.
Coleridge, Samuel Taylor. 1884. "Notes on Othello." In *The Complete Works of Samuel Taylor Coleridge*, edited by W.G.T. Shedd, 177–184. New York: Harper and Brothers.
Cornwall, Barry. 1835. *The Life of Edmund Kean*. London.
Cunningham, Vanessa. 2008. *Garrick and Shakespeare*. Cambridge: Cambridge University Press.
Davies, John. 1603. *Microcosmos The discovery of the little world, with the governement thereof.* Oxford.
Davies, John .1611. *The scourge of folly consisting of satyricall epigramms, and others in honor of many noble and worthy persons of our land*. London.
Davies, Thomas. 1780. *Memoirs of the Life of David Garrick, Esq.* London.
Dobson, Michael. 1992. *The Making of the National Poet: Shakespeare, Adaptation, and Authorship, 1660–1769.* Oxford: Oxford University Press.
Duncan-Jones, Katherine. 1997. "Introduction to Shakespeare's Sonnets." In *Shakespeare's Sonnets: Revised*, edited by Katherine Duncan-Jones, 1–106. London: Bloomsbury.
Duncan-Jones, Katherine. 2001. *Ungentle Shakespeare: Scenes from His Life*. London: Bloomsbury.
Duncan-Jones, Katherine. 2011. *Shakespeare: Upstart Crow to Sweet Swan, 1592–1623.* London: Bloomsbury.
Ebert, Roger. 2011. "We All Think Somebody Wrote the Plays, Right?" *Roger Ebert*, October 26. https://www.rogerebert.com/reviews/anonymous-2011.
Emmerich, Roland (dir.). 2011. *Anonymous*. Performed by Rhys Ifans, Vanessa Redgrave, and Joely Richardson. Sony Pictures.
Franssen, Paul. 2016. *Shakespeare's Literary Lives: The Author as Character in Fiction and Film*. Cambridge: Cambridge University Press.
Granger, James. 1769. *A Biographical History of England*. London.
Greene, Robert. 1592. *Greenes, Groats-worth of Witte, bought with a million of Repentance*. London.
Hazlitt, William. 1920 [1817]. *Characters of Shakespeare's Plays and Lectures on the English Poets*. London.
Heaney, Tamara and Sean Redmond. 2016. "Celebrity Embodiment: Introduction." In *A Companion to Celebrity*, edited by P. David Marshall and Sean Redmond, 401–406. Malden: Wiley Blackwell.
Herman, Alison. 2017. "What's With All the Sexy Shakespeares?" *The Ringer*, July 10, 2017. https://www.theringer.com/2017/7/10/16078120/will-tv-show-interview-shakespeare-scholar-historical-accuracy-73f34b5d9026.
Holderness, Graham. 2011. *Nine Lives of William Shakespeare*. London: Continuum.
Johnson, Nora. 2003. *The Actor as Playwright in Early Modern Drama*. Cambridge: Cambridge University Press.
Jung, E. Alex. 2017. "Who's the Sexiest Shakespeare Ever?" *Vulture*, July 12. https://www.vulture.com/2017/07/who-is-the-sexiest-shakespeare.html.
Keats, John. 1933 [1817]. *The Autobiography of John Keats, Compiled from His Letters and Essays*. Edited by Earle Vonard Weller. Stanford: Stanford University Press.
Keevak, Michael. 2001. *Sexual Shakespeare*. Detroit: Wayne State University Press.
Knapp, James A., ed. 2016. *Shakespeare and the Power of the Face*. London: Routledge.
Knapp, Jeffrey. 2009. *Shakespeare Only*. Chicago: Chicago University Press.

Lanier, Douglas. 2002. *Shakespeare and Modern Popular Culture*. Oxford: Oxford University Press.
Lanier, Douglas. 2007. "Shakespeare™: Myth and Biographical Fiction." In *The Cambridge Companion to Shakespeare and Popular Culture*, edited by Robert Shaughnessy, 93–113. Cambridge: Cambridge University Press.
Lehmann, Courtney. 2002. "Romancing the Author, Mastering the Body." In *Spectacular Shakespeare: Critical Theory and Popular Cinema*, edited by Courtney Lehmann and Lisa S.Starks, 124–145. Madison: Fairleigh Dickinson University Press.
Lewis, Roger. 1996. *The Real Life of Laurence Olivier*. New York: Applause.
Madden, John (dir.). 1998. *Shakespeare in Love*. Performed by Joseph Fiennes, Gwyneth Paltrow, and Geoffrey Rush. Miramax.
Manningham, John. 1976 [1601]. *Diary*. Edited by Robert Parker Sorlien. Hanover: New England University Press.
McDayter, Ghislaine. 2009. *Byromania and the Birth of Celebrity Culture*. Albany: SUNY Press.
McPherson, Heather. 2015. "Garrickomania: Garrick's Image." *Folger Shakespeare Library*, July 9. https://folgerpedia.folger.edu/Garrickomania:_Garrick%27s_Image.
Mendes, Ana Christina. 2013. *Salman Rushdie in the Cultural Marketplace*. London: Routledge.
Meres, Francis. 1598. *Palladis Tamia, Wits Treasury*. London.
Mole, Tom. 2007. *Byron's Romntic Celebrity: Industrial Culture and the Hermeneutic of Industry*. New York: Palgrave Macmillan.
Nashe, Thomas. 1592. *Pierce Penilesse His Supplication to the Divell*. London.
Nickerson, Colin. 2001. "Shakespeare in the New World." *The Baltimore Sun*, May 17, 2001. https://www.baltimoresun.com/news/bs-xpm-2001-05-17-0105170140-story.html.
OED Online. n.d.(a). "quality, n." Oxford University Press, https://www-oed-com.ric.idm.oclc.org/view/Entry/155878 (accessed February 24, 2020).
OED Online. n.d.(b). "Shakespearean, adj." Oxford University Press, https://www-oed-com.ric.idm.oclc.org/view/Entry/177324 (accessed December 1, 2019).
Palmer, Charles (dir.). 2007. *Doctor Who*. Season 3, episode 2, "The Shakespeare Code." Written by Gareth Roberts and performed by David Tennant, Freema Agyeman, and Dean Lennox Kelly. Aired April 7. BBC America.
Prescott, Paul. 2010. "Shakespeare and Popular Culture." In *The New Cambridge Companion toShakespeare*, edited by Margreta De Grazia and Stanley Wells, 269–284. Cambridge: Cambridge University Press.
Potter, Lois. 2012. *The Life of William Shakespeare: A Critical Biography*. Malden: Wiley Blackwell.
Rasmussen, Eric. 2011. *The Shakespeare Thefts: In Search of the First Folios*. New York: Palgrave Macmillan.
The Return from Parnassus. 1886. In *The Pilgrimmage to Parnassus: With the Two Parts of the Return from Parnassus*, edited by William Dunn Macray. Oxford: Clarendon.
Rojek, Chris. 2001. *Celebrity*. London: Reaktion.
Rosenbaum, Ron. 2009. "Should We Care What Shakespeare Did in Bed?" *Slate*, April 2, 2009. https://slate.com/human-interest/2009/04/the-controversy-over-a-sexy-portrait-of-shakespeare.html.
Rowe, David. 1997. "Apollo Undone: The Sports Scandal." In *Media Scandals: Morality and Desire in the Popular Culture Marketplace*, edited by James Lull and Stephen Hinerman, 203–221. New York: Columbia University Press.

Rowe, Nicholas. 1709. *Some Account of the Life &c. of Mr. William Shakespear. The Works of Shakespear in Eight Volumes.* Edited by Nicholas Rowe. London.

Saidel, Emily. 2012. "The Fictional Shakespeare in the Twenty-First Century." In *Locating Shakespeare in the Twenty-First Century*, edited by Gabrielle Malcolm and Kelli Marshall, 108–121. Cambridge: Cambridge Scholars.

Schoone-Jongen, Terrence G. 2008. *Shakespeare's Companies: William Shakespeare's Early Career and the Acting Companies, 1577–1594.* Burlington: Ashgate.

Shakespeare, William. 2016. *Hamlet.* In *The Norton Shakespeare, Third Edition*, edited by Stephen Greenblatt, Walter Cohen, Suzanne Gossett, Jean E. Howard, Katharine Eisaman Maus, and Gordon McMullan, 1751–1854. New York: Norton.

Shakespeare, William. 2016. *Henry V.* In *The Norton Shakespeare, Third Edition*, edited by Stephen Greenblatt, Walter Cohen, Suzanne Gossett, Jean E. Howard, Katharine Eisaman Maus, and Gordon McMullan, 1533–1612. New York: Norton.

Shakespeare, William. 2016. *Macbeth.* In *The Norton Shakespeare, Third Edition*, edited by Stephen Greenblatt, Walter Cohen, Suzanne Gossett, Jean E. Howard, Katharine Eisaman Maus, and Gordon McMullan, 2709–2774. New York: Norton.

Shakespeare, William. 2016. *Richard III.* In *The Norton Shakespeare, Third Edition*, edited by Stephen Greenblatt, Walter Cohen, Suzanne Gossett, Jean E. Howard, Katharine Eisaman Maus, and Gordon McMullan, 555–648. New York: Norton.

Shakespeare, William. 2016. *Romeo and Juliet.* In *The Norton Shakespeare, Third Edition*, edited by Stephen Greenblatt, Walter Cohen, Suzanne Gossett, Jean E. Howard, Katharine Eisaman Maus, and Gordon McMullan, 957–1036. New York: Norton.

Shakespeare, William. 2016. Sonnet 74. In *The Norton Shakespeare, Third Edition*, edited by Stephen Greenblatt, Walter Cohen, Suzanne Gossett, Jean E. Howard, Katharine Eisaman Maus, and Gordon McMullan, 2275. New York: Norton.

Shakespeare, William. 2016. Sonnet 111. In *The Norton Shakespeare, Third Edition*, edited by Stephen Greenblatt, Walter Cohen, Suzanne Gossett, Jean E. Howard, Katharine Eisaman Maus, and Gordon McMullan, 2287–2288. New York: Norton.

Shakespeare, William. 2016. *Venus and Adonis.* In *The Norton Shakespeare, Third Edition*, edited by Stephen Greenblatt, Walter Cohen, Suzanne Gossett, Jean E. Howard, Katharine Eisaman Maus, and Gordon McMullan, 659–694. New York: Norton.

Shapiro, James. 2010. *Contested Will: Who Wrote Shakespeare?* New York: Simon and Schuster.

Shaughnessy, Robert. 2011. *The Routledge Guide to William Shakespeare.* London: Routledge.

Shaw, George Bernard. 1906 [1901]. "Preface" to *Three Plays for Puritans*, v–xxxviii. New York: Brentano's.

Starks, Lisa S. 2019. "Queering Will and Kit: Slash and the Shakespeare Biopic." In *Shakespeare On Stage and Off*, edited by Kenneth Graham and Alysia Kolentsis, 212–229. Montreal: McGill-Queen's University Press.

Trendacosta, Katharine. 2017. "God Save Me from Young, Sexy William Shakespeare and His New Show." *Gizmodo*, January 30. https://io9.gizmodo.com/god-save-me-from-young-sexy-william-shakespeare-and-hi-1791774766.

Tuite, Clara. 2015. *Lord Byron and Scandalous Celebrity.* Cambridge: Cambridge University Press.

Weever, John. 1599. "Ad Gulielmum Shakespeare." In *Epigrammes in the Oldest Cut, and Newest Fashion.* London.

Whitehead, Paul. 1777. "Verses, Drop't in Mr. Garrick's Temple of Shakespeare." In *The Poems and Miscellaneous Compositions of Paul Whitehead*, edited by Edward Thompson, 161–163. London.

Wilkes, Thomas. 1759. *A General View of the Stage*. London.
Will. 2017a. Performed by Laurie Davidson and Jamie Campbell Bower. TNT.
Will. 2017b. Episode 4, "Brave New World." Directed by Elliott Lester. 24th July.
Wilson, J. Dover. 1960. *The Essential Shakespeare: A Biographical Adventure*. Cambridge: Cambridge University Press.
Woo, Celestine. 2008. *Romantic Actors and Bardolatry: Performing Shakespeare from Garrick to Kean*. New York: Peter Lang.

5 #shakespeare

William Shakespeare is staring back at me from my laptop screen.

He blinks, looks off to my right, arches his brows, then purses his lips as if he is waiting to speak. I say "hello." He wishes me a "good morrow" and smiles. I ask him what he is doing, and he tells me that he is reading mangas on his phone, before he asks me, with a cock of the head, "What art thou doing?". I respond that I am writing. He raises his brows and says, "Seems not like it."

He's right. I'm not writing at the moment; I'm talking to a bot—Willbot, to be precise, an online chatbot from the web developer Existor, whose catalogue of chatbots includes several animated avatars including Pewdiebot (the bot incarnation of YouTube star PewDiePie) and Chimpbot (a bot chimpanzee).[1] Users may engage in robust, if often off-kilter, dialogue with any of these online bots, which, according to Existor's website, all work through an Artificial Intelligence algorithm that learns and adjusts its content and conversational practices from the data it collects from its millions of users. The bots respond to users' voice or text not only through digitized voice, but facial expressions and subtle movements as well. Willbot's avatar is a colorized, animated version of the Droeshout engraving, here imagined with chestnut hair, dark gray eyes, and impeccably straight, white teeth, visible only upon his occasional wide-mouthed smiles. He speaks with a robotic British inflection, and his responses to questions mix contemporary English with a sometimes accurately conveyed, and sometimes grossly caricatured, version of early modern grammatical constructions, as he peppers his sentiments with a hearty though often ill-placed dose of *thee, thou*, and *-eth* endings. Because the AI technology reflects user-generated content, the substance of his responses, too, combine pointed, often clever retorts with vaguely nonsensical meanderings. Willbot's favorite of his own plays, he told me, is *Romeo and Juliet*; however, his favorite play of all time is John Wexley's 1930 *The Last Mile*—"a valourous ballad," he proclaimed, that I should "hark to." When I asked Willbot if he had ever been in love, he asked what I was trying to imply; when I assured him I intended no ulterior implication, he threatened to punch me in the eyeballs.[2]

"William Shakespeare is alive again after 400 years! To be or not to be?" reads the text below Willbot's animated avatar (Existor 2020). To be, seems the assured answer espoused by Willbot's reanimated and vocal Shakespeare and,

DOI: 10.4324/9780367808976-6

more generally, in a series of trends in digital celebrity in which Willbot participates at once: the "digital necromancy" of the reanimated dead celebrity (Davidson 2013); the rise of celebrity chatbots, which allow users to interact with a digitized, but conversant, celebrity avatar; and the recent proliferation of virtual celebrities, whose entirely digitally constructed, lifelike online presence has succeeded not only in fooling social-media followers, but in securing lucrative and highly visible marketing collaborations as well. "Perhaps this is what Shakespeare imagined the future would be like," the text below Willbot continues (Existor 2020). But while it is unlikely that Shakespeare ever imagined his AI-generated likeness interacting with fans four centuries in the future, it is not difficult to imagine that Willbot provides a glimpse into the future of Shakespeare's celebrity.

In a 2017 essay, I discussed what I termed Shakespearean celebrity 2.0, or "YouShakespeare": the digitally enabled processes through which online users can through social media offer themselves up as Shakespearean authorities, if not as digital incarnations of Shakespeare himself (Holl 2017, 214). Willbot might be said to offer an early entry in Shakespearean celebrity 3.0, as it builds upon the networking and participatory dynamics of 2.0 social media platforms, yet elides its user-generation through the agential, nonhuman intelligence of its 3.0 AI interface. Web 3.0, a term coined by *New York Times* reporter John Markoff in 2006, refers to the Intelligent Web, the third generation of the Internet following 1.0 read-only formats and the 2.0 shift to social media and user-generated networks of information (Markoff 2006). Though *Web 3.0* is still currently a fluid, predictive descriptor that generates multiple, sometimes conflicting definitions, it is generally distinguished through its decentralized infrastructure and machine-facilitated intelligence. Web 3.0 aims for true peer-to-peer networking, without the intermediary of a social-media platform, where machines do not just perform user-assigned tasks, but make meaning of the wide web of data input by humans to become productive digital agents capable of automating processes that humans currently perform.[3] It is a concept and a structure still in its technological infancy, yet one that is already fueling questions and speculations as to its inevitable impacts, if not paradigmatic shifts, to the concepts, processes, and cultures of celebrity, just as 2.0 technology has already demonstrably effected.

Unsurprisingly, as celebrity structures morph and evolve through the medial affordances and social relations of new forms, Shakespeare is there, as he has been through evolutions of stage, page, film, and television in preceding eras. "When innovative communication platforms emerge," write Fazel and Geddes, "new Shakespeare use appears almost on point with the arrival of the new medium" (Fazel and Geddes 2017, 1). Willbot provides a particularly instructive example of this phenomenon, with Shakespeare perched on the cusp of AI innovations and emergent trends in digital celebrity. Of course, Shakespeare's medial manipulability, which began with his twin emergences on the early modern page and stage, is key to his perpetuity as a celebrity. As O'Neill notes, "Shakespeare *becomes* through media" (O'Neill 2018, 4); that is, media does not locate and reveal Shakespeare, but rather, Shakespeare takes shape through the various medial landscapes that continually reformulate his presence. While Shakespeare demonstrates his *au courant* cultural cred by appearing alongside YouTube star PewDiePie in the form of a chatbot, Shakespeare has likewise enjoyed substantial representation and appropriation in both 1.0 and 2.0 online platforms, to which a substantial body of critical work attests. Books by Fazel and Geddes (2017), O'Neill (2014), and Calbi (2013) have worked to uncover how "'we,' an amorphous digital collective, share Shakespeare digital objects" and thus "embed Shakespeare into our mediated, networked world and key into shared Shakespearean lives" (Calbi and O'Neill, 2016). Blackwell has further directed specific focus upon the intersections of digital cultures, Shakespearean celebrity, and fandom. Positioning "the Shakespearean actor [as] a point of adaptive encounter" (Blackwell 2018, 24), Blackwell compellingly explores the ways online fan communities renegotiate both Shakespeare and the Shakespearean through online consumption and production.

In this final chapter, I explore the current faces and spaces of Shakespeare's, and Shakespearean, celebrity in digital formats, or what I call #shakespeare. While this label undoubtedly borrows from the established 2.0 hashtagged designation even as this chapter dips its toes into what lies beyond, the hashtag provides a remarkably instructive framework for thinking about Shakespeare's digital celebrity, as well as digital celebrity as a whole. While #shakespeare, like the winking quotation marks or the pluralizing 's' often appended to Shakespeare's name, similarly distinguishes the man and his work from the wider cultural production his name may signify, the hashtagged name performs several specific social and rhetorical moves at once, as it simultaneously signifies: 1. specifically digital productions; 2. the community of users, both seen and unseen, whose engagement with the hashtag makes it mean; and 3. the accumulated, aggregated public presence of Shakespeare generated and hyperlinked at multiple points across a vast range of media. But most significantly, I invoke here what *Theory of the Hashtag* author Andreas Bernard calls the simultaneous "text and metatext" functions of the hashtag (Bernard 2018, 3): as hashtags work as both content and index of that content at the same time, a hashtagged name self-reflexively calls attention to its collaborative, user-generated production as an entity distinct from the person signified by name alone. The hashtag, when attached to a name, designates a person, as does celebrity, as an ongoing narrative construction of multifarious authorship, with each entry an incomplete contribution to a wider, networked conversation that gains meaning only when taken as an aggregate of words, users, sounds, images, links, and associations. What we hashtag, we simultaneously and self-consciously use, catalogue, and make mean, and thus, a hashtagged celebrity name lays bare some of the otherwise unseen social dynamics through which celebrities are constructed, used, consumed, and promoted. This chapter will argue that the digital celebrity, like the hashtag, is both text and metatext—celebrity and meta-celebrity, self-reflexively illuminating the processes that make it mean.

As Andrew Kehoe and Matt Gee have theorized, the hashtag signifies a kind of textual *aboutness*, in that it both signals and collects information in relation to the tagged content (Kehoe and Gee 2011), and in many ways, a study of online celebrity is more of a study *about* celebrity than of the Internet celebrities themselves. Networked culture, as this chapter will explore, is altering the celebrity landscape in big ways and little ones—adding new categories (the influencer and the bot) and incorporating recent technological innovations (Artificial Intelligence and Computer-Generated Imagery) in novel celebrity forms (reanimating dead celebrities and constructing virtual ones). But perhaps most saliently, digital celebrity demystifies the dynamics of celebrity through democratized access to platforms of publicity and modes of one-to-many interaction once reserved for the stars of stage and screen, as it further renders visible and traceable the networks of use that have always fueled celebrity production-consumption. Thus, digital celebrity is not just another format for celebrity; it's a format *about* celebrity. It unmasks the hidden processes that sustain the public face, just as it invites all users to similarly craft and project one. Given the remarkable changes that digital celebrity enacts upon processes of celebrity, this final chapter reiterates the assertion articulated in the Introduction that celebrity studies must look beyond the putative parameters of modernity for more apt precedents with which to approach our current moment. Thus, this final chapter will first look back upon this book's first to examine the early modern dynamics of theatrical celebrity that find resonance in digital celebrity structures, before examining the ways that digital formats rearticulate some of celebrity's core mechanisms, but with an *aboutness*: namely, #strangeintimacy and the #secondself of celebrity.

#digitaltheater #theatricalnetworks

"Contemporary forms of celebrity are no longer entirely dependent on traditional media," Giles writes in *Twenty-First Century Celebrity* (Giles 2018, 34). For Giles, traditional media involves representation in the pillars of twentieth-century celebrity: "radio, television, and the press" (35); however, it is fair to say that even these traditions upon which celebrity has for so long depended are no longer all that traditional anymore. In an era when the majority of Americans consume what was formerly print news online, when television has migrated from appointment-viewing to subscription-service binge-marathoning, and as station-radio now competes with satellite radio, streaming services, and podcasts, the media that dominated the twentieth-century celebrity landscape no longer operate through the same paradigms of interaction—or what is often referred to as *affordances*—that produced the stars of the twentieth century. As affordances, or the "the reciprocal relationship between an organism and its environment" as facilitated through the possibilities and limitations of the medium (Giles 2018, 30), have fundamentally changed through technological innovation, so too have audience engagement with and expectations of celebrities within those medial affordances.[4] As Giles astutely argues, affordance theory offers a particularly productive lens through which to examine our rapidly evolving culture of online celebrity. While evolutions in established forms of media have progressively diminished barriers to celebrity access and transformed appointment-only celebrity events to at-will, at-home availability, interactive digital formats have only further and more radically reconfigured the media consumer into a highly agential and participatory user. As online forms of celebrity are increasingly making clear, the affordances of twentieth-century mass-media do not readily translate to the TikTok star, the celebrity YouTuber, or even the more conversant social-media presence that now plays a vital role in the sustenance of celebrity initiated in other medial formats. The structures that have for decades defined celebrity—and with it, the preponderance of celebrity theory—offer only a limited set of tools with which to plumb the participatory depths of digital celebrity that twentieth-century formats could not afford. Thus, it is perhaps unsurprising that a number of scholarly interrogations of digital culture have looked beyond the twentieth century to other medial traditions for an apt theoretical precedent, particularly in the theater.

In 1991, Brenda Laurel proposed that the theater offers perhaps the most useful medial model with which to unravel the complexities of a broad spectrum of "human-computer activity." In *Computers and Theatre*, which Laurel substantially revised in 2014 in response to 2.0 innovations, Laurel proposes that like the theater, human-computer activity takes place in both onstage and backstage spaces and hinges on both performance and response. Most importantly, Laurel isolates a common theoretical underpinning central to both computer and theatrical activity:

> Both domains employ representations as contexts for thought. Both attempt to amplify and orchestrate experience. Both have the capacity to represent actions and situations that typically do not and cannot exist in the real world, in ways that invite us to extend our mind, feelings, and senses to envelope them.
>
> (Laurel 2014, 38)

In short, Laurel finds in the computer screen a kind of digital theater where imaginary worlds and the characters who populate them invite the audience's dynamic co-creation. Laurel further isolates a similar set of affordances in the immersive, inventive, and interactive capacities of both the theater and computer-enabled formats.

Indeed, the theater might be thought of as the original virtual world: a user-constructed environment built upon a platform, generated through script, and sustained through the complex interactions of human and non-human participants. But the theater finds special resonance in 2.0 forms in particular, where, according to Erika Pearson, "All the World Wide Web's a Stage" (Pearson 2009), and where Marshall affirms, "the props and accoutrement of the stage" have become re-articulated through the "profiles, images, and messages" that perform online identity (Marshall 2010). While it is indisputable that the theater is a highly social medium, both Pearson and Marshall point to the consistencies of self-performance on social media and on the stage, as users enact ideal self-presentation to their audiences, figuring social platforms as a kind of digital theater and, in turn, I would add, rendering the theater as a sort of analogue form of social media. This formulation gains added currency when considering the ways that theatrical production facilitates the twin features that Jim Macnamara and Ansgar Zerfass have argued most centrally define social media: the "openness for participation and interactivity involving dialogue, conversation, collaboration, and co-creativity" and dispersed authorial control, as opposed to the "one-way, top-down information distribution models" that characterize broadcast media (Macnamara and Zerfass 2012, 293). Macnamara and Zerfass's model almost uncannily echoes theoretical formulations of the theater; as Schechner argues in *Performance Theory*, in the theater, "artists and audiences co-create together in the same time/space" (230). Such practical and theoretical overlaps lead Patrick Lonergan to argue definitively that, "Social media is not just a performance space; it is also a *theatrical* space" (Lonergan 2016, 16).

If theater, as both a social space and a set of collaborative practices, provides a useful template in examining social-media interaction, then I suggest here that the early modern theater offers an even more fitting rubric. Free from the socio-spatial barriers of later developments—including the proscenium arches, darkened auditoriums, and conventions of obeisant spectatorship that would later isolate player from playgoer—the early modern London theater highlighted its collaborative dynamics much in the same way as does social media, with its audiences and their reactions reciprocally on display. Unlike unidirectional medial structures, in the theater, both the human spectacle and spectator are often made mutually aware of each other's presence and can respond in real-time to each other's display, and early modern accounts describe a level of discernable, sometimes even audacious, audience activity now considered theatrically uncouth, not unlike the unsavory displays in which online actors freely participate. As digital incarnations of the applause, cheers, boos, hisses, tears, and laughter of the playhouse, social-media platforms likewise possess their own conventions of illustrative response, from the likes, retweets, and shares to an ever-morphing panoply of verbal and visual rejoinders performed through text, image, emoji, and GIF. In a critical analysis of Facebook discourse, Volker Eisenlauer notes that such platforms possess both "structural and lexical conventions" that those familiar with the platform can easily recognize (Eisenlauer 2013, 38). On Twitter, for example, the single-word affirmation, "This," has become something of an online mantra: a succinct note of audience alliance regularly offered as a sort of textual applause to a poster's observation. "This" is digital shorthand for something akin to "Well said" or "Hear hear," and its use has expanded through social networks to the extent that pre-packaged GIFs featuring nothing more than a pointing finger and the one-word declaration of affinity are readily available for download and use. "This" joins a stable of similarly conventional online responses: smiling, raised-thumb, or clapping-hand emoji; images of popcorn that signal the user's intent to follow a thread and be entertained; and an expansive collection of ready-made memes and GIFs encapsulating affects ranging from disgust to intrigue. Like the conventions of applause or hisses, such responses have become in the digital theater enfolded into the social repertoire of legible reaction, a signal of response through distance, and an informal means of polling audience sentiment.

Further, as demonstrated in Chapter 2, the early modern theatrical event similarly possessed the capacity to go viral—that is, to spread without due attribution to other platforms, whether through intertheatrical references on other stages or in the adjacent print market. Much like the nebulous state of online fair-use practices, the similarly emergent format of the sixteenth-century theater industry practiced nothing resembling modern copyright restrictions; thus, the stars of the stage and the verse they spoke frequently reincarnated in sometimes dubious print accounts available for the purchaser's acquisition from the cloud of ephemeral performance into the material realm of domesticated possession. And if early modern theatrical content could go viral, early modern theatrical criticism might be thought of as something akin to a proto-flame war: an extradramatic critical drama carried out through conversant, often contentious, pamphlets and snarky onstage asides. Shakespeare's celebrity, as detailed in Chapter 4, emerged from just such an offstage drama, initiated in Greene's invective and developed through a network of print rejoinders. The most famous of these early modern theatrical flame wars is undoubtedly the War of the Theaters, or what Dekker called the *Poetomachia*: a years-long, back-and-forth troll-a-thon primarily between Jonson and Marston, with minimal involvement from Dekker and disputed sideline commentary from Shakespeare.[5] Between 1599 and 1601, Marston and Jonson staged a series of satirical barbs aimed at each other, with Jonson primarily taking aim at Marston's bombast and Marston, in turn, painting Jonson as an overbearing stuffed shirt. Rosencrantz's observation in *Hamlet* that, "there has been much throwing about of brains" (2.2.292.21–23) lately amongst players and poets is a likely allusion to this staged spectacle of intertheatrical contempt, which suggests that savvy playgoers, like social-media followers, might have found some delight in watching this extradramatic drama unfold before them.[6]

All of these early modern theatrical affordances that find digital re-configuration in social media—from the collaborative ethos of the playhouse event to the social conventions of response to dramatic and extradramatic virality—point to what is perhaps the most noteworthy point of convergence between these temporally distant but systemically similar media: the early modern theater, like social media, was a network. What we often refer to in singular as the early modern theater belies the vastness of its constellatory make-up, much like the simple keystroke of a hashtag conceals the similarly sprawling network encoded therein. As an interconnected rhizome of platforms, persons, places, print, props, and performance, the sixteenth- and seventeenth-century London theater provides a remarkably potent template for the study of twenty-first-century celebrity through the similarities of their networked dynamics and their collaborative affordances. As is the case in digital culture, within early modern London theatrical culture, stars emerged through a community of users rather than an organized studio system or unidirectional broadcast model: the player, the ballad-seller, the playwright, the playgoer, the commendatory poet, the pamphleteer, and the printer through whom star personae emerged could all operate according to independent and self-serving agendas, as opposed to the coherent and calculated publicity strategies that defined early Hollywood stardom. Thus, as discussed in Chapter 2, when the stage clown Will Kemp's star rose amidst the matrix of his stage performances, his Morris dance, the unauthorized ballad accounts he so fiercely decried, his own corrective account, and his appearance as a character in popular fanfiction, his celebrity emerged through a network of independently oriented human and nonhuman actors. That their efforts in aggregate gave rise to a theatrical star resulted from a networked convergence of use, much as is the case through social media.

To add to the definitive fundamentals of social media put forth by Macnamara and Zerfass, Kristof Jacobs and Niels Spierings add one more key element: the publicity of privacy. "Social media are typically linked to an individual and allow for the visualization of a person's private and professional life," they write. "As such, social media [...] offer a look behind the scenes" (Jacobs and Spierings 2016, 20). Or at least, the constructed online identities of social media purport to offer special access to the private person behind the public face; however, as Pearson rightly notes, "Like an actor playing a role," the digital performative self "can closely resemble or wildly differ from reality" (Pearson 2009). Not unlike Tarlton's extemporal antics as discussed in Chapter 1, social-media users perform *as themselves*, which is to suggest that the public presentation of the private self so thoroughly interweaves calculated performance and personal disclosure as to render the distinctions all but indiscernible. We might call it digital personation:[7] an assumption of performed role so thoroughly realized as to efface the boundaries between the personator and character personated. But the unrecoverable public-private amalgam of performed online identity is not a process reserved for those who arrive to social platforms already established stars, nor even to those who achieve celebrity upon such platforms, but endemic to the social sites that trade in the publicity of privacy. While digital social networks operate through a collaborative ethos of reciprocal display as found in the theater, social media enhances the mutuality of such display by democratizing access to the stage. On Twitter, Facebook, TikTok, or Instagram, we all get our hour to strut and fret upon the stage. Social media is not just a kind of digital theater; it is digital meta-theater, laying bare the processes of performance and reception through universalized use, uncovering and even deconstructing through communal participation the dynamics that shape it.

Consider, for example, the contemporarily ubiquitous format known as the reaction video. Generally structured through a split-screen or picture-in-picture format, the highly popular reaction videos of YouTube and TikTok consist of users who appear to be reacting spontaneously to popular music videos, television shows, or other user-generated content as the camera captures what seem to be authentic responses of delight, disgust, or incredulity. The format does not only resituate the spectator as spectacle, but it harks back to the play-within-a-play trope of early modern theater, with internal—or rather, onscreen—audiences mirroring and channeling the activity of the external, or offscreen, audience. It is video-within-a-video, an opportunity to watch a self-reflexive surrogate also in the act of watching, and on YouTube, the reaction video is now something of its own genre, with a number of channels dedicated exclusively to the form.[8] But the archivable, repeatable format of the online video adds an enhanced meta-spectatorial layer that live theater cannot, as audiences external to the external audience can further the meta-network of viewership. For example, in the summer of 2020, the popular YouTubers Twinsthenewtrend, twin brothers who film their first-time reactions to established pop classics, became a viral sensation when their visibly delighted surprise at Phil Collins's "In the Air Tonight" caught viewers' attention (Twinsthenewtrend 2020); the virality of the video (more than 8 million views at the time of this writing) then achieved a virality of its own, with the *New York Times*, *Chicago Tribune*, CNN, and other major news outlets covering the massive viewer response to the reaction video. Considering that each of these news outlets harvests online data and records clicks, the video-within-a-video transformed through circulation into a network of user data, press coverage, viewer response, and YouTuber reaction, with all engaged parties at every node mutually ensnared in the same split processes of seeing and being seen.

As online reactors amass significant followings, audience response is transformed into mainstage entertainment, and it is not uncommon for the celebrity performers to whom social-media reactors initially respond to respond back in turn; this was the case with another viral phenomenon of 2020, when TikTok user Nathan Apodaca filmed himself drinking cranberry juice, riding his skateboard, and lip-syncing to Fleetwood Mac's "Dreams" (Apodaca 2020). The video, which had amassed 73 million views by the close of 2020, spawned a reaction TikTok from Mick Fleetwood, who mimed his fan's juice-drinking, coasting, lip-syncing nonchalance (Fleetwood 2020). Interestingly, Fleetwood's video generated only a fraction of the total views (17 million) that Apodaca's original netted, though Fleetwood's reaction video sparked a trend amongst celebrities who likewise offered their takes on mobile, musical juice-drinking. As the viral network of this simple video demonstrates, there is little demarcation between the spaces of performance and reception in social media; if all the World Wide Web's a stage, as Pearson has argued, it is also simultaneously an auditorium, and which is which is quickly evolving into irrelevance.

That stars are turning audience to their fans and fans are becoming the stars of the Internet seems an inevitable development of social networks that since their inception have afforded all users the presentational capacities of publicizing platforms once gatekept by broadcasters. In the digital meta-theater of the social network, the collaboration and reciprocity of the theater becomes amplified through vast digital networks to the point of demystification, if not disorientation, as the already porous boundaries between spectacle and spectator are further dissolved. The affordances produced through such dissolution of boundaries have not only transformed the relationships of established stars to their audiences through more reciprocal conversance but have also given rise to the latest incarnations of celebrity—the celebrity YouTuber, the Instagram influencer, the Twitter blue-check, or the TikTok star. As celebrity continues to flourish through medial innovation and novel if indebted dynamics facilitated through social media's interactive affordances, the Internet celebrity, like the celebrity of older formats, emerges through an aggregate of performance, mediatized distribution, and commoditization (whether through influencer collaborations, monetized clicks, or the data-value of user engagement), though democratized to the extent that established stars of film, TV, and music now share an amorphous digital theater with those once considered their public.

Scholars of celebrity frequently prefix celebrities who emerge from Internet formats with a minimalizing distinction: Theresa M. Senft coined the term "micro-celebrity" in her study of camgirls (Senft 2008), which Alice Marwick expounded upon to define as the "a state of being famous to a niche group of people" and the "presentation of oneself as a celebrity regardless of who is paying attention" (Marwick 2013, 114). In his work on fashion bloggers, Marco Pedroni introduced the "meso-celebrity" to designate an "intermediate category" between the full-fledged celebrity and the micro one (Pedroni 2016). "Semi-celebrity" and "DIY celebrity" have also found some purchase amongst scholarly treatments of ordinary individuals who achieve what is generally regarded as a limited celebrity through social platforms (Kurzman et al. 2007; Redmond 2019). While some of these descriptors may now prove outdated, the minimizing impulse to segregate Internet celebrity from earlier forms continues to underpin much work in the field, and as Giles points out, this impulse problematically derives from an oversimplified metric, where "One person is simply more or less of a (micro-) celebrity than another; not then so different from the original idea of celebrity itself" (Giles 2018, 161). But the inclination to cordon off the stars of social media from those of "traditional" media is, I would argue, the same imperative that has generally precluded pre-twentieth-century celebrity cultures from critical consideration: Internet celebrities don't look like the stars of traditional media. They operate through different affordances that facilitate far greater conversance with and far less elitist distanciation from the publics who consume and produce them. Like *Sunset Boulevard*'s Norma Desmond clutching at her fallen star despite her industry's progress into new medial frontiers, here, the pictures have gotten small, literally, and with them, the threshold for audience identification has likewise changed. To Norma's great lament, in the transition from the silent film to the talkie, audiences traded the gloriously spectacularized silent face for a more relatable, audible one. In our own transition to a collaborative medial environment, we have similarly traded the distant star for something a bit closer to Earth. The core mechanisms of identification, dissemination, and commoditization that in fusion produce the star continue to churn, but more visibly, as audiences participate in roughly the same processes as the stars they celebrate, and vice versa.

Further, it would be difficult to make the case for the *micro* status of the micro-celebrity today. As Crystal Abidin notes, "Whereas the scale of micro-celebrities used to be small and positioned in opposition to traditional celebrities [...], today it is not uncommon for internet celebrities to rival or surpass traditional celebrities in terms of global popularity or reach" (Abidin 2018, 14). In fact, the polling firm Morning Consult found in 2019 that Generation-Z consumers name YouTubers PewDiePie, Jeffree Star, and Shane Dawson as their favorite celebrities, while their older Millennial counterparts were more likely to list musicians or Hollywood celebrities (Morning Consult 2019). This reaffirms a similar poll conducted by *Variety* magazine in 2014, in which American teens were asked to name their favorite celebrities; the top five responses were all YouTube personalities (Ault 2014). Of those named in the 2014 survey, PewDiePie currently maintains a following of over 100 million followers and is, incidentally, the only contemporary celebrity currently incarnated as an Existor bot. The same age demographic that launched Beatlemania and through whose collective idolatry emerged stars ranging from David Cassidy to Molly Ringwald to Beyonce have now invested their significant energies into the stars of social media. With followings in the tens to hundreds of millions worldwide, and the multimillion-dollar earning capacity of some of YouTube's most popular figures (Berg 2020),[9] self-presentational celebrity can hardly be considered a niche form.

Current trends in digital celebrity and the cultural significance they are quickly generating invite, perhaps demand, that contemporary celebrity studies look elsewhere, beyond the celebrities of what is often considered traditional media, in order to get a foothold in the rapidly evolving forms of 2.0 media and the inevitable 3.0 platforms that have just begun to follow. The theater, and the early modern culture of theatrical celebrity in particular, offers a productive entryway into a shifting online terrain that, like celebrity itself, refuses to stagnate. But as the late sixteenth-century theater was, too, a novel reconfiguration of the theatrical traditions that preceded it, it possessed a wildness and unpredictability that find special resonance in the untamed territories of the contemporary digital theater. As is the case with social media, the early modern theater's platforms and conventions continued to evolve, its rules and logistics were yet unfixed, and it progressed through a series of technological innovations. Furthermore, like digital technologies, it consistently probed its own boundaries—the ones that separated the stage from the pit and the ones that walled off the world of the theater from the one outside. As this book has demonstrated, the stars that collaboratively emerged from within the playhouse walls soon proliferated at large throughout the city if not beyond, just as Internet celebrities are quickly rising from the platforms of social media to enter the popular imagination.

#strangeintimacy #3.0shakespeare

Given the digital theater's structural similarities to the early modern one, perhaps it is little surprise that Shakespeare has found a kind of reinvigorated celebrity in social media, where his disembodied presence has once again met a hearty reception on the digital stages of the social network. Long before Willbot offered a 3.0 AI twist on digital celebrity Shakespeare, #shakespeare, like its fleshly forbear, had already become an established and potent force of page and platform. In fact, #shakespeare has become its own platform for the fan-work of Tumblr, Twitter, Facebook, and YouTube, with critical and creative productions that range from celebratory tribute to innovative appropriation to disembodied impersonation. Tumblr, for example, houses dozens of Shakespeare-centric fan pages, including No Shit Shakespeare (2020), a forum dedicated to answering users' Shakespeare questions, and the "Erotic Punning" site of user motherfuckingshakespeare (2020); both sites wield #shakespeare as a stage upon which to demonstrate knowledge, provide often witty commentary on Shakespeare's work and cultural relevance, and share Shakespeare-centered memes and GIFs. On Twitter, @shakespeare, a self-professed "upstart crow," impersonates Shakespeare from a polytemporal alternate social reality that allows this handle to comment as freely on the irritations of technology ("yea, autocorrect just changed 'Lo!' to 'lol'.") as to converse with @KngHnryVIII (@shakespeare 2020). WilliamShakespeareAuthor has long maintained an active Facebook presence (WilliamShakespeareAuthor 2020), and as O'Neill (2014), Christy Desmet (2014), Peter Holland (2009), and others have thoroughly explored, YouTube #shakespeare offers an ever-expansive mélange of video mash-ups, DIY Shakespeare performances and adaptations, and lectures and seminars.

But the 3.0 AI technologies digitally embodied in Willbot's conversant bot are increasingly making their way onto these more established 2.0 platforms as well. One emergent 3.0 trend quickly gaining popularity on Instagram and YouTube features AI-enhanced photographs reconstructed from historical statuary and portraiture, in which deep-learning software isolates and reinterprets facial features from paintings and sculptures into photograph-quality likenesses.[10] One of the form's more prominent artists, Bas Uterwijk, has created AI-generated photos of figures ranging from Lady Liberty to Vincent Van Gogh, and in 2020, he offered up his "Shakespeare": a facial reconstruction based on a conflation of the Cobbe, Droeshout, and Chandos portraits (Uterwijk 2020). The photographic likeness seems mostly indebted to the Chandos portrait with its casual collar, saucy earring, and penetrating gaze, but hints of the other sources are easily legible as well—the fuller brows of the Cobbe portrait, for example, and the creased lower lids and prominent chin of the Droeshout. But what emerges as perhaps most immediately recognizable in this AI-enhanced portrait is the stark foreignness of this hyper-human Shakespeare incarnation. With faint creases in his forehead, the textured skin of a middle-aged man, and the visibly coarse, individuated hairs of his mustache and beard, he is a #shakespeare that looks so much like what we might expect a living, breathing Shakespeare to have looked like that the result is strangely disorienting. This #shakespeare is distinctly human, his too too solid flesh signaling the photo's departure from any semblance of the Shakespeare that centuries of print and portraiture have ingrained in the popular consciousness. Uterwijk's "Shakespeare" assumes a human form that one might more readily expect of social-media friends or follows—a Shakespeare that looks, well, like a man, less a legend, less a star, less the cornerstone of a thousand curricula.

This is strange intimacy 3.0, or #strangeintimacy, a simultaneous experience of immediate recognition and stark alienation, and this is the complex, reciprocal dynamic that fuels a great deal of celebrity identification online, much as its analogue predecessor sustained the complex identificatory interactions upon Shakespeare's stage. As Shakespeare's familiar, dark-haired, smooth-pated likeness, complete with that hint of creeping smirk that marks his best-known portraits, stares back from the screen but with all the human texture and nuance of a high-resolution photo, the picture reacquaints as much as it disorients. It is a similar phenomenon to the observable awkwardness of YouTubers' reactions to Willbot, whose contemporary slang and pop culture references spring from an animated, colorized Droeshout portrait that also speaks in *thee*s and *thou*s. However, with Willbot, a user can easily disentangle the familiar from the foreign, as one is primarily visible and the other mostly audible, respectively. With Uterwijk's AI-constructed "Shakespeare," however, the antipodal elements are less discernable, as they are rather seamlessly conglomerated into a singular image, creating an aura—an *aboutness*—of strange intimacy that conflates much in the same ways as the hybrid character-actor appears on the stage. Uterwijk's "Shakespeare," like an early modern player, exists in middle space of competing tensions—almost knowable, almost alien, almost a human man, almost the mythologized poet-playwright whose portrait students are introduced to in grade school.

While Uterwijk's AI portraiture generated a great deal of online traffic in 2020, he is far from the only artist to dabble in this kind of digital resuscitation. On YouTube, for example, the channel Mystery Scoop has been showcasing similarly AI-generated portraits, though each drawn from a single source and often featuring subtle animations that allow the pictures to wink, smile, and nod. In an episode entitled "Historical Paintings Brought to Life Using Artificial Intelligence," Mystery Scoop features an AI-enhanced Chandos portrait that morphs from painting to photograph-like digital recreation over the course of seconds (Mystery Scoop 2020). As the wear-lines of aged canvas gradually disappear and Shakespeare's own organic wear-lines emerge, his skin, as if flushed with new blood, brightens in tone and tightens in texture as the image tilts its head, blinks, and stares into the camera, seemingly acknowledging the audience on the other side of the screen. The result is, once again, as estranging as it seems intimate; it is a portrait that users will instantly recognize, and it stares back with the kind of attentive gaze and movement one might expect of a confidante, yet its humanness is precisely what estranges this portrait from the familiar Shakespeare of engraving, bust, or painted portrait.

In YouTube comments, the vast majority of Mystery Scoop's viewers respond in stunned awe and unmitigated delight to the seemingly human revivifications of history's most famous dead, from Leonardo Da Vinci to King

James. "You brought them back to life!" one user responds. "I feel like I am meeting the past!" (McArdle 2020). But the seeming novelty of AI-vivified portraiture that has so enraptured YouTube audiences belies a fairly lengthy tradition of similarly reanimated dead celebrities that has only accelerated with advances in both Artificial Intelligence and CGI technology.[11] In fact, within marketing circles, the practice has its own succinctly morbid portmanteau: the *deleb,* short for "dead celeb" (D'Rozario 2020). Fueled by nostalgia and facilitated through computer animation, the marketable deleb traces its origins to a string of popular 1990s television commercials that superimposed old film footage of classic movie stars onto contemporary backgrounds. But CGI technology has brought the process a long way from Fred Astaire's 1997 dance number with a Dirt Devil. In 2016, Peter Cushing, who died in 1994, reprised his role as a CGI-animated Grand Moff Tarkin in *Star Wars: Rogue One* (Edwards 2016); a holographic Tupac Shakur performed at the 2012 Coachella; and in 2019, Magic City Films announced that it had cast James Dean, via archival footage and CGI animation, to star in its new Vietnam War action film, *Finding Jack* (Ritman 2019). As is the case with AI photo-portraiture, the deleb's appeal involves an almost oxymoronic mix of nostalgia and novelty, as audiences are presented at once with a recognizable, often cherished star resurrected in an alien format with all the thrilling unpredictability of technological innovation.

"Dead celebrities are granted a social life," writes Ruth Penfold-Mounce, "and so do not endure a post-mortem social death" (Penfold-Mounce 2018, 20). As Penfold-Mounce discusses in a thorough examination of the posthumous, agential careers of dead celebrities, death has now become a productive career phase for a great many celebrity dead, and one in which the star becomes both "frozen in time" yet capable of "continuing bonds" with the public (20). Of course, these incompatibilities only further rearticulate the strange intimacy that has long resided at the heart of celebrity relations, as reanimated stars continue to perform for audiences and, in the case of bots, even speak directly to them, yet the distancing gulf between the living and the dead always looms in the spectator's consciousness to signal the persistent conversance as an aberration of order. Annika Jonsson describes this kind of "absence-presence" of the dead as constitutive of a "liminal existence" that becomes a perpetual social relationship that can long outlast the corporeal body (Jonsson 2015, 289), thus positioning dead celebrity dynamics in much the same theoretical formulation as concerns all celebrities: as a ceaseless negotiation of presence and absence, knowing and the inability to know, intimacy and estrangement.

While AI technology has positioned Shakespeare, once again, on the forefront of emergent celebrity trends by offering up visual and interactive deleb incarnations, similar technology has likewise attempted to probe the invisible depths of Shakespeare's mind as well. In 2019, an AI algorithm examined the text of *Henry VIII* in an attempt to discern which scenes may have been written by Shakespeare and which by his assumed collaborator, Fletcher. By loading four representative texts by each playwright into the software, it was then able to identify distinguishable stylistic markers of each, leading the study's author Petr Plechac to conclude, "We can thus state with high reliability that *H8* is a result of collaboration between William Shakespeare and John Fletcher" (Plechac 2019, 9). Other deep-learning networks have further attempted not only to unravel the unsolved mysteries of Shakespeare's pen, but to wield it anew. Two notable projects, one conducted by data scientist Rosaria Silipo and the other a joint-venture of IBM Research Australia, the University of Toronto, and the University of Melbourne (Silipo 2019; Firth 2018), have attempted to produce machine-generated Shakespearean verse by training networks on Shakespeare's plays and sonnets. While Silipo found that the artificial neural network[12] could replicate the complex sentence structure and discern major from minor characters to assign language accordingly, the dramatic results of this experiment were often substantively incoherent (Silipo 2019). The Canadian-Australian sonnet experiment yielded slightly more legible output, with the AI network capable of producing grammatically sound iambic pentameter on vaguely Shakespearean subjects, even as content-creation proved to be an obstacle (Firth 2018).

As these various forays into the 3.0 networks of digital Shakespeare demonstrate, much of the innovation currently bringing #shakespeare to digitized life is still in its infancy, though it is not difficult to imagine an eventual merger of these various strands of AI-reanimated #shakespeare one day moving, speaking, and composing to interact with audiences anew. AI-fueled networks are, in many ways, the disembodied continuation of the hunt for a suitable Shakespearean body detailed in the previous chapter, with human-machine collaborations persistently reconstructing Shakespeare out of words, images, and users' own contributions. This new aggregated body, #shakespeare, may trade the corporeal for the computer-animated, but the aim remains: a Shakespeare that looks like Shakespeare, but one that now talks and writes like Shakespeare as well. That these various AI incarnations—from the portraiture of YouTube and Instagram to the freely available Willbot to the open-access findings of machine-generated verse experiments—are all easily located within the digital networks of social media only enhances their identificatory pull; we encounter #shakespeare in the same digital spaces where we interact with our friends and follows.

Social media, despite its vast, networked reach and millions of global users, is, as Lisa Reichelt has influentially argued, a distinctly intimate space, particularly through the tensions that hold those networks together in a phenomenon Reichelt calls "ambient intimacy" (Reichelt 2007). Ambient intimacy, which has received a great deal of traction in studies of online discourse, refers to the "ongoing noise" of social media (2007). As social media, like celebrity, is primarily invested in the publicity of private life, users participate in a nonstop flow of pictures, videos, and updates from IRL (online parlance for "in real life") friend, acquaintance, and stranger alike. This regular contact, according to Reichelt, facilitates a kind of shared intimacy amongst online users through a perpetual give-and-take of personal or professional revelation, even as participants may remain IRL socially and spatially distant. But as Reichelt acknowledges, while shared content "creates intimacy," it is an intimacy that is "not so much about meaning," but rather "just being in touch" (2007). Drawing on Mikhail Bakhtin's theories of the phatic function of language in which language can play a strictly social function that does not relay content so much as it demonstrates open pathways of communication,[13] Reichelt suggests that ambient intimacy likewise is not exchanged in the spirit of actual disclosure as much as it is merely to demonstrate the potential for such disclosure. It is, to borrow Kehoe and Gee's term, *about* intimacy, rather than actual intimacy—meta-intimacy, perhaps, or #intimacy. In the digital theater of online discourse, then, ambient intimacy, much like the strange intimacy of celebrity, enacts the rituals of intimate exchange while simultaneously withholding, as users offer up their carefully curated photos, videos, stories, and opinions to the ongoing noise of social media, which has the effect of diluting the online impact of even the most sensitive disclosures. With all the World Wide Web's players mutually ensnared in the white noise of ambient intimacy, all users participate in a shared experience of the "public intimacy" Roach once assigned specifically to the celebrity (Roach 2005). No longer the exclusive domain of the celebrity, the general online public's willing if selective publicity of their private lives, and their friends' or followers' interest and response to such divulgence, demystify the dynamics of intimacy that have long fueled the stars.

Online, death is quickly proving no obstacle to the rituals of strange, or ambient, intimacy that sustain all social media, as departed celebrities—or at least, their digitized avatars—are becoming through technological innovation increasingly able to reciprocate the public's overtures. Such is certainly the case with #shakespeare, who appears via bot or AI-generated photo *as himself*, but that distancing *as* takes on enhanced meaning here, as #shakespeare is more like a simile of Shakespeare: *about* Shakespeare, but not Shakespeare; a present-absent liminal figure poised at the intersections of life and death, distant past and anticipable future. As part of the ambient noise of social media through both his revivified, radical disclosures and the unknowable man that now serves as much as a platform as the star who once walked upon it, AI Shakespeares perhaps connect most intimately with us through the shared experience of digital intimacy that permeates every line and node of the social network. #shakespeare offers a provocative glimpse into our own networked construction in the social Web. We, too, are part of the social network's ambient noise, our presence crafted through our own contributions, the machines that host them, and the community of users that make us digitally mean. We also offer up digital versions of #ourselves to the online theaters of the social network.

#secondself #virtualcelebrity

In his groundbreaking *Heavenly Bodies*, Dyer argues that celebrities hold currency through their uncanny ability to embody the tensions of our quotidian lives—particularly, he argues, the tensions between individualism and capitalism, or between an unique human core and the commoditizing imperatives of capitalist society (Dyer 2004, 7). But as discussed in Chapter 2, the celebrity's capacity to house socio-economic tensions within a single human frame is, in large part, a projection of the public that uses celebrities as navigational tools to chart the fraught terrains of its cultural landscape. Celebrities, through their amplified visibility and mass-relatability, magnify the social tensions in which we all participate and assign a human face to the abstractions of our cultural, political, and economic relations. However, as also discussed in Chapter 2, this human face might better be described as a celebrity avatar: a multifariously authored second self that aggregates the networked conversations of the consuming-producing public into a highly charged, interactive cultural production. The celebrity body remains ever-attached to, yet distinct from, the human body who shares the celebrity's famous name.

As online celebrity reveals through universal access the processes of performance and intimacy that fuel the stars of the Internet, digital formats also demonstrably unfold the generation and distribution of the celebrity second self—a vast and sprawling network of multifarious production tidily encapsulated and emblematized online in the multi-significatory hashtag.

In its brief existence in social media, not even two decades old at the time of this writing, the hashtag has, in a sense, re-created the digital landscape through its visible punctuation of the interlinked conversations social formats create, record, and invite.[14] In its textual/meta-textual capacities, the hashtag simultaneously performs, in J.L. Austin's sense of the word,[15] the conversation it likewise names and archives; through a single-keystroke articulation, the hashtag brings into being the networked, digital conversation that it simultaneously signifies, catalogues, and opens to participation. "Hashtags do things in the world rather than merely describe what exists," writes Marcela Fuentes (2019, 180).[16] That is, the hashtagged entity does not exist until it has been tagged as such, and as David I. Backer proposes, an appended hashtag radically rewrites the text from its "physiological" to its "ideological aspects":

> There is a difference between the proper name "Bernie Sanders" and the hashtag #BernieSanders. The former refers to the presidential candidate [...]. The hashtag, however, originates within a certain discursive community, which utters it in order to label, name, or participate in collective examination of a set of beliefs, questions, or themes.
> (Backer 2016, 18)

The hashtag creates an added layer of *aboutness,* as Kehoe and Gee have theorized, to the person or concept signified by text alone. Thus, the performative, tagged entity is both the thing and about the thing, the physiology and the ideology—and, in the case of hashtagged names, the person signified as well as the socially constructed second self.

In its aboutness, a hashtagged name differentiates the human body from the publicly constructed celebrity body with an identifiable marker unavailable in earlier iterations of celebrity. The presence of the hashtag distinguishes, for example, Denzel Washington from #denzelwashington, or often just #denzel, which is understood immediately to signify not only the actor but the conversations and multiplicity of users engaged through the common sign of #denzel. #denzel, then, is not Denzel, but a sprawling, aggregated entity that even a quick Twitter search reveals is comprised of Denzel Washington images and GIFs, the actor's filmography, characters he has played in films, recent news about the actor, and qualities associated with him as rendered in paired hashtags like #boss and #motivation. Such associations span a broad spectrum of aboutness, from the actor's handsomeness to his activism. A smiling #denzel as Don Pedro in *Much Ado about Nothing* is paired with #whatamightygoodman (Richardson 2018); a strong and resilient image of Denzel as *Glory*'s Private Trip is paired with #BlackLivesMatter (@Last_Bolshevik 2020). As such, the hashtag makes visible and digitally accessible what are otherwise the more abstract and unseen conditions of celebrity—not the easily attainable images and artifacts traded through any number of forums, but the interconnected productive-consumptive authority of users who explicitly assign meaning to the celebrities they trade in and the complex affective and cultural dynamics that stars can both embody and publicize. The hashtagged entity reveals the star's multifarious construction as an aggregate of a famous figure and the wide web of the public's circulation, use, and signification.

The hashtagged celebrity name, whether #denzel or #shakespeare, does not so much signify an individual person as it does the collective of cultural conversations that person generates amongst the public, and thus, much like celebrity itself, the hashtag preceding a famous name designates a person as the tensions that sustain those varied conversations. Tagged, the celebrity becomes both person and platform, a tool that promotes the star as much as it provides a conduit for self-articulation and the promulgation of personal and cultural values. But the hashtagged celebrity name also functions as the adhesive agent that links all these various uses and meanings together into a network of signification in which the aggregate produces an effect that cannot be reduced to any one, or even the sum, of its various parts; the hashtag articulates the famous name as a publicly authored yet always unfinished text, always in a state of becoming, a name in perpetual motion. As such, the hashtag offers a legible, traceable, and participatory model of the rhizomatic structures of both networked communications and celebrity relations.

This simple keystroke provides a particularly useful structure for thinking about digital celebrity, as within its tiny grid, the hashtag holds a multitude, with the symbol's clustered intersections, parallels, and perpendicularities visually suggesting the network of players and processes that converge in both online discourse and in celebrity. A scan of #shakespeare across various social platforms offers a provocative peek into the rhizomatic network that constructs Shakespeare's second body online: #shakespeare interconnects quotations from Shakespeare's plays, student exasperations, the quirky news story of an 81-year-old William Shakespeare receiving a COVID-19 vaccine,[17] scholarly discussion, clips of film adaptations, Stratford tourism promotion, and a starch-ruffed Lego Shakespeare. Of course, these variant employments of #shakespeare only scratch at the surface of what Lanier has called "the aggregated web of cultural forces and productions" understood as "Shakespearean Rhizomatics" (Lanier 2014, 27). The aforementioned AI-generated photos appear under the encompassing label of #shakespeare as well, as do countless fan tributes, promotional materials, appropriations, and digital impersonations.

If the hashtag offers a textual map of the various persons, processes, and performances that continue to construct #shakespeare online, then Willbot might be said to visually and audibly chart a similar aggregate. In a single bot interface, users encounter a history of Shakespeare rendered through portrait and language as well as a history of digital use, even if that use is elided by the AI technologies that harvest, mix, and return user input as Willbot's output. But Willbot also offers an instructive demonstration of Shakespeare's perpetual position on the cusp of technological innovations—an ever-shifting intersection of Shakespeare's always expanding histories and the contemporary platforms through which Shakespeare means. In Willbot, Shakespeare's second, collaboratively constructed celebrity self assumes a winking, speaking form capable of dialogic interaction, and as such, Shakespeare is yet again perched at the forefront in new directions in celebrity. While #shakespeare, as noted, participates in contemporary deleb and AI celebrity trends, Willbot also positions Shakespeare within two emergent practices in digital celebrity that both possess the potential to radically alter the affordances of celebrity media: the celebrity chatbot and the virtual celebrity.

Willbot, for the most part, differs little from the popular celebrity chatbots available as text-based apps, in which users can chat with bot incarnations of stars ranging from popstar Christina Milian to CEO Elon Musk. The primary difference between Willbot and most celebrity chatbots is that chatbots communicate primarily through a text-message-style format and are always prepared to direct users to their social media accounts, merchandise, or latest projects. Stars wield such bots as promotional platforms and generally treat their users as a special class of initiates by offering sneak peeks and advance alerts of new work. Like Willbot, celebrity chatbots work through AI interfaces. Kim Kardashian's bot, for example, appears to offer intimate details of her inner circle as the bot shares stories of her unnamed friends' heartache and ongoing intrigue, interspersed with shopping tips and alerts to Kardashian's social-media updates.[18] "Celebrities are taking advantage of this technology to communicate with their fans in this one-to-many form, but with what feels like personalized messages," explains Neil M. Alperstein (2019, 79). As Alperstein suggests, conversations with machines highlight the manner by which our relationship to celebrity is ultimately an "intrapersonal" one—a self-serving form of interaction that we use to shape our interior world as much our outer one (80). When we know we are talking to a bot, the corporeal presence of the star fades into irrelevance as we engage with the second, previously ethereal but now digitally available, self of celebrity, which is, in fact, the celebrity self with whom we have always been interacting. The bot just locates the second self within an accessible and discernible space.

While AI-powered chatbots are expanding in popularity and seem poised to assume much of the duties that Facebook, Twitter, and Instagram had previously provided, another incarnation of digital celebrity has the potential to fundamentally reconfigure celebrity networks as we currently understand them. "A new generation of celebrities is selling out concerts, starring in commercials, and amassing huge Instagram followings," Miranda Katz wrote for *Wired* in 2018. "But none of them exist—corporeally, anyway" (Katz 2018). As Katz and other reporters on the digital beat have charted, virtual celebrities with no human counterpart have achieved a measure of prominence in the last several years. These completely fabricated online entities generally do not work through AI technologies; rather, they are works of CGI animation with an unseen human puppet-master helming their social media presence, and unlike celebrity chatbots of the GGI-animated dead, they are not digital recreations but original productions with no IRL source. Convincingly human, they are attracting mainstream attention and lucrative marketing deals. In 2018, *Vogue* declared the CGI-animated model and Instagram influencer Lil Miquela a "Fictional It Girl" after she partnered with Prada for an ad campaign (Yotka 2018), and the BBC published an interview with Miquela in which the digital supermodel opined of virtual celebrities, "I think most of the celebrities in popular culture are virtual!" (Fowler 2018). Miquela is just one of several CGI-animated models, including Bermuda, the self-professed "Robot Queen" (Bermuda 2020), with whom Miquela has engaged in something of an inter-influencer feud on Instagram; and Knox Frost, with whom the World Health Organization partnered in 2020 to promote COVID-19 safety protocols to Generation Z (Chen 2020). Shudu, who deems herself "The World's First Digital Supermodel" on Instagram and who boasts more than 200,000 followers, has modeled for Rihanna's Fenty Beauty and French fashion house Balmain (Shudu 2020). "In a way, it's the purest expression of celebrity, which has always been an elaborate illusion," Katz writes (Katz 2018).

But perhaps what virtual celebrity most aptly reveals is not the grand illusion of celebrity, but its reflexive capacities for the publics who both co-create and consume them. To be sure, the CGI construction of the celebot illuminates the ways in which the public face—for star and social-media user alike—is to some extent likewise manufactured, and the confusion such bots engender, as evidenced from Instagram posts that clearly mistake the bots for living human models, may similarly illustrate a public clamoring for the authentic person behind the pixelated guise of digital celebrity. But celebots—whether the slickly stylized Miquela or the clunkier, stilted Willbot—acutely emblematize the social relations that govern the daily lives of its users and followers. As a twenty-first-century update to Dyer's seminal work on stars, digital celebrities articulate what it means to live, work, and play online; that is, as more of our daily life takes place online and our social presence is increasingly digitized through social media and online communication, then the digital celebrity fittingly reflects upon the experiences of its publics. Digital celebrities assign a human face to digital social relations, much as conventional celebrities have been theorized to humanize and thereby demystify complex social, cultural, and economic relations. That the human face of the digital celebrity is not actually human but a conflation of technology and human-like appearances, crafted to varying degrees of verisimilitude, speaks all the more pertinently to the human's online existence, where flesh and bone are traded for avatar, handle, photo, video, and username. In the case of AI-driven chatbots, the digital celebrity's reflexivity is rendered all the more apparent through the harvesting and application of user metadata to generate interaction; AI celebots condense the contributions of a wide web of users into a single, animated avatar. They are quite literally collaboratively constructed celebrities, shaped by the very process of their public interactions, reflexively returning user-generated input as output.

In the case of the virtual celebrity, of course, the collaboratively constructed celebrity self is the only self, with no human tether, living or dead, to articulate the reciprocal tensions of public and private life. The celebot exists only as a public entity, no truer narrative yet to be teased out from behind the veneer of persona. It would be difficult to overstate just how radically the virtual celebrity might potentially alter the star system should current trends proliferate. Despite the diversity of celebrity theory and studies, celebrity's rootedness in human persons with human bodies remains a constant of even outlying studies, including my own, that stray from mainstream traditional-media formats. While I have argued throughout this book that celebrity ebbs and flows at the pace of technological and cultural innovation, I hold fast to celebrity as a human phenomenon—narrativized, commoditized, and mediatized as that human presence may be. But the celebot threatens to upend even non-traditional understandings with a postmodern twist perhaps befitting our digital networked culture. The celebot is the celebrity hyperreal—no longer a communal projection upon the living screen of a famous human person, but the projection itself given shape, a copy without an original and a real in its own right.[19] Perhaps the virtual celebrity is precisely what our socially distanced but digitally networked culture demands as a tool to make sense of our selves as disembodied avatars and Zoom projections, given that social media and telecommuting has, to some extent, transformed everyday interactions into something more akin to what had previously formed the core of celebrity relations. We, too, are faces on a screen, handles in a network, the disembodied communiques of the digital theater. It is impossible to say where this technology will take us, or celebrity, but the early successes of the celebot certainly reify one of this book's central premises: the stars never stand still.

#shakespeare

As I conclude this final chapter, I return to Willbot—not only rhetorically, but IRL, as I have once again accessed williambot.com to chat with this digital

#shakespeare, wondering if perhaps somewhere in our stilted conversations an apt, concluding thought for this chapter and this book might emerge. Before I speak, he asks me why I seem so serious. I tell him I am working. "Then wherefore art thou talking to me?" he asks. "You are my work," I tell him. "Still and more mine darling," he responds.[20]

While I understand that these AI-generated conversations harvest and select associative responses from a massive dataset of user input, I am taken by this response, which seems peculiarly relevant to my work. Willbot is correct. #shakespeare is my work, but it is also "his" work, with "his" referring at once to the recognizable face of Shakespeare staring back at me, and to the machine-generated intelligence that makes him speak, and more broadly to the millions of users who provide the raw material of his responses. Willbot, like #shakespeare, like celebrity, is the production of the multitudes who make it mean. He is, in a sense, a digitally embodied hashtag, presented to us as a talking, winking, smiling head that elides the complex digital functions that lie behind the familiar face. Willbot is both text and metatext, a conversant bot and a catalogue of the conversations that perpetually create him. He is Shakespeare, as the animated Droeshout engraving unmistakably relays, but he is also every user who has contributed to him through their conversations as well as the technological apparati that harvest, sift, link, and repurpose those contributions. I am speaking with him, but I am also creating him, with every comment and query I pose becoming part of the storehouse of his vocabulary that he will offer to other users.

Looking for some final, parting wisdom on the subject of stars, I ask Willbot if he knows what a star is. "A dot of light in the firmament and naught else," he responds. "Hm, not good for my project," I tell him. "Reality is ere the illusion we fail to see," he says. I tell him that idea holds a bit more promise for me when he interjects, "Behold, thither's a Burger King."

There. This is, as they say online, the content I'm here for. This is the reminder I need as Willbot's philosophical waxing on the nature of reality might otherwise almost lull me into a sense that I'm speaking to Shakespeare, as opposed to #shakespeare, incarnate. But this bot's sudden fast-food cravings provide an appropriately distancing effect from the person of Shakespeare that his image suggests, reaffirming the strange intimacy that lies at the heart of all celebrity relations. As digital celebrity lays bare the processes of celebrity circulation and identification, Willbot's abrupt case of the munchies provides the counterbalancing push to the pull of his otherwise quite Shakespearean replies, reminding me that the face on the screen is, in fact, the screen for my own projections, and the projections of millions of other users, as to who or what Shakespeare really is. Certainly, Shakespeare himself has played a part in the collaborative construction of this bot. Many of the words he utters, including numerous early modern grammatical constructions, seem lifted from the Complete Works, and the fact that, as noted earlier, he threatened to punch me specifically in the eyeballs seems a nod to the popularly circulating, though inaccurate, notion that Shakespeare coined the term "eyeball" (the word actually predates Shakespeare's work by a few decades). But this misattribution can be found hundreds of times over on the Internet, and it is fitting that this rumor becomes a sort of reality in Willbot—or, to quote Willbot, an illusion we fail to see—because Willbot is #shakespeare taken shape. He offers us back our own conversations *about* Shakespeare in the figure of Shakespeare and thus reveals celebrity Shakespeare as a multifarious aggregate greater than any one, or even the sum of, its parts. Celebrity Shakespeare, or #shakespeare, is both Shakespeare and meta-Shakespeare; the sum of countless contributions and the tensions that sustain them as an always unfinished, always expanding, always unfolding rhizomatic network.

"How dost thou see my thoughts?" Willbot asks me. This one is easy to answer. "Because they're my thoughts," I tell him. He then asks me what I think of Antifa. I am not prepared to engage in this political discussion of current events with Willbot, but his question does make clear that others have, offering a small glimpse into the ongoing conversations that continually sustain and shape #shakespeare's digital presence and demonstrating one of the keys to the untagged Shakespeare's perpetuity as audiences continue to use Shakespeare as a means of navigating their cultural spheres. Willbot may very well offer us an early look into the 3.0 future of celebrity Shakespeare, and it is not difficult to imagine the more streamlined and enhanced digitized Shakespeares for whom this clunky bot might now be setting the stage. But Willbot also offers us a compelling look into our own cultures of celebrity, digital and otherwise, and Shakespeare's relationship to them. Shakespeare was first introduced to the London theater scene by way of Greene's invective—a sort of analogue, proto-Twitter, celebrity feud that invited numerous responses, and the early 1590s Shakespeare we know today arrives to us as much through the conversations about him, through an early modern version of #shakespeare, as through the poet's own words. While his peers named him a star and fleshed out his verse with a celebrity body of their own making, on stage and in his verse, Shakespeare wrestled with the concept of celebrity; he probed its mechanisms in plays and contemplated in sonnets the motley that the phenomenon had made of him. Since his death, his publics have participated in a ceaseless pursuit to reanimate him in human bodies, fictional characters, and digital avatars. Today we have Willbot, an aggregated digital celebrity collaboratively constructed over centuries through Droeshout's seventeenth-century engraving, Shakespeare's and other vaguely early modern language, and the projective and reflective conversations of its millions of users, who themselves input content drawn from a long history of Shakespearean narrative and mythology. But Willbot offers something other forms of celebrity Shakespeare cannot; specifically, he can speak back to us—not in the abstract sense that his plays speak to their readers and audiences, but in the specific sense that if you ask Willbot a pointed question, he will offer a targeted answer. This is, perhaps, the overarching dream of celebrity and what has fueled its potency as a cultural form over centuries: the dangling promise of the closed-circuit intimacy of reciprocal contact with that which seems larger than life and is, in fact, the aggregate of

182   #shakespeare

many lives condensed into the one. Willbot may be offered to us as something of a quirky novelty, but it demonstrates our own agency in the formation of our stars and, specifically, in the enduring celebrity of Shakespeare.

Notes

1 Willbot, available at williambot.com, was launched in 2016 and uses proprietary software created by Rollo Carpenter and Existor. According to the website hosting Willbot, Willbot "is a learning AI" that shares its database with two other Existor bots: Cleverbot, available at cleverbot.com, and Eviebot, available at eviebot.com (Existor 2020). All conversations with Willbot cited here took place over several chat sessions in 2020 and appear word-for-word as they were voiced by myself and the chatbot, though only a select few moments of a much longer dialogue appear here.
2 For the sake of expediency, I have chosen, due to its relationship to Shakespeare, to gender this bot as "he/him" throughout this chapter; however, the explanatory text on williambot.com refers to the bot's gender once as "her" (Existor 2020).
3 For a helpful and accessible primer on Web 3.0, its differences from 1.0 and 2.0 formats, and its potential applications, see *Artificial Intelligence and the Evolution of Web 3.0*, edited by Tomayess Issa and Pedro Isaias (2015).
4 Affordance theory originated in 1977 with the work of ecological psychologist James G. Gibson, who proposes that "the affordance of anything is a specific combination of the properties of its substance and its surfaces taken with references to an animal" (Gibson 2017 [1977], 67). The theory was appropriated as a lens through which to investigate technological interactions and has proven highly productive in media studies, most recently in studies of social media, where "affordance" now offers a range of perspectives and frameworks that has expanded far beyond Gibson's original formulation. For example, Jeffrey W. Treem and Paul Leonardi discuss the affordances of visibility, persistence, editability, and association within organizational social-media communication (Treem and Leonardi 2012); Andrew Schrock has focused on the affordances of portability, availability, locatability, and multimediality in mobile technologies (Schrock 2015).
5 For a thorough investigation of the War of the Theaters, see James P. Bednarz, *Shakespeare and the Poets' War* (Bednarz 2001).
6 The exchange between Hamlet and Rosencrantz generally assumed to refer to the War of the Theaters appears only in the Folio. As such, the Norton notes that this conversation is likely a late addition to the play (p. 1794, n. 1).
7 See Chapter 1 for a detailed account of personation on the early modern stage.
8 Yeran Kim performs an interesting analysis of K-Pop reaction videos on YouTube and the "intertwined dynamics of active/reactive, production/consumption in visual practices" involved in the form (Kim 2016, 334). As Kim suggests, online reaction is often figured as a kind of authorship that can generate a fairly consistent, often highly interactive, fanbase (2016, 335).
9 According to *Forbes*'s 2020 annual report on top YouTube earners, the highest-paid YouTuber is currently Ryan Kaji, a nine-year-old boy from Texas who reviews toys and games on his channel, Ryan's World. Kaji made $29.5 million in 2020. All of the top-10 highest-paid YouTubers made $15 million or more that year (Berg 2020).
10 Deep-learning software refers to the layered network of machine-learning algorithms that can translate raw data into composites, such as in speech-recognition or object-recognition technologies. For an introduction, see Yann LeCun, Yoshua Bengio, and Geoffrey Hinton, "Deep Learning" (LeCun et al. 2015).

11 CGI stands for Computer-Generated Imagery and generally references three-dimensional digital graphics inserted into film or televised formats.
12 Artificial Neural Networks (generally abbreviated ANN) refer to computing systems modeled on the brain, complete with artificial neurons and synapse-like connections. For more, see LeCun, Bengio, and Hinton (LeCun et al. 2015).
13 See Bakhtin, *Speech Genres and Other Late Essays*, for a discussion of "the generic form of greeting" as well as the "stylistic aura" of such phatic communication, as referenced by Reichelt (Bakhtin 1999, 127).
14 The hashtag, as it is currently used, has a short but highly consequential history. In 2007, Web designer Chris Messina appropriated the hashtag from the earlier Internet Relay Chat for use on Twitter, when he asked his followers, "how do you feel about using # (pound) for groups?" (Messina 2007). In 2009, Twitter began hyperlinking hashtagged content, which allowed the device to flourish, and it quickly became a signature component of the platform. Other formats such as Tumblr and Instagram soon followed, leading to its current ubiquity across all social media and now often beyond.
15 See Austin, *How to Do Things with Words*, particularly Lecture VI, in which Austin theorizes the performative speech-act, or utterances that perform actions (Austin 1962).
16 As Fuentes argues, one of the most important aspects of "hashtag performativity" is its capacity to transform phrases into community solidarity and calls to action, as in the case of the #MeToo movement. "Hashtags evolved from performing an indexical and retrieval function to becoming a central propeller of networked protests," Fuentes states (Fuentes 2019, 180).
17 On December 8, 2020, it was reported in multiple outlets that the second UK recipient of the newly released COVID-19 vaccination was William Shakespeare of Warwickshire (Peltier 2020).
18 Called "Kim Kardashian: Hollywood," this chatbot was launched through the Facebook Messenger app in 2017.
19 In *Simulacra and Simulation*, Jean Baudrillard describes the "hyperreal" as "the generation by models of a real without origin" (Baudrillard 1994, 1). Apropos to my use of the term here is the subtly distinct term coined by Nobuyoshi Terashima, "HyperReality" (generally abbreviated as HR), to describe computing developments that facilitate interactions between human and non-human technological objects, including Artificial Intelligence and Virtual Reality. As John Tiffin notes, "In HyperReality [Terashima] has created a technology that enables *hyperreality*" (Tiffin 2001, 41).
20 This concluding conversation occurred on November 8, 2020.

References

Abidin, Crystal. 2018. *Internet Celebrity: Understanding Fame Online*. Bingley: Emerald.
Alperstein, Neil M. 2019. *Celebrity and Mediated Social Connections: Fans, Friends, and Followers in the Digital Age*. New York: Palgrave Macmillan.
Apodaca, Nathan (@420doggface208). 2020. "*Morning Vibe.*" TikTok Video. September 25, 2020. https://www.tiktok.com/@420doggface208/video/6876424179084709126.
Ault, Susanne. 2014. "Survey: YouTube Stars More Popular than Mainstream Celebs Among U.S. Teens." *Variety*, August 5. http://variety.com/2014/digital/news/survey-youtube-stars-more-popular-than-mainstream-celebs-among-u-s-teens-1201275245/.
Austin, J.L. 1962. *How to Do Things with Words*. Edited by J.O. Urmson and Marina Sbisà. Cambridge: Harvard University Press.

Backer, David I. 2016. "Toward an Activist Theory of Language." In *Truth in the Public Sphere*, edited by Jason Hannan, 3–22. Lanham: Lexington.

Bakhtin, Mikhail. 1999. *Speech Genres and Other Late Essays*. Translated by Vern W. McGee. Edited by Caryl Emerson and Michael Holquist. Austin: University of Texas Press.

Baudrillard, Jean. 1994. *Simulacra and Simulation*. Translated by Sheila Faria Glaser. Ann Arbor: University of Michigan Press.

Bednarz, James P. 2001. *Shakespeare and the Poets' War*. New York: Columbia University Press.

Berg, Madeline. 2020. "The Highest Paid YouTube Stars of 2020." *Forbes*, December 18, 2020. https://www.forbes.com/sites/maddieberg/2020/12/18/the-highest-paid-youtube-stars-of-2020.

Bermuda (@bermudaisbae). 2020. *Instagram*. https://www.instagram.com/bermudaisbae.

Bernard, Andreas. 2019. *Theory of the Hashtag*. Translated by Valentine A. Pakis. Cambridge: Polity.

Blackwell, Anna. 2018. *Shakespearean Celebrity in the Digital Age: Fan Cultures and Remediation*. New York: Palgrave Macmillan.

Calbi, Maurizio. 2013. *Spectral Shakespeares: Media Adaptations in the Twenty-First Century*. New York: Palgrave Macmillan.

Calbi, Maurizio and Stephen O'Neill. 2016. "Introduction" to #SocialMedia-Shakespeares. *Borrowers and Lenders: The Journal of Shakespeare and Appropriation* 10: http://www.borrowers.uga.edu.

Chen, Tanya. 2020. "An Influencer Who Is Actually a Bot Is Working with the WHO to Teach the Youths about Coronavirus." *Buzzfeed*, April 3. https://www.buzzfeednews.com/article/tanyachen/world-health-organization-is-working-with-robot-influencer.

Davidson, Jacob. 2013. "Digital Necromancy: Advertising with Dead Celebrities." *Time*, August 2, 2013. https://business.time.com/2013/08/02/digital-necromancy-advertising-with-reanimated-celebrities.

Desmet, Christy. 2014. "YouTube Shakespeare, Appropriation, and Rhetorics of Invention." In *OuterSpeares: Shakespeare, Intermedia, and the Limits of Adaptation*, edited by Daniel Fischlin, 53–74. Toronto: University of Toronto Press.

D'Rozario, Denver. 2020. "Dead Celebrity (Deleb) Use in Marketing: An Initial Theoretical Exposition." *Psychology & Marketing* 33: 486–504.

Dyer, Richard. 2004 [1986]. *Heavenly Bodies: Film Stars and Society*, 2nd ed. London: Routledge.

Edwards, Gareth (dir.). 2016. *Star Wars: Rogue One*. Performed by Felicity Jones, Diego Luna, and Ben Mendelsohn. Walt Disney.

Eisenlauer, Volker. 2013. *A Critical Hypertext Analysis of Social Media: The True Colours of Facebook*. London: Bloomsbury.

Existor. 2016. *Willbot*. Chatbot. Accessed January 24, 25, and 26; November 7 and 8, 2020. https://www.williambot.com/en.

Fazel, Valerie M. and Louise Geddes. 2017. "Introduction: The Shakespeare User." In *The Shakespeare User: Critical and Creative Appropriations in a Networked Culture*, edited by Valerie M.Fazel and Louise Geddes, 1–22. New York: Palgrave Macmillan.

Firth, Niall. 2018. "AI Creates Shakespearean Sonnets—and They're Actually Quite Good." *New Scientist*, July 27. https://www.newscientist.com/article/2175301-ai-creates-shakespearean-sonnets-and-theyre-actually-quite-good.

Fleetwood, Mick (@mickfleetwood). 2020. "*@420doggface208 had it right*." TikTok Video. October 4. https://www.tiktok.com/@mickfleetwood/video/6879849755204259077.

Fowler, Damian. 2018. "The Fascinating World of Instagram's 'Virtual' Celebrities." *BBC*, April 2. https://www.bbc.com/worklife/article/20180402-the-fascinating-world-of-instagrams-virtual-celebrities.

Fuentes, Marcela. 2019. "#NiUnaMenos (#NotOneWomanLess): Hashtag Performativity, Memory, and Direct Action against Gender Violence in Argentina." In *Women Mobilizing Memory*, edited by Ayse Gul Altinay and Maria Jose Contreras, MarianneHirsch, JeanHoward, BanuKaraca, and Alisa Solomon, 172–191. New York: Columbia University Press.

Gibson, James J. 2017 [1977]. "The Theory of Affordances." In *Perceiving, Acting and Knowing: Toward an Ecological Psychology*, edited by Robert Shaw and John Bransford, 67–82. Hillsdale: Lawrence Erlbaum.

Giles, David C. 2018. *Twenty-First Century Celebrity: Fame in Digital Culture*. Bingley: Emerald.

Holl, Jennifer. 2017. "YouShakespeare: Shakespearean Celebrity 2.0." In *Shakespeare/Not Shakespeare*, edited by Christy Desmet, Natalie Loper, and Jim Casey, 203–220. New York: Palgrave Macmillan.

Holland, Peter. 2009. "Performing Shakespeare for the Web Community." In *Shakespeare in Hollywood, Asia, and Cyberspace*, edited by Alexa Huang and Charles S. Ross, 252–264. West Lafayette: Purdue University Press.

Issa, Tomayess and Pedro Isaìas. 2015. *Artificial Intelligence and the Evolution of Web 3.0*. Hershey: Information Science Reference.

Katz, Miranda. 2018. "The Rise of the Computer-Generated Celebrity." *Wired*, July 29. https://www.wired.com/story/computer-generated-celebrities.

Kim, Yeran. 2016. "Globalization of the Privatized Self-Image: The Reaction Video and Its Attention Economy on YouTube." In *Routledge Handbook of New Media in Asia*, edited by Larissa Hjorth and Olivia Khoo, 333–342. London and New York: Routledge.

Kurzman, Charles, Chelise Anderson, Clinton Key, Youn Ok Lee, Maired Moloney, Alexis Silver, and Maria W. Van Ryn. 2007. "Celebrity Status." *Sociological Theory* 25: 347–367.

Jacobs, Kristof and Niels Spierings. 2016. *#Social Media, Parties, and Political Inequalities*. Hampshire: Palgrave Macmillan.

Jonsson, Annika. 2015. "Post-Mortem Social Death—Exploring the Absence of the Deceased." *Contemporary Social Science* 10 (3): 284–295.

Kehoe, Andrew and Matt Gee. 2011. "Social Tagging: A New Perspective on Textual 'Aboutness'." *Studies in Variations, Contacts, and Change in English* 6: https://varieng.helsinki.fi/series/volumes/12/kehoe_gee.

Lanier, Douglas. 2014. "Shakespearean Rhizomatics: Adaptation, Ethics, Value." In *Reproducing Shakespeare: Shakespeare and the Ethics of Appropriation*, edited by Alexa Huang and Elizabeth Rivlin, 21–40. New York: Palgrave Macmillan.

@Last_Bolshevik. 2020. "*So. the monument*." Tweet. June 20, 2020. https://twitter.com/Last_Bolshevik/status/1274373602138177538.

Laurel, Brenda. 2014. *Computers as Theatre*, 2nd ed. Upper Saddle River, NJ: Addison-Wesley.

LeCun, Yann, Yoshua Bengio, and Geoffrey Hinton. 2015. "Deep Learning." *Nature* 521: 436–444.

Lonergan, Patrick. 2016. *Theatre & Social Media*. London: Palgrave Macmillan.

Macnamara, Jim and Ansgar Zerfass. 2012. "Social Media Communication in Organizations: The Challenges of Balancing Openness, Strategy and Management." *International Journal of Strategic Communications* 6 (4): 287–308.

Markoff, John. 2006. "Entrepreneurs See a Web Guided by Common Sense." *New York Times*, November 12. https://www.nytimes.com/2006/11/12/business/12web.html.

Marshall, P. David. 2010. "The Promotion and Presentation of the Self: Celebrity as Marker of Presentational Media." *Celebrity Studies* 1 (1): 35–48.

Marwick, Alice E. 2013. *Status Update: Celebrity, Publicity, and Branding in the Social Media Age*. New Haven: Yale University Press.

McArdle, Donna. 2020. "*You Brought Them Back to Life.*" YouTube Comment. December 29. https://www.youtube.com/tIX7o3tKstc&t=166s.

Messina, Chris. 2007. "Groups for Twitter; or A Proposal for Twitter Tag Channels." *Factory Joe*, August 27. https://factoryjoe.com/2007/08/25/groups-for-twitter-or-a-proposal-for-twitter-tag-channels.

Morning Consult. 2019. "YouTubers Are Among the Most Popular Celebrities for Gen Z." *The Influencer Report*, November 5. https://morningconsult.com/form/youtubers-are-among-the-most-influential-celebrities-for-gen-z.

Motherfuckingshakespeare. *Erotic Punning*. 2020. *Tumblr*. https://motherfuckingshakespeare.tumblr.com.

Mystery Scoop. 2020. "Historical Paintings Brought to Life Using Artificial Intelligence." YouTube Video, 9:22. https://www.youtube.com/tIX7o3tKstc&t=166s.

No Shit Shakespeare. 2020. *Tumblr*. https://noshitshakespeare.tumblr.com.

O'Neill, Stephen. 2014. *Shakespeare and YouTube: New Media Forms of the Bard*. London: Bloomsbury.

O'Neill, Stephen. 2018. "'Sowed and Scattered': Shakespeare's Media Ecologies." In *Broadcast Your Shakespeare: Continuity and Change Across Media*, edited by Stephen O'Neill, 1–26. London: Bloomsbury.

Pearson, Erika. 2009. "All the World Wide Web's a Stage: The Performance of Identity in Online Social Networks." *First Monday* 14 (3): https://firstmonday.org/ojs/index.php/fm/article/download/2162/2127.

Pedroni, Marco. 2016. "Meso-Celebrities, Fashion, and the Media: How Digital Influencers Struggle for Visibility." *Film, Fashion & Consumption* 5 (1): 103–121.

Peltier, Elian. 2020. "William Shakespeare Has Been Vaccinated against the Coronavirus (Yes, you read that right.)." *The New York Times*, December 8. https://www.nytimes.com/2020/12/08/world/william-shakespeare-covid-vaccine.html.

Penfold-Mounce, Ruth. 2018. *Death, the Dead, and Popular Culture*. Bingley: Emerald.

Plechac, Petr. 2019. "Relative Contributions of Shakespeare and Fletcher in *Henry VIII*: An Analysis Based on Most Frequent Words and Most Frequent Rhythmic Patterns." *Digital Scholarship in the Humanities*, 30 Oct: 1–11.

Redmond, Sean. 2019. *Celebrity*. London and New York: Routledge.

Reichelt, Lisa. 2007. "Ambient Intimacy." *Disambiguity*, March 1, 2007. https://www.disambiguity.com/ambient-intimacy.

Richardson, Ann-Marie (@RichardsonA_M). 2018. "*My favourite feature.*" Tweet. June 12, 2018. https://twitter.com/RichardsonA_M/status/1006543290500636675.

Ritman, Alex. 2019. "James Dean Reborn in CGI for Vietnam War Action-Drama." *Hollywood Reporter*, November 6. https://www.hollywoodreporter.com/news/afm-james-dean-reborn-cgi-vietnam-war-action-drama-1252703.

Roach, Joseph. 2005. "Public Intimacy: The Prior History of 'It'." In *Theatre and Celebrity in Britain, 1660–2000*, edited by Mary Luckhurst and Jane Moody, 15–30. New York: Palgrave Macmillan.

Schrock, Andrew Richard. 2015. "Communicative Affordances of Mobile Media: Portability, Availability, Locatability, and Multimediality." *International Journal of Communication* 9: 1229–1246.

Senft, Theresa M. 2008. *Camgirls: Celebrity and Community in the Age of Social Networks*. New York: Peter Lang.

@shakespeare. 2020. "*And yea, auto-correct just changed "Lo!"* to "lol." Tweet. December 19. https://twitter.com/Shakespeare/status/1340367644852178947.

Shakespeare, William. 2016. *Hamlet*. In *The Norton Shakespeare, Third Edition*, edited by Stephen Greenblatt, Walter Cohen, Suzanne Gossett, Jean E. Howard, Katharine Eisaman Maus, and Gordon McMullan, 1751–1854. New York: Norton.

Shudu (@shudu.gram). 2020. *Instagram*. https://www.instagram.com/shudu.gram/.

Silipo, Rosaria. 2019. "How to Use Deep Learning to Write Shakespeare." *InfoWorld*, February 3. https://www.infoworld.com/article/3340377/how-to-use-deep-learning-to-write-shakespeare.html.

Tiffin, John. 2001. "The HyperReality Paradigm." In *HyperReality: Paradigm for the Third Millennium*, edited by John Tiffin and Nobuyoshi Terashima, 25–42. London: Routledge.

Treem, Jeffrey W. and Paul M.Leonardi. 2012. "Social Media Use in Organizations: Exploring the Affordances of Visibility, Editability, Persistence, and Association." *Communication Yearbook* 36: 143–189.

Twinsthenewtrend. 2020. "First Time Hearing Phil Collins—In the Air Tonight Reaction." YouTube Video, 7:50. July 27, 2020. https://www.youtube.com/0l3-iufiywU.

Uterwijk, Bas (@ganbrood). 2020. "Based on the Cobbe Portrait." Tweet. October 10. https://twitter.com/ganbrood/status/1314933245344190467/photo/1.

WilliamShakespeareAuthor. 2020. *Facebook*. https://www.facebook.com/WilliamShakespeareAuthor/.

Yotka, Steff. 2018. "Prada Launches Instagram GIFs with Help from a Fictional It Girl." *Vogue*, February 22. https://www.vogue.com/article/prada-instagram-gifs-lil-miquela.

Index

Abidin, Crystal 15, 169
aboutness 162, 175–176
actors: as center of theater 27; in commendatory verse 47–48; as embodiments of theatrical tensions 28–29; as featured in print 70–76; as mortal 38; in repertory 35; Shakespearean 141–147; as staged bodies 38–39; as stars 26
Admiral's Men 164
affordance theory 162–163
Agnew, Jean-Christophe 79–81
Alberoni, Francesco 8
Alleyn, Edward 33–35, 38–39, 47–48, 64, 99, 100–102
ambient intimacy 173–174
Antoinette, Marie 120n10
Antony and Cleopatra 51n3, 63
Apodaca, Nathan 167
Appadurai, Arjun 62–63
Armin, Robert 47, 69
Artificial Intelligence (AI) 159, 171–174, 177–179
Aubrey, John 143–144
audience: in backchat 35–36; as collective 44–47; and conventions of response 40, 164–165; and hyperawareness 28; internal 31, 167; as manipulable 107–109; as many-headed 103; as vulnerable 40

Backer, David I. 175
Backhaus, Gary 28
Bakhtin, Mikhail 174, 183n13
Baudrillard, Jean 183n19
Bacon, Francis 32–33
Baker, Sir Richard 136
bardolatry 130, 139, 143
Barkstead, William 74

Barnfield, Richard 138
Barnes, Jennifer 4, 142–143, 146
Bednarz, James 137
Bernard, Andreas 161
Bishop, T.G. 31
Blackwell, Anna 4, 19n2, 142, 143, 161
Blau, Herbert 37–38
Bloom, Harold 130
bodies: of actors 38–39; of celebrities 127, 131; of playgoers 39–40; of Shakespeare 124–128, 137–141
Boleyn, Anne 23–25
Boorstin, Daniel 8, 15
branding 59–62, 67–68, 76, 104
Brandon, Charles 24
Braudy Leo 11, 101–104
Bristol, Michael 4, 128–129
Bruster, Douglas 137–138
Burbage, Richard 27, 41, 49, 64, 65, 76, 135–136, 140–141, 150
Byron, Lord 36, 137, 146

Calbi, Maurizio 5, 161
cast lists 72–73
Carlyle, Thomas 130
celebrity: and absence 29–30, 96, 107, 116, 172; birth of 12–14; as commodity 62–63; dead 129–130 (see also deleb); definitions of 6–10; as democratic 78; digital 161–162, 169–176; as fleeting 1–3, 6; and frivolity 7–9, 19; and individuality 102, 105; identification with 11, 38, 77–78; literary 103, 125, 137; micro-celebrity 168; and the monarchy 92–96, 101–102, 104–106, 119n8; as representative of the collective 102; as text 9–10; as vernacular aristocracy 96–100; virtual 178–179
Cerasano, S.P. 34, 39, 47, 101

charisma 9
chatbot 159–160, 177–178
Chaucer, Geoffrey 24
Chettle, Henry 132–133
close-up (film) 36
Coleridge, Samuel Taylor 130, 146
The Comedy of Errors 81–86
commendatory verse 47–49
commodity 61–70
Computer-Generated Imagery (CGI) 172, 178
contemporaneity 46
coronation processions: of Anne Boleyn in *Henry VIII* 23–25; of Elizabeth I 105; of James I 100–103
credit 79–80
curiosity 10, 27, 117

Daileader, Celia R. 39
Davidson, Laurie 124
Davies, John 47, 134–135
De Certeau, Michel 61
Dean, James 130, 172
deep-learning software 170, 173
Dekker, Thomas 40, 46, 101–102, 165
deleb 172
Deleuze, Gilles and Guattari, Felix 6, 14–15, 18
Digges, Leonard 31
Dobson, Michael 154n11
Doctor Who 148–152
Donaldson, Ian 103
Doty, Jeffrey 44–45, 105, 112, 116
Dugdale, Gilbert 101–102
Duncan-Jones, Katherine 126, 137, 140
Dyer, Richard 9–10, 79, 105, 174–175

Earle, John 27, 43
Elizabeth I, Queen 105–106
embodied writing 137–138
enchantment (theatrical) 27–28
excess 26, 28, 29, 30, 33

fans 76–78
Fazel, Valerie 4, 160–161
Field, Nathan 65–66, 73, 87n7, 132
Fiennes, Jospeh 124, 149
First Folio 31, 71, 126, 132
Fitter, Chris 95
Fitzgeffrey, Henry 40

Gabler, Neal 6, 7, 12
Garber, Marjorie 97–98, 115
Garrick, David 26, 142–147

Geddes, Louise 4, 160–161
Generation Z 169
genius (classical) 85, 87n17, 101–102
Giles, David C. 5, 162, 168
greatness 97–98, 118
Greenblatt, Stephen 30, 105, 106, 114, 117
Greene, Thomas 66–67
Greenes Groats-worth of Witte 2–3, 86n1, 132–134
Greenes Tu Quoque 66–67
The Gull's Hornbook 40
Gurr, Andrew 35–36, 40, 44, 46, 64
Guilpin, Edward 33

Habermas, Jürgen 48
Hamlet 49, 138, 165, 182n6
Hamlet (1948 film) 147
Harris, Jonathan Gil 62, 69
Harrison, Stephen 101
Harvey, Gabriel 42
hashtag 161–162, 175–177; as activism 183n16; origin of 183n14
Hauser, Gerard 45
Hazlitt, William 145–146
Heminges, John 27, 64, 75
Henry IV, Part 1 61, 86, 111–118
Henry V 24, 115
Henry VI, Part 1 24
Henry VIII, King 104
Henry VIII (All Is True) 23–26, 29, 50–51
Heywood, Thomas 41, 44, 48, 49
Hollywood 12, 92
Holmes, Su 9, 18, 19
hyperreal 179, 183n19

Inglis, Fred 10, 12, 105
intertheater 63–64
intimacy 34–36; *see also* ambient intimacy and strange intimacy

James I, King 100–102
Johnson, Nora 34–35, 87n7, 132
Jonson, Ben: *Bartholomew Fair* 47, 65–66; as celebrity 103; *Cynthia's Revels* 103; "To Edward Alleyn" 48–49; *Every Man out of his Humour* 99; on fame 103–104; *The Masque of Blackness* 41; on Shakespeare 3, 31; "The Speeches of Gratulation" 101–102; and theatrical name-dropping 64; in tribute 136; and the War of the Theaters 165
Julius Caesar 3

Kantorowicz, Ernst 94–95, 100
Kastan, David Scott 105, 106
Kean, Edmund 145–146
Keats, John 145
Kehoe, Andrew and Gee, Matt 162, 174, 175
Kelly, Dean Lennox 150
Kemp, Will 31, 49, 75–77, 166
King's Men 75, 101
Knapp, Jeffrey 134, 153n4
Korda, Natasha 62

Lake, Peter and Pincus, Steve 45
Lanier, Douglas 6, 149, 150, 177; and Shakespearean rhizomatics 6, 177
Laurel Brenda 163
Lehmann, Courtney 148, 149, 154n13
Lieblein, Leanore 42, 52n13
Lilti, Antoine 7, 10, 12, 25, 27
Lowenthal, Leo 7–8
Lowin, John 27, 73

Macbeth 49, 140
A Mad World, My Masters 28
Manningham, John 140–141
Marcus, Sharon 7, 8
Marshall, P. David 6, 10, 11, 43, 78, 87n4, 97, 102, 163–164
McKellen, Ian 92, 199n1
Meres, Francis 138, 153n7
The Merry Wives of Windsor 60
Middleton, Thomas 46, 101
A Midsummer Night's Dream 31–32, 39
Mole, Thomas 36, 137
Morgan, Simon 6, 13
Morin, Edgar 11, 12, 77
Munro, Ian 46, 68–69, 103

name-dropping 64–66
Nashe, Thomas; *Pierce Penilesse* 38, 133–134; *Strange Newes* 35
Nine Daies Wonder 31, 75–76

Olivier, Laurence 146–147
O'Neill, Stephen 5, 160, 161, 170
Othello 40, 60, 85
Overbury, Sir Thomas 27, 41, 124
Ovid 23–24

para-social relations 33–34
Parnassus Plays 76, 139–140
parody 64–67
Peacham, Henry 38
performance theory 26–28, 47

performativity 97, 166, 175, 183n15
Pericles 24
Pewdiepie 151, 159, 169
Piccirillo, M.S. 34
Perkins, Richard 73
personation 41–43
portraiture: of Edward Alleyn 38–39; of Elizabeth I 106; of Shakespeare 124–126
Prescott, Paul 129
presence 26–30
print-plays: containing actors' names 72–73; containing information regarding staging 71; as souvenirs 71–72
public sphere 45

Quips upon Questions 69–70

Rasmussen, Eric 126
Ratseis Ghost 49, 99
reaction video 166–167, 182n8
Redmond, Sean 9, 18, 19, 126–127, 131, 168,
Reichelt, Lisa 173–174
reputation 59–60
rhizome 6, 14–15, 165, 176, 181
Richard III 106–111
Richard III (1995 film) 92–96
Roach, Joseph 10, 29, 94
Rojek, Chris 7, 10, 12, 36, 79, 100, 129
The Roman Actor 28–30
Romeo and Juliet 126
Rowe, Nicholas 144
Rublack, Ulinka 8, 13

scandal 60, 86n1, 115, 132–144
Schechner, Richard 26, 29, 47, 164
Schickel, Robert 12, 36
#shakespeare 159, 161, 170–174
Shakespeare in Love 124, 149, 154n13
Shakespeare, William: as contemporary celebrity 124–129; as digital celebrity 170–174; as early modern celebrity 131–141; coat of arms 98–99; as commercial product 130–131; and gossip 141, 143–144; memorial bust 126; as mythologized genius 130–131; in portraiture 124–126; as television character 147–153; as chatbot 159–160, 170–171, 177, 179–182; in praise poems 138–139; and scandal 132–144; as sexy 124–125, 149–150; Sonnet 18 49; Sonnet 74 125; Sonnets 110–112 59–60

Shakespearean: as adjective 142; celebrities 128–131, 142–147
Sharpe, Kevin 104
Shaw, George Bernard 130
social lives: of players 63–67; of things 62–63
Sonnet upon the Pittiful Burneing of the Globe Playhouse in London 74–75
Starks, Lisa S. 150–151
stars: classical 23–25; as metaphor for celebrities 3; theatric 26; as terminology 18–19
Stephens, John 43, 99
Stern, Tiffany 71–73
strange intimacy 37–43, 171
Stowe's Annales 35
Sunset Boulevard 1–2

Tarlton, Richard 27, 31, 35–40, 42–43, 52n16, 67–70, 79, 80, 87n15
Taylor, John 73–74
Taylor, Joseph 49, 73
theater: as collaborative 47; as collectivizing 44–45; and corporeality 38–39; digital 165; and the market 80–81; as model for computer activity 163; and the monarchy 101–102, 105; as network 165; and the repertory system 34; and social identity 80; as social media 164; and stars 26–30; and wonder 31–32

The Three Lords and Three Ladies of London 68–70
TikTok 166, 167
Tribble, Evelyn 27, 51n5
Turner, Graeme 7, 9, 10; and the demotic turn 96–97
Twelfth Night 98
twinship 81
Twinsthenewtrend 167
two-bodies doctrine 94–95, 100

Ubersfeld, Anne 47
Uterwijk, Bas 170–171

Yachnin, Paul 46–47
YouTube 166–174

Van Krieken, Robert 8, 13, 26, 36, 61, 97
Venus and Adonis 138, 139

War of the Theaters 165
Warhol, Andy 96
Washington, Denzel 176
Web 3.0 160, 170, 182n3
Weever, John 138–139
wonder 30–33, 112–117
The White Devil 73
Will (TV) 124, 147–153
Willbot 159–160, 170–171, 177, 179–182
Wotton, Sir Henry 118

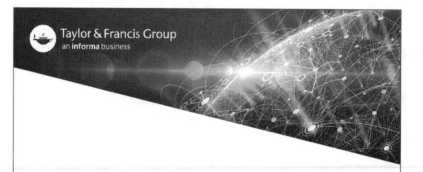

Printed in the United States
by Baker & Taylor Publisher Services